# KRAUTROCK

# TRACKING ✳ POP

SERIES EDITORS: JOCELYN NEAL, JOHN COVACH, AND ALBIN ZAK

German
Music
in the
Seventies

# KRAUTROCK

Ulrich Adelt

University of Michigan Press • Ann Arbor

Published in the United States of America by the
University of Michigan Press
Manufactured in the United States of America
♾ Printed on acid-free paper

2019   2018   2017   2016      4   3   2   1

A CIP catalog record for this book is available from the British Library.

Library of Congress Cataloging-in-Publication Data

Names: Adelt, Ulrich, 1972– author.
Title: Krautrock : German music in the seventies / Ulrich Adelt.
Description: Ann Arbor : University of Michigan Press, 2016. | Series: Tracking pop |
    Includes bibliographical references and index.
Identifiers: LCCN 2016006365 | ISBN 9780472073191 (hardcover : alk. paper) | ISBN
    9780472053193 (pbk. : alk. paper) | ISBN 9780472122219 (e-book)
Subjects: LCSH: Krautrock (Music)—History and criticism. | Rock music—Germany
    (West)—1971–1980—History and criticism.
Classification: LCC ML3534.6.G3 A34   2016 | DDC 781.660943/09047—dc23
LC record available at http://lccn.loc.gov/2016006365

# Acknowledgments

First, I want to thank Hörfuß Allstars (Hanno Kiehl, Dirk Reimers, and Sascha Krück), my on-and-off band for many years. We were making krautrock and didn't even know it.

I am extremely grateful for the unique and friendly environment in the American Studies program at the University of Wyoming. I especially want to thank Eric Sandeen and Frieda Knobloch, the two directors in recent years. Other Wyoming faculty that have greatly helped me with this book include John Dorst, Isadora Helfgott, Gregg Cawley, and Kerry Pimblott. Of course I cannot leave out our wonderful office assistant, Sophie Beck. I have also had many hardworking graduate assistants at Wyoming, so thank you, Glen Carpenter, Julian Saporiti, Robin Posniak, Rie Misaizu, Jascha Herdt, Kiah Karlsson, David Loeffler, Maggie Mullen, and Susan Clements.

In preparation for this book, I was able to spend a research semester in Germany, and I would like to thank the Deutscher Akademischer Austauschdienst (DAAD), Sabine Broeck from the University of Bremen, and Ulrich Duve of the Klaus Kuhnke Archiv für Populäre Musik.

Thanks to everybody at the University of Michigan Press, especially Chris Hebert and the anonymous reviewers. I'm also grateful to Joel Rudinow for recommending the press.

For answering questions about my research, I want to thank Jean-Hervé Péron and Zappi Diermaier of Faust, Giorgio Moroder, Rusty Egan, Rudi Esch, and the *Pitchfork* writers Brian Howe, Dominique Leon, Nick Neyland, Brent Sirota, Nick Sylvester, Joe Tangari, and Douglas Wolk. For inviting me to talk about my research in Germany, Great Britain, and the Netherlands, I want to thank Uwe Schütte, Hans Bak, Frank Mehring, and Barry Shank.

And finally, thanks to God and my wonderful family, without whom I would be nothing: my wife Ursula and my children Maya, Luna, Stella, and Noah.

# Contents

# Introduction

West German popular music from the late 1960s and early 1970s, commonly referred to as "krautrock" today, has had an astonishing renaissance in the last decade. Reissues of long out-of-print albums, eagerly anticipated live appearances by formerly obscure artists like Faust, and the ongoing references to bands like Kraftwerk, Can, and Neu! in the music of post-rock, indie, and electronica artists have prompted a renewed interest in musicians who deliberately operated outside the Anglo-American mainstream. However, this book is not an attempt to celebrate the essential Germanness of artists like Klaus Schulze or Amon Düül II. Instead, I investigate how national identity gets transformed when it has become impossible to defend (as in the case of post-Nazi Germany). As I argue throughout the book, krautrock represents a process in which the nation-state becomes deterritorialized, hybridized, and ironically inverted, as well as increasingly cosmopolitan, communal, and imbued with alternative spiritualities.

I situate krautrock within its particular context of national identity and globalization and address krautrock's intersections of transnational musical production and the reshaping of the globalization of US popular culture within this framework. Although it emerged with an emphasis on a specific white West German counterculture, krautrock's expressions of sonic identity proved to be varied and conflicted. The transnational focus of my analysis within the context of globalization demands a broader definition of the term *krautrock* that is inclusive of developments on the periphery of any German "mainstream," in particular in terms of gender, "race," and nationality. Therefore, unlike other accounts of the music, this book prominently features artists like Donna Summer and David Bowie.

Generally, krautrock is used as a catch-all term for the music of various white West German rock groups of the 1970s that blended influences of African American and Anglo-American music with the experimental and electronic music of European composers. Many krautrock bands arose out of the West German student counterculture and connected leftist political activism with experimental rock music and, later, electronic sounds. There are no precise dates for krautrock, and while the heyday of the movement was roughly from 1968 to 1974, one could also argue that it lasted well into the 1980s. Krautrock was primarily a West German art form and differed significantly from East German *Ostrock*, with the latter's emphasis on more traditional song structures. Krautrock and its offshoots have had a tremendous impact on musical production and reception in Great Britain and the United States since the 1970s. Genres such as indie, post-rock, techno, and hip-hop have drawn heavily on krautrock and have connected a music that initially disavowed its European American and African American origins with the lived experience of whites and blacks in the United States and Europe. At the same time, while reaching for an imagined cosmic community, krautrock, not only by its name, stirs up essentialist notions of national identity and citizenship.

Despite being frequently mentioned in magazines and on Internet blogs, krautrock continues to be a much-understudied topic among popular music scholars (a notable exception is a special issue of *Popular Music and Society* from December 2009). Apart from a few publications that merely list individual performers and bands, the only books about the topic available in English are David Stubbs's journalistic overview *Future Days: Krautrock and the Building of Modern Germany* (2014) and Nikos Kotsopoulos's coffee-table tome *Krautrock: Cosmic Rock and Its Legacy* (2010).[1] Both books offer many interesting details but not much in-depth analysis. Finally, there is Julian Cope's out-of-print *Krautrocksampler* (1996), a highly subjective account by a fellow musician and self-proclaimed fan.[2] Unfortunately, English-language accounts of krautrock by well-known musicians and journalists like Julian Cope and Lester Bangs oftentimes engage a fascination with what they perceive as the Germanness of the music as an exotic Other—for instance, although many krautrock musicians explicitly distanced themselves from the past, the Germany chapter in Jim DeRogatis's seminal book about psychedelic rock is entitled "The Krautrock Blitzkrieg."[3] The only two German-language monographs are journalist Henning Dedekind's meandering *Krautrock: Underground, LSD und kosmische Kuriere* (2008) and Alexander Simmeth's doctoral dissertation *Krautrock transnational* (2016).[4]

## Krautrock and Spatiality

I hesitate to call krautrock a "genre" or "movement" and would rather describe it as a "discursive formation" or a "field of cultural production." According to Michel Foucault, "the unity of a discourse is based not so much on the permanence and uniqueness of an object as on the space in which various objects emerge and are continuously transformed."[5] Foucault applies this instability of seemingly fixed systems of classification to medical science, economics, and grammar, but it also informs the fragmented relationships between different musical expressions discussed in this book under the contested term *krautrock*. Connected merely by their destabilizing of the seemingly coherent notion of national identity, krautrock musicians rarely worked with each other (or even knew of each other) and did not form local scenes that expressed larger issues in regional ways. Indicative of a discursive formation, "influences" on and by krautrock artists did not operate in linear ways, a central figure did not emerge, and even the term *krautrock* was only retroactively applied from outside Germany. For Foucault, discursive formations are an attempt to apply some regularity to "systems of dispersion" (like krautrock), to describe "series full of gaps, intertwined with one another, interplays of differences, distances, substitutions, transformations."[6] Unlike Foucault, Pierre Bourdieu locates economic power relations of cultural production outside discursive formations and prefers the term *field*. Viewed as a field of cultural production, krautrock requires an analysis that does not differentiate between its aesthetic value and social context, between its "internal" and "external" meanings.[7]

Rather than providing a purely musicological or historical account, I discuss krautrock as being constructed through performance, articulated through various forms of expressive culture (among them, communal living, spirituality, visual elements but, most importantly, sound) by people not even directly interacting with each other but still structurally related. This explains how krautrock succeeded through time and space and does not merely reflect historical events. Barry Shank has recently addressed the complex and dynamic relationship between music and identity in which real politics can emerge: "The act of musical listening enables us to confront complex and mobile structures of impermanent relationships—the sonic interweaving of tones and beats, upper harmonics, and contrasting timbres—that model the experience of belonging to a community not of unity but of difference."[8] Shank goes on state that, rather than reifying identity, musical forms help "capturing an emergent sense of the world."[9] While Shank's examples are mostly Anglo-American, krautrock serves to illustrate the transnational dimension of the politics he so aptly describes.

One of the weaknesses of current accounts of krautrock is that none of them engage any deeper analysis of krautrock's context of globalization. By employing a derogatory term for Germans in its name, krautrock is clearly linked with national identity, but, particularly in times of increased globalization, the nation-state appears as the mediator between the local and the global.[10] Scholars like Arjun Appadurai, Fredric Jameson, John Tomlinson, and Anthony Giddens have argued that globalization as a communicational concept works dialectically as both economic standardization and cultural pluralism.[11] "Creolization" (Hannerz), "indigenization" (Robertson), and "hybridization" (Canclini) are cultural processes that allow movements not just from the center to the periphery but also from the periphery back to the center.[12] My analysis follows Jonathan Xavier Inda and Renato Rosaldo's call for an anthropologically motivated study not just of what Gilles Deleuze and Félix Guattari have called "deterritorialization" but also of "reterritorialization," a relocalizing of culture in new or changed contexts.[13]

Néstor García Canclini describes the process of deterritorialization and reterritorialization as "the loss of the 'natural' relation of culture to geographical and social territories and, at the same time, certain relative, partial territorial relocalizations of old and new symbolic productions."[14] Canclini's context is 1990s Latin America, but with the disruption of World War II, krautrock artists also expressed a fragmented, porous transnational identity that, in Canclini's words, lacked "consistent paradigms" and experienced the loss of "the script and the author."[15] Krautrock's deterritorialization, its negation of the nation-state as a stable identifying force, plays with national identity through expressing an international or cosmic non-German Germanness and through ironically invoking older, seemingly stable forms of Germanness. The latter reterritorialization also involves non-German subjects identifying with a transformed and transmogrified Germanness as evidence of krautrock's "globalization."

In addition to deterritorialization, hybridization helps to understand the transnational dimension of krautrock. Despite critiques of biologism and the obviation of issues like class and gender, cultural hybridity can be useful for describing the exchanges that take place between the center and the periphery or between different peripheries.[16] Hybridity can function as a form of resistance but does not necessarily entail oppositional politics. Canclini warns of reducing the study of hybridized popular culture to either deductivist or inductivist notions, for example, assuming either that cultural production is exclusively determined by hegemonic sectors or that subaltern forces are solely responsible for shaping popular culture. As with the term "globalization," "hybridization" can be used in an inflationary way (after all, there are no "pure" cultures anyway). Yet when contrasted with essentialist forces, hybrid culture becomes more specific and identifiable. Krautrock's hybridity appears in a variety of ways, from the blurring of "man" and "machine" to linguistic slippages and syncretic spirituality.

It should not come as a surprise that the spatiality of popular music is one of the major factors that create its hybridity. As George Lipsitz has noted in describing a poetics of place:

> Recorded music travels from place to place, transcending physical and temporal barriers. It alters our understanding of the local and the immediate, making it possible for us to experience close contact with cultures from far away. Yet precisely because music travels, it also augments our appreciation of place. Commercial popular music demonstrates and dramatizes contrasts between places by calling attention to how people from different places create culture in different ways.[17]

Lipsitz's description of popular music as both transcending and reaffirming a sense of place applies to krautrock's double discourse of the national and the transnational. In a different approach, Josh Kun has developed the notion of "audiotopias," in which music itself appears as a spatial practice: "Music is experienced not only as sound that goes into our ears and vibrates through our bones but as a space that we can enter into, encounter, move around in, inhabit, be safe in, learn from."[18] One might add that as an alternative space, music is not always safe but disruptively appears in what Lipsitz calls "dangerous crossroads." Josh Kun goes on to argue that political citizenship does not necessarily equate cultural conformity, and that "music can be of a nation, but it is never exclusively national; it always overflows, spills out, sneaks through, reaches an ear on the other side of the border line, on the other side of the sea."[19]

It follows from the ability of music to transgress and trespass invoked by Kun and Lipsitz that the relationship between national identity and music is always interpenetrative.[20] In their seminal book on popular music, identity, and place, geographers John Connell and Chris Gibson talk about the contested enterprise of linking music and nation-states when "boundaries are porous, constantly being broken, necessitating new national anthems and new attempts to sustain imagined communities in the face of transnational flows."[21] I disagree with Connell and Gibson's assessment that national sounds are by definition "retrospective and nostalgic"[22] and want to show that unlike national anthems, krautrock allows for a more flexible expression of nationality that necessitates moving across borders, as well as questioning essentialist and fixed notions of what it means to be German.

## Germany after World War II

The impact of the Nazi era, not just on the generation that survived it but also on subsequent generations of Germans, cannot be overestimated. Initially devastated by the allied bombings, West Germany in particular recovered quickly and underwent a complex process of Americanization.[23] In the long run, the direct influence of US foreign policy through prescribed "denazification" proved much less successful than the influx of American popular culture, leading to what a character in Wim Wenders's film *Im Lauf der Zeit* (*Kings of the Road*, 1976) calls "colonizing the subconscious."[24] The 1950s youth movement, the *Halbstarken* (the "half strongs"), which was comprised of Americanized adolescents fed on rock'n'roll, chewing gum, and the films of Marlon Brando and James Dean, was an early example of this colonization. Instead of critically investigating their Nazi past, West Germans after World War II tended to focus on "economic recovery, social reconciliation, and rebuilding Germany's international standing."[25] While many former Nazis remained in powerful positions, the United States helped to sponsor the *Wirtschaftswunder* ("economic miracle") of the 1950s through the Marshall Plan, named after US secretary of state George Marshall, which provided 1.5 billion dollars for West Germany between 1948 and 1952. Yet Americanization always met structures of localization, and in some cases, as the belated success of some krautrock groups in the United States proves, West German culture was successfully exported and globalized. In addition, the proximity of East Germany with a cultural ideology from the opposite spectrum of the Cold War provided an ever-present alternative to the American model. Resistance against Americanization has taken shape in various forms of anti-Americanism, in particular in the late 1960s with protests against the Vietnam War.

The student protests that swept West Germany in the late 1960s had many commonalities with those in other industrialized Western countries (like the United States, France, and Great Britain) and those of the Prague Spring, but the Nazi past posed a specific challenge, oftentimes referred to by the problematic concept of *Vergangenheitsbewältigung* ("mastering of the past"). In psychological terms, it was not just the first generation that had survived the terror of National Socialism but also their children and grandchildren that would suffer from the trauma of the Third Reich, albeit in different ways.[26] Although many former Nazis had remained silent, the next generation began the slow process of coming to terms with the collective guilt of a wounded nation. The social movements of the late 1960s in West Germany or the *68er Generation* ("Generation of 1968") consisted of a number of different organizations and causes, among them higher education reform, mass media criticism, as well as protests against nuclear arms and the Vietnam War, all of which could be connected to a critique of fascism. Yet the actors in the transition from World War II to the *Wirtschaftswunder* of the 1950s to the protests of the 1960s cannot easily be separated into "Nazis" and their "children."[27]

The West German counterculture positioned itself as an agent in dealing with an unfinished Nazi past. It was propelled by the fatal shooting of student Benno Ohnesorg by a plainclothes police officer during a demonstration in West Berlin in 1967 and the passing of the *Notstandsgesetze* ("Emergency Laws") by a grand coalition of the two major political parties in 1968, which allowed for the curtailing of civil liberties in times of national crisis. These developments led to the founding of the Außerparlamentarische Opposition (APO, "Extra-Parliamentary Opposition") with prominent leaders like Rudi Dutschke, who was shot in 1968 by a right-wing extremist and seriously wounded, dying twelve years later.[28] Fueled by the theories of Theodor W. Adorno, Herbert Marcuse, and Antonio Gramsci, APO members aimed at radically breaking with fascist ideology.[29] Other groups like the Sozialistischer Deutscher Studentenbund (SDS, "German Socialist Student Union") pursued similar ideas. In their critique of authorities, mass media, and imperialist anticommunism and in their focus on critical thinking and participatory democracy, APO and SDS had long-term effects on West Germany's political culture. They influenced communes; the women's, gay liberation, and environmentalist movements; civil rights organizations; and support groups for ethnic minorities, but they also had ties to the terrorist organization Rote Armee Fraktion (RAF, "Red Army Faction"), which became notorious for violent activity in the 1970s.[30]

Although the social movements of the late 1960s brought intellectual challenges to West Germany, it should be noted that, as with the United States, rather than pursuing noble political ideals, the majority of the counterculture was much more interested in experimenting with recreational drugs and exploring sexuality, two areas that could be easily commodified. As Jakob Tanner has cheekily observed about West German hippies, "it was surprisingly easy to integrate the subcultural impulses into the universal spiral of commercialization which deepened consumer society and globalization under the banner of the American Dream."[31] Yet a specific, localized form of West German counterculture had begun to develop out of the rubble of World War II as well, and popular music was one of the most significant ways through which this counterculture was expressed.

## The Essen Song Days

In both drawing on and departing from standard Anglo-American rock music, krautrock positioned itself in the midst of debates about globalization and national identity right from its earliest appearance at the Essener Songtage (Essen Song Days). As the first public forum for krautrock, the Essen Song Days signaled the beginning of the music's history. They took place from September 25 to September 29, 1968, in the West German city of Essen, part of the industrial Ruhrgebiet (Ruhr region). The urban environment contrasted sharply with West Germany's earliest open-air festivals at rural Waldeck, which had taken place annually since 1964 and featured mainly singer-songwriters. The Essen Song Days were the first major pop festival in Europe with eight venues, forty-three events, more than two hundred musicians and an audience of forty thousand, and performances, among others, by international stars like Frank Zappa and the Mothers of Invention, the Fugs, and Alexis Korner, but also West German groups Amon Düül I, Tangerine Dream, and Guru Guru.[32] Main sponsor for the festival was the city of Essen's Department of Youth, which provided 300,000 Deutsche Mark for an event that, despite only paying the artists a per diem allowance, ended in a financial disaster with a loss of DM 80,000.[33] One of the reasons may have been the relatively low ticket prices of DM 3 to DM 7.

The Essen Song Days were organized by a team led by the eccentric Rolf-Ulrich Kaiser, a music journalist who later founded the krautrock labels Ohr and Kosmische Kuriere before suffering a mental breakdown and retreating from the scene. He was inspired by the Monterey Pop Festival of the previous year but wanted to mix pop and politics more overtly at Essen, invoking the New Left, quoting Herbert Marcuse in the booklet for the festival, and stating that "songs don't make a revolution but songs accompany revolutions."[34] In another article for the booklet, the cover for which showed a stylized version of the iconic image of Frank Zappa on the toilet, Kaiser talked about a "festival that is uncompromisingly open in particular to the political and social aspects of the new music," where "protest songs and new pop songs" catered to the "involved generation."[35] The transnational politics of the Essen Song Days were meant to blend Marcuse and Zappa in covering diverse aspects of a burgeoning counterculture.[36]

Despite some setbacks—Pink Floyd and Phil Ochs had to cancel, French musicians were invited but their union did not allow them to play for free, and musicians from the Soviet Union and Czechoslovakia were denied visas—the Essen Song Days represented "a key transnational moment of the late-sixties, signaling the birth of an international youth culture with popular music as its soundtrack."[37] While krautrock was featured at the festival, much of its political bent was more focused on direct action rather than musical experimentation. For instance, a banner calling for Americans to get out of Vietnam was put up behind the stage on the opening night. The Song Days also included a number of discussion panels and political theater by groups like Floh de Cologne and the Fugs. Finally, protesters who viewed the festival as a government ploy disrupted an event with Wilhelm Nieswandt, the mayor of Essen.

The krautrock groups that appeared at the Essen Song Days were less engaged with direct political action but arguably had a more profound impact through their deterritorialized sonic force, which would still reverberate decades later. Krautrock groups were prominently featured at two of the festival's events. The first was *Deutschland erwacht: Neue Popmusik aus Deutschland* ("Germany Awakes: New Pop Music from Germany") on Thursday at 3 p.m., repeated the following day at the same time. It showcased free jazz by Peter Brötzmann and Time Is Now, a group led by German Gunter Hampel but also featuring aspiring British fusion guitarist John McLaughlin. More importantly, the event premiered krautrock groups Amon Düül, Tangerine Dream, and Guru Guru (the latter still as "Guru Guru Groove"). Newspaper accounts varied but agreed on the extreme volume and a crowd of fewer than 300 national and international freaks and hippies.[38] Amon Düül's cacophonous jamming, Tangerine Dream's avant-garde experiments, and Guru Guru's psychedelic rock shocked and invigorated a small but devoted audience. The three groups returned, among many others, for the Saturday night event "Let's Take a Trip to Asnidi" (the title had been switched from the more overt drug reference "Hashnidi" to the city of Essen's medieval name). An audience of twelve thousand watched and danced to bands on two stages, accompanied by projections, stroboscopes, and underground films. The event lasted until 7 a.m. and was the first exposure of krautrock groups to a larger crowd.[39]

In the course of the following decade, krautrock became more varied than the music that Amon Düül, Tangerine Dream, and Guru Guru presented at the Essen Song Days and engaged with national identity and globalization in more complex ways, but, as Timothy Brown notes, "the Songtage helped solidify a new linkage between musical experimentation and cultural-political experimentation."[40] With the Essen Song Days, krautrock groups had found an audience, mostly West Germans who could be described as "the politically active and militant leftists, the peacefully stoned hippies, the curious middle-class liberals, adolescents fed up with their fathers' generation, musicians trying out new paths."[41] At the time, none of the German musicians performing at the Essen Song Days thought of their music as "krautrock," but it was the place-specific moniker that would retroactively define their careers.

## The Term *Krautrock*

Viewed as a genre, krautrock seemingly points to a specific national identity, but, as I will argue throughout this book, it continuously transgresses spatial borders and defies rigid classifications.[42] Historically, the term itself was only one among many describing West German popular music from the 1970s. Until about 1973, the music magazines *Musikexpress* and *Sounds* used *Deutsch-Rock* ("German Rock") to label the new groups from West Germany. The term *krautrock* was introduced by the British DJ John Peel and taken up by the British music press, which interchangeably also used other terms like *Teutonic rock* or *Götterdämmer rock*. The West German music press initially used *krautrock* as a term to dismiss specific artists. In an ironic move, the band Faust had already called the first song on their 1973 album *Faust IV* "Krautrock." Amon Düül had recorded a song called "Mama Düül und ihre Sauerkrautband spielt auf" ("Mama Düül is Playing with her Sauerkraut Band") back in 1969, but it should be noted that the German word *Kraut* is short for "sauerkraut" only in its English translation—in German it refers to, among other things, herbs, weeds, and even drugs. Although it has become fairly common to describe German popular music from the 1970s as krautrock, many performers associated with the music continue to reject the term, and it remains disputed to this day.

The positive spin on the term *krautrock* originated with the British music press. The publications *Melody Maker* and *New Musical Express* raved about West German bands, some of which, like Faust and Amon Düül II, became more successful in Great Britain than in their home country; Tangerine Dream's *Phaedra* even reached the UK Top Ten in 1973. As a consequence of krautrock's success in Great Britain, the term became more acceptable in West Germany. In 1974, the label Brain issued a triple-album compilation of West German music under the title *Kraut-Rock*. In his liner notes, Winfried Trenkler wrote: "Rock from the Federal Republic [of Germany] doesn't have to hide behind Anglo-American rock, in particular when German musicians don't even try to sound like their famous colleagues from the U.S.A. and England."[43] Since the 1990s, krautrock has been successfully rebranded as a genre in countries that include Germany and Great Britain, but also the United States and Japan. For instance, in April 1997, *Mojo* magazine ran a thirty-page special under the title "Kraftwerk, Can and the Return of the Krautrockers."

Another term commonly used for some German music from the 1970s is *kosmische Musik* ("cosmic music"). It was introduced by Rolf-Ulrich Kaiser to market krautrock artists like Ash Ra Tempel, Tangerine Dream, and Klaus Schulze. Although also rejected by many artists associated with it, *kosmische Musik* remains a somewhat useful term to describe the synthesizer-heavy, meditative anti-rock of some West German musicians of the 1970s. Like *krautrock*, the term has remained popular in particular with British music critics, who often simply abbreviate it as the grammatically incorrect *kosmische*.

Because of the music's hybridity, a musicological definition of the term *krautrock* is equally difficult than a semantic or historical definition. The influence of music traditionally perceived as German, such as the compositions of Bach, Beethoven, and Brahms, on what would evolve around 1968 as krautrock is negligible (the history of any distinctively "German" music mostly dates back to the nineteenth century and is more a product of writers and politicians than of classical composers[44]). Krautrock also stood in stark opposition to popular forms like *Volksmusik* ("people's music"), traditional regional styles mostly from Bavaria, or *Schlager* (literally "hit"), German-language pop songs with simple melodies and sentimental lyrics.[45] Finally, krautrock rejected heavily Anglo-Americanized or African American-derived forms of postwar popular music like the toned-down German-language rock'n'roll of Peter Kraus and the early 1960s German beat bands like the Rattles and the Lords.

Despite its rejection of Anglo-American influences, krautrock did pay tribute to some of the psychedelic rock bands and other countercultural artists from Great Britain and the United States, namely Pink Floyd, Frank Zappa, and Jimi Hendrix. Yet instead of merely developing another replication of the major Anglo-American and African American styles that dominated the airwaves, krautrock artists also drew from two distinctive musical developments that were outside mainstream rock's framework, both geographically and structurally: experimental composition and free jazz.

The Darmstadt Summer Courses, "instituted in 1946 to bring young Germans [ . . . ] up to date with music unheard under the Nazis,"[46] became increasingly international over the years and involved composers like Edgar Varèse, Karlheinz Stockhausen, and Pierre Boulez. The Darmstadt school's embrace of total serialism and resistance to neoclassicism foreshadowed many of krautrock's developments. Stockhausen, who taught two of the musicians who later founded the krautrock group Can, collaborated with the Studio for Electronic Music in Cologne as early as 1953 and began "sampling" and electronically manipulating non-Western music and national anthems in his compositions *Telemusik* (1966) and *Hymnen* (1966/1967). Another vital influence on krautrock clearly outside Anglo-American traditions were German free jazz musicians like Peter Brötzmann, Manfred Schoof, and Alexander von Schlippenbach, part of a central European (Scandinavian/German/Dutch) scene that was departing from the harmonic and rhythmic conventions still retained in American free jazz.

Sonically, krautrock came to encompass a range of styles, from the electronic music of Klaus Schulze and the jazz rock of Kraan to the political songs of Floh de Cologne, the folk rock of Witthüser & Westrupp, and music that is even harder to classify but had a long-lasting impact, like that of Faust, Cluster, or Popol Vuh. Krautrock was influenced by African American music but also involved the conscious departure from blues scales.[47] Unlike psychedelic rock groups in the United States, many krautrock performers had a background in European classical music and ties to the electronic music of "serious" composers. Krautrock's embrace of the dilettante, abstract, and experimental contrasted with British progressive rock's focus on composition and romantic themes. The early use of synthesizers, nontraditional song structures, and the employment of a steady, metronomic beat (generally referred to as *motorik*) instead of rock'n'roll's backbeat also set krautrock apart from Anglo-American music of the 1970s. Through their connections to the avant-garde art world, through their more intellectual approach, and through abandoning traditional song structures, krautrock bands were in some aspects more daring and radical than comparative groups in Great Britain and the United States like Pink Floyd, the Beatles, or the Beach Boys.

As the music scene in West Germany was flourishing in the 1970s, it became increasingly harder to make generalizations about krautrock. While many groups included classically trained musicians, diverted from the blues scales of American psychedelic rock groups like the Grateful Dead, released albums on small labels like Ohr, Pilz, and Brain, moved to the country to live in communes, and employed electronic instruments, none of these characteristics applied to all krautrockers. Among the many different and unconnected local scenes were Düsseldorf, with the slick electronics of Kraftwerk, Neu!, and Wolfgang Riechmann; Hamburg, with the experimental rock of Faust; Cologne, with the groove-heavy minimalism of Can; Munich, with the psychedelic progressive rock of Amon Düül II; and West Berlin, with the synthesizer drones of Klaus Schulze, Ash Ra Tempel, and Tangerine Dream. While I engage with each of these local scenes in this book, I do not discuss those German bands from the 1970s that were almost indistinguishable from their British and American counterparts. These bands included the internationally successful Scorpions, Nektar, and Triumvirat.

Krautrock was an exclusively West German phenomenon. To explain the absence of the music in East Germany, it is useful to consider the differences of the counterculture between East and West. Students in East Germany had more fundamental needs, which were expressed by singer-songwriters, many of whom were harassed or banned by the Communist government. Rock groups like the Puhdys mostly imitated British and American bands while adding German lyrics.[48] Since Marxism was part of the establishment in the East, many young people viewed the United States as a potential liberator, and there was not the same urge to reject Anglo-American and African American influences as in krautrock.[49] Jazz and rock were sought after as a "window to the West."[50] With the difficulty of obtaining and accessing music from Western countries, krautrock was also simply not big enough to make it over to East Germany. Despite the absence of krautrock in East Germany, understanding the divided nation is crucial for the politics of the music, in particular West Berlin groups like Tangerine Dream and Ton Steine Scherben, who were tied to West Germany ideologically but not geographically.

## Chapter Overview

This book consists of six chapters. I have chosen to focus on a number of major performers who represent specific themes particularly relevant for a discussion of national identity and globalization. The narrative moves from a broader application of the argument to a specific analysis of communal strategies and alternative spiritualities. After a brief excursion into cinematic representations, I turn the gaze from inward to outward by looking at musicians on the fringes and outside German national identity. I conclude by discussing the impact krautrock had as a transnational force on later developments. I am fully aware that, since this book is a critical study and not a popular history, there are a number of important krautrock performers whom I do not discuss at length and a number of popular anecdotes that I do not relate. A more comprehensive popular account of krautrock in English has yet to be published.

The first chapter introduces the major argument of the book by comparing the different ways the groups Can, Kraftwerk, and Neu! created a postwar German identity that engaged with and set itself apart from the Nazi past and the influx of Anglo-American music. Both Can and Kraftwerk employed technological inventions and blended man-made and machine-made music. Whereas Can was still a traditional rock formation and looked beyond Germany's borders for musical influences, Kraftwerk gradually became an all-electronic outfit and deliberately emphasized their seemingly distinct German heritage in a semi-ironic fashion. Through a critical engagement with consumer culture and advertising, Neu!'s mostly instrumental music signaled a forward movement and had transnational appeal. In their later work with Harmonia and La Düsseldorf, the musicians of Neu! turned to more specific localizations.

The second chapter connects the music of three krautrock bands to the history of communes and explores how notions of community and conflict, while responding to similar modes of oppression, were expressed in vastly different ways. Amon Düül came out of the highly politicized urban *Kommune 1* but espoused politics only indirectly in their psychedelic rock; Faust founded a rural avant-garde commune with the backing of a major record company and radically broke with popular music traditions; Ton Steine Scherben arose from West Berlin's squatter movement and expressed the most overt political agenda of the krautrock scene, an agenda that eventually also included gay rights.

The third chapter recounts the rise and fall of *kosmische Musik*. Performers like Ash Ra Tempel, Tangerine Dream, Klaus Schulze, and Popol Vuh helped to promote postnational notions of New Age cosmic identity, which involved the consumption of psychedelic drugs and the invention of new sounds, in particular through the employment of the synthesizer. Whereas Klaus Schulze's solo work involved a return to the national, Florian Fricke's work with Popol Vuh pushed the alternative spiritualities of *kosmische Musik*'s New Age approach toward a redefined Christianity.

Engaging closer with the visual aspects of the music, the fourth chapter turns to parallels between krautrock and the New German Cinema of the 1970s and discusses the connections between the landscapes of Werner Herzog's highly acclaimed films and the soundscapes provided by the krautrock group Popol Vuh. The failings of colonialism, the ecstatic experience of nature as culture, and the reimagining of the national as the universal in Herzog's *Aguirre (The Wrath of God)*, *Fitzcarraldo*, and *Nosferatu* were augmented by Popol Vuh's soundtracks to these films and reveal more general trends in West German postwar artistic expression.

In the fifth chapter, I discuss Italian-German producer Giorgio Moroder's collaborations with African American soul singer Donna Summer as well as the three years British pop star David Bowie spent in West Berlin in the 1970s. Despite a similar experimentation with synthesizer-generated sounds to that of many krautrock groups, Summer and Moroder are generally labeled as disco, and their connections to German national identity are deemphasized. Challenging narrow confines of proper Germanness in terms of gender, race, and sexuality, songs like "Love to Love You Baby" and "I Feel Love" can help to foster a transnational and less phallocentric understanding of krautrock. David Bowie's "Berlin Trilogy" also engaged with krautrock's latent queerness. Bowie's preconceived notions of 1920s and 1930s Germany were replaced by the reality of 1970s West Berlin, and its fragmented identity was expressed on the albums *Low*, *"Heroes"*, and *Lodger*.

The last chapter traces some of krautrock's national and transnational impact. The short-lived but massively successful *Neue Deutsche Welle*, new wave and post-punk from the early 1980s, continued some of krautrock's trends but more narrowly focused on German themes and lyrics. Subsequently, NDW was quickly commodified and had only minor long-term effects outside West Germany. Meanwhile, krautrock was picked up by post-rock, hip-hop, and electronica artists. Most striking was the renewed interest in West German music from the 1970s among American indie rock communities. The popular music webzine *Pitchfork Media* exemplifies the rearticulation and reappropriation of German transnational identity by writers and fans culturally removed from its origins.

# 1 A Musical *Stunde Null*

## The Recordings of Can, Kraftwerk, and Neu!

Asked about influential krautrock bands, many contemporary critics and fans would agree that three names top the list: Can, Kraftwerk, and Neu!. For instance, in 2004 the widely read music webzine *Pitchfork Media* included six albums by the three groups in their "Top 100 Albums of the 1970s." In many ways representative of krautrock, Can, Kraftwerk, and Neu! envisioned a reterritorialized postwar German identity that both engaged with and set itself apart from the Nazi past and the influx of Anglo-American music. As West Germany had lost its political foundation and was looking ahead by embracing consumer culture, Neu! signaled forward movement by ironically invoking a commodified "newness" and by daring to leave their music sounding as unfinished as German identity after World War II, a time period sometimes referred to as *Stunde Null* ("Zero Hour").[1] For Neu!, Can, and Kraftwerk, a new German identity was explicitly connected to playing around with technological inventions and hybridizing man-made and machine-made music. All three bands strove to gain control over their musical production, album art, and tour schedules in order to make art that reflected an unstable national identity.

However, there were also significant differences in the way Can, Kraftwerk, and Neu! articulated Germanness. Can, whose creative peak years were from 1968 to 1974, were a standard rock formation (drums/bass/guitar/keyboards/vocals) and looked beyond Germany's borders for musical influences. Kraftwerk, on the other hand, had their creative peak years from 1974 to 1983, after krautrock proper, gradually became an all-electronic outfit, and deliberately emphasized their seemingly distinct German heritage in a semi-ironic fashion. Finally, Neu!, who began as an offshoot from Kraftwerk, also captured a specific West German zeitgeist but more directly expressed a critique of consumer capitalism. In their later work, Neu!'s two musicians, Michael Rother and Klaus Dinger, turned to a more specific localization: Rother with Hans-Joachim Roedelius and Dieter Moebius of Cluster in the krautrock "supergroup" Harmonia and later on his solo albums, Dinger with the band La Düsseldorf, which, in contrast to Rother's pastoral music and his embrace of rural northern Germany, celebrated the city of Düsseldorf as the harbinger of new wave globalization.

## Can

In an interview, Can keyboarder Irmin Schmidt stated: "We come from a generation that, when beginning to notice art, was standing in a pile of rubble in a country whose entire culture looked like the cities: destroyed, discontinued."[2] Schmidt also called Can a "band of 1968" to emphasize their connection to the student demonstrations in Paris.[3] Can was, in fact, formed in 1968 in Cologne and belonged to a group of early krautrock pioneers that also included Tangerine Dream, Guru Guru, and Xhol Caravan. At its core an instrumental outfit, the band worked with different singers over the years. The four key members of Can, with the exception of guitarist Michael Karoli, were no traditional rock musicians. Irmin Schmidt (born 1937) had studied music with Karlheinz Stockhausen and György Ligeti and had worked as a piano teacher and conductor. His innovative keyboard technique included rapid-fire karate chops. Holger Czukay (born 1938 as Holger Schüring) had also studied with Stockhausen. He reduced his bass playing to simple runs but also edited the music of the band after and even while it was being recorded and added other sounds from radios and tapes to the mix. Michael Karoli (born 1948) might have been the most conventional rock musician in the band, but he made his Stratocaster sound like a violin, integrated his solos well into the overall structure, and did not dominate the sound like other rock guitar players. Finally, Jaki Liebezeit (born 1938) had a background as a free jazz drummer but returned to repetitive rhythms for Can ("I was a living loop," he said in an interview[4]), using his drums as a melodic instrument, playing a motorik beat with subtle variations, and generally inventing a new rhythm for each Can song.

Can recorded their first album *Monster Movie* (1968) with the African American sculptor and singer Malcolm Mooney (born 1944), whom Irmin

Schmidt had met in Paris. Mooney's improvised singing, in which he drew on nursery rhymes ("Mary Mary, So Contrary") and a letter from his girl-friend ("You Doo Right"), was influenced by rhythm and blues and inter-locked with Jaki Liebezeit's hypnotic beats. On their first album, Can already worked with their concept of what Irmin Schmidt has called "spon-taneous or collective composition"[5] (rather than "improvisation"), creating songs on the spot but giving them a clear structure, remixing them, and adding overdubs later on. Holger Czukay has described a major difference between Can's collective compositions and a more jazz-derived form of improvisation:

> Most of the bands I know that improvise, if at all, follow a certain pattern. You hear exactly which direction they're going in and it's very consistent. Then they get to a point where they have the chance to destroy every-thing and develop completely new ideas. But at this exact point, which is so crucial, almost all groups go back to the theme! It's all over right there. What's different about us compared to almost all other bands is that at that point we keep playing.[6]

Because the overall sound of the group was more important than its indi-vidual parts, Czukay also referred to Can as an "orchestra" rather than as a "band" and compared their musical approach to passing the ball in soccer.[7] David Stubbs describes Can's collective spirit, which extended to royalties being distributed evenly among the band members, as a conscious move away from fascism and quotes Jaki Liebezeit saying that Can deliberately had no "*Führer.*"[8]

An important aspect of Can's sound concept was their approach to tech-nology. *Monster Movie*, like most of the band's albums, was not recorded in a conventional studio but live in Schloss Nörvenich, an old castle the band had permission to use (they would later set up their own Inner Space Studio in an abandoned movie theater). The recording equipment consisted only of two stereo tape decks, four microphones, two small speakers, and a few mal-functioning amplifiers, in addition to the band's instruments. Can's inven-tiveness and unusual production methods made up for their lack of funding, which was also true for later recordings by the band. As Holger Czukay explained: "If there's a lot to do, I play short notes or an empty string, so I can turn a few knobs during the break. If the soundboard requires a lot of work, I slam the strings every four bars, so I can regulate the sound in the remaining bars. That way we can do without a sound engineer."[9] Because Can could not attract a record label, they initially released *Monster Movie* on their own with only 500 copies. When the album sold well, it was picked up by Liberty Records.

Malcolm Mooney had to leave the band shortly after recording *Monster Movie* because of his mental instability and returned to the United States. Can's second album, *Soundtracks* (1970), featured the music for TV and movie productions with which the band financed their other music. It still had Mooney singing on two tracks (one of them Can's most conventional song, the melodious "She Brings the Rain") but also introduced their new vocalist Kenji "Damo" Suzuki (born 1950), a Japanese hippie Holger Czukay and Jaki Liebezeit had encountered busking in Munich and hired on the spot as their new lead singer. Whereas Mooney's singing had a rhythmic, earthy quality, Suzuki's approach was more melodic and "spacey" and interlocked with Michael Karoli's breezy guitar riffs. This could be evidenced on *Soundtracks'* epic "Mother Sky," a song that disrupted the psychedelic rock narrative by starting with the climax instead of ending with it. Irmin Schmidt called Mooney a "vocalizing drumkit" and Suzuki an "inventor of melodies."[10] Karoli added: "The sound of the band altered, from a group that had a screaming singer to one that had a whispering singer."[11]

Damo Suzuki's lyrics, an occasionally incomprehensible mix of English, Japanese, and invented languages, were rich with linguistic slippages and further removed Can's sound from African American influences.[12] The odds-and-ends compilation album *Unlimited Edition* (1976) revealed that, as early as 1968, Can had dabbled in Vietnamese, North African, and Spanish flamenco music, and they would continue experimenting with what was later called "world music" until they disbanded. Some of these experiments were released as numbered pieces of the humorously titled "EFS," the "Ethnological Forgery Series" (including New Orleans jazz, various forms of aforementioned world music, and even a version of Jacques Offenbach's "Can Can"). Holger Czukay stated: "We never came off as particularly German. We focused more on international music scenes."[13] Can's deterritorialized, international approach was reflected in their English band name and song titles, their Japanese lead singer, and their early touring and success in Great Britain, but in many ways the core band members were responding to a specific demand to create a more multicultural German identity against the mainstream of Americanization after World War II. This multicultural identity was far from stable, as it brought "international" elements in conflict with the band's Germanness. Irmin Schmidt noted: "We didn't want to pretend we were born in Nashville, Memphis, Brooklyn, or Manchester when we were really from Berlin, Munich, or Straubing."[14] The self-reflexivity of the "EFS" recordings was a testament to Can's critique of authenticity, whether this notion was rooted in German classical music or world music.

Can recorded their three most important albums with Damo Suzuki as their lead singer: *Tago Mago* (1971), *Ege Bamyasi* (1972), and *Future Days* (1973). Named after a privately owned island close to Ibiza, *Tago Mago* was a double album and, with a reference to Satanist Aleister Crowley (on "Aumgn"), Suzuki's cryptic lyrics, and more radical sound experiments than on earlier recordings, presented the group as shrouded in magic and mystery. The album cover, which depicted one orange and one green silhouette of a man with an oversized brain and a speech bubble or smoke with brain tissue emanating from the mouth, could be interpreted as a drug reference. The song "Mushroom," with the line "when I saw mushroom head I was born and I was dead," could be as well but, with its detonation at the end, could also have been a reference to the atom bomb. "Mushroom" was one of the three somewhat more conventional songs on the album's first side, which also included the enigmatic "Oh Yeah" with backwards vocals and some Japanese lyrics by Damo Suzuki. The song "Halleluwah" made up all of side two. It consisted of rhythm samples by Jaki Liebezeit and elaborate editing by Holger Czukay, who treated the track like a movie, with fade-ins, fade-outs, and cross-fades. Side three and four of *Tago Mago* featured highly experimental pieces the band came up with in between recording the songs for the first record. On "Aumgn," one could hear Irmin Schmidt trashing a chair and imitating Japanese gagaku singers in a slowed-down voice, a dog accidentally coming in and barking, and Holger Czukay righting a fallen microphone stand and adjusting the vocal. "Peking O" had Damo Suzuki shouting gibberish over electronic drums. Only the closing song "Bring Me Coffee or Bring Me Tea" returned to a somewhat more traditional structure.

Can's radical experimentation and departure from rock structures continued on their next album. *Ege Bamyasi* took its name and self-referential pop art cover from a Turkish can of okra (signaling a non-Western response to Andy Warhol's Campbell's soup cans). Side one opened with a fade-in of Jaki Liebezeit playing Afro-Cuban percussion on another "instant composition," the hectic avant-garde funk of "Pinch," over nine minutes long and largely absent of melody. Damo Suzuki's incomprehensible spoken-word delivery was interjected with a slide whistle and splashes of keyboards and guitar feedback. In contrast, the acoustic-guitar-driven "Sing Swan Song" was slower and hypnotic, and "One More Night" featured a 7/4 beat with minimalist, interlocking bass and drums and whispered vocals added on top. Side two was equally experimental, beginning with "Vitamin C," dominated by drums and a bass ostinato and occasionally erupting into Suzuki shouting the cryptic line: "Hey you, you're losing, you're losing, you're losing, you're losing your vitamin C!" "Soup" began similar to "Pinch" but after five minutes dissolved into another four minutes of overdriven keyboards and call-and-response patterns between drums and vocal shrieks. *Ege Bamyasi* closed with two shorter and more conventional songs. The hit single "Spoon," which incorporated a drum machine and had a verse-chorus structure, reached number six on the German charts after it had been used for the soundtrack of a TV movie. Yet, the commercial potential of even this song was less pronounced than its experimentation with sound.

*Ege Bamyasi* was followed by *Future Days*, which Can recorded after a four-week vacation to southern Europe. The album, which featured the I Ching symbol of the cauldron on the cover, had a laid-back, ambient feel and contained only four songs. It opened with the title track on which syncopated drumming emerged out of white noise, with flourishes of jazz guitar, single-note bass, and "lead" vocals that were buried deep in the mix. "Future Days" segued into the aptly titled "Spray," which, as many of Can's songs, placed drums and percussion squarely in the foreground. The track also featured Irmin Schmidt's tone clusters and only allowed vocals and guitar, standard rock's central elements, to appear at the end. *Future Days'* first side ended with the tight groove of "Moonshake," which consisted of sixteenth notes on the drums and a two-note figure on the bass. With a length of three minutes and the resemblance of lead vocals, the song almost had a rock format, but the featured "solo" consisted of off-kilter keyboard and percussion sounds. "Bel Air," the twenty-minute atmospheric soundscape of side two, began with a reggae rhythm and slowly increased in tempo, started off twice more with heavily layered drums, returned to the first part and again slowly increased in tempo before fizzling out altogether except for a short reprise.

In addition to Can's incorporation of non-Western musical styles and highly experimental elements, it was their engagement with technology that helped to create their unique sound. The emphasis on Western technology created a deliberate conflict with the group's world music sound. For Can, technology was not a means to control the music but rather another mode of experimentation. Long before it became common practice, Can were remixing their own music (as when they used the same bass line for different songs in their live performances, for which they radically revised their recorded repertoire). Mixing and editing were hugely important for Can's recorded output. Holger Czukay remarked: "You play for the machines in the studio, and the machines really like to listen. They have a heart and a soul; they are living beings."[15] Can's engagement with technology would later be echoed by Kraftwerk's concept of the "man-machine" hybrid, and Irmin Schmidt's comment that "our music was sandwiched somewhere between organic and machine-made"[16] also applied to the band from Düsseldorf. The major difference would be that Kraftwerk claimed to happily let the machines take over, whereas Holger Czukay held on to some concept of authorial intention when he warned: "I love machines but they should never get the upper hand."[17]

After Damo Suzuki's departure to become a Jehovah's Witness, Can unsuccessfully tried out different singers. *Soon Over Babaluma* (1974), *Landed* (1975), and *Flow Motion* (1976) featured Michael Karoli and Irmin Schmidt trading off vocals, which echoed some of Suzuki's linguistic slippages and vocal experimentation. *Soon Over Babaluma* introduced Michael Karoli's fiery violin playing and was the last album the band recorded without a multitracking machine. Different group members have admitted that the more advanced technology ruined the concept of "instant composition." *Landed* occasionally sounded like glam rock (as on the opener "Full Moon on the Highway") but also included the two-chord jam "Vernal Equinox" and the lengthy, improvisational "Unfinished" that covered all of side two. *Flow Motion* contained the surprise disco hit "I Want More," which Can even performed to the prerecorded track on the British chart show *Top of the Pops* (the performativity of this event was underscored when a roadie for the band took Michael Karoli's place). This commercial success coincided with the band's final and least experimental phase, as they had settled for a mix of reggae, Latin rock à la Santana, and progressive rock, which they continued on their following three albums.

*Saw Delight* (1977), *Out of Reach* (1978), and *Can* (1979) saw Holger Czu–

kay gradually retreating. He still participated by editing and "playing" the radio, which meant that he provided ready-made samples. Czukay's contributions were not only prefiguring later DJ techniques but were also in remarkable unison with Kraftwerk's fascination for the radio as an acoustic man-machine. When Czukay gave up playing bass for the band, they added former Traffic members Rosko Gee from Jamaica (bass guitar, vocals) and Rebop Kwaku Baah from Ghana (percussion, vocals). While more overtly infusing their sound with world music, the group largely abandoned the radical sound experiments of their earlier records. Can consequently disbanded, only to get together once more in 1989 for the album *Rite Time*, with Malcolm Mooney on vocals. Michael Karoli died in 2001, making another reunion of the band unlikely.

Traces of Can's music could be heard most clearly on the post-rock albums of Public Image Limited, Sonic Youth, the Fall (who even recorded a song entitled "I Am Damo Suzuki"), and Tortoise. Their impact on electronic music was acknowledged by the artists who remixed Can songs for the 1997 double CD *Sacrilege*, but their approach to sound also foreshadowed the works of Brian Eno, the Orb, and Bill Laswell. Can's impact even extended to mainstream hip-hop when Kanye West sampled their "Sing Swan Song" for his 2007 track "Drunk and Hot Girls."

Can were not the only krautrock artists whose search for an alternative to both European classical music and Anglo-American rock made them seek out international connections. Embryo, Agitation Free, and Popol Vuh drew from Indian and North African traditions; groups like Nektar, Xhol Caravan, and Amon Düül II featured British and American musicians; Tangerine Dream and Klaus Schulze initially had more success in France than in their home country. Much of krautrock's transnationalism was a response to the impossibility of defending German national identity after World War II. With their non-German lead singers, their English name, and their interest in a border-crossing, cosmopolitan, but also unfinished and conflicted soundscape, Can epitomized one approach to address a problematic past. Another major krautrock group, Kraftwerk, represented a different approach.

## Kraftwerk

Kraftwerk was formed in 1970 in Düsseldorf by two students of classical music, Ralf Hütter (born 1946) and Florian Schneider-Esleben (born 1947), who later dropped the second part of his last name. The two multi-instrumentalists recorded the fairly typical krautrock album *Tone Float* under the name Organisation before switching to the German name Kraftwerk ("power plant"), using German titles for their songs and albums, and finally even singing in German. As Hütter recalled:

> There was really no German culture after the war. Everyone was rebuilding their homes and getting their little Volkswagens. In the clubs when we first started playing, you never heard a German record, you switched on the radio and all you heard was Anglo-American music, you went to the cinema and all the films were Italian and French. That's okay but we needed our own cultural identity.[18]

The group's first two albums, simply titled *Kraftwerk* (1970) and *Kraftwerk 2* (1972), were sprawling electronic experiments and sounded more like Can's music than the succinct and meticulously crafted songs the band later became famous for. At the same time, Kraftwerk's early music did have some machine-like qualities, such as the staccato rhythm of the flute on "Ruck-zuck" ("Very Quickly") and the use of electronic percussion, which was unusual for the time.[19] For *Ralf und Florian* (1973), Hütter and Schneider tightened their sound and began to highlight nonorganic elements of their music even more, in particular for the electro pop of "Tanzmusik" ("Dance Music"). They also introduced vocoder-generated lyrics on "Ananas Symphonie" ("Pineapple Symphony").

Although Florian Schneider's processed flute had dominated much of Kraftwerk's early music, both Schneider and Hütter eventually settled for keyboards and synthesizers as their preferred instruments. Influenced by Karlheinz Stockhausen and other pioneers of electronic music, and by *musique concrète*, Kraftwerk gradually became an all-electronic group without relinquishing romantic elements in their music. A number of "organic" musicians passed through the band in their earlier years, including Michael Rother (electric guitar) and Klaus Dinger (drums), who left to form Neu!. They eventually made way for two electronic percussionists, Wolfgang Flür (born 1947) and Karl Bartos (born 1952). Kraftwerk used their Kling Klang Studio in Düsseldorf as a laboratory to invent new instruments and sounds. The band members also talked about "playing the studio" and "taking the studio on tour." Like Can's Inner Space Studio, Kling Klang was the key for developing Kraftwerk's unique sound. Collaborator Maxime Schmitt described Kraftwerk's studio work the following way:

> Often, they would all sit behind the console, letting the machines run by themselves for one or two hours, the sequencers, everything. From time to time Florian would stand up and go to another machine and start or launch another sequence. It was almost closer to a traditional jam session than to studio work. The following day they would listen back to the tape.[20]

Kraftwerk's manufactured jam sessions, as Schmitt described them, make for an interesting comparison with Can's "instant compositions." Despite some significant differences, like Kraftwerk's reliance on the multitrack recording techniques that hindered Can's creativity, both groups had the freedom and time to work in their own studios and develop spontaneity in their conversations between man and machine.

Kraftwerk released their breakthrough album *Autobahn* in 1974. The title track was over twenty-two minutes long, but, in contrast to the symphonic rock of groups like Yes and King Crimson, it was flat, straightforward, and simple. The song "Autobahn" was intended to aurally evoke driving on a German freeway and included electronic simulations of honking, speeding, and a car radio. Emil Schult's cover art depicted an autobahn with two German cars representing different class backgrounds—a Volkswagen Beetle and a Mercedes. In a similar way, the song "Autobahn" emphasized Kraftwerk's national identity.[21] It contained German-language lyrics, notably the chorus "wir fahr'n, fahr'n, fahr'n auf der Autobahn" ("we are driving on the freeway"), which was influenced by the Dadaist poetry of Kurt Schwitters but also reminded some listeners of the Beach Boys song "Fun, Fun, Fun." The Beach Boys sang about driving as well ("she'll have fun, fun, fun 'til her daddy takes the T-Bird away"), but for them, as for other American artists like Chuck Berry and Bruce Springsteen, cars symbolized freedom, independence, and excitement, whereas "'Autobahn' reflected the connection between the concrete monotony of the highway and daily life."[22] John T. Littlejohn has juxtaposed Kraftwerk and the Beach Boys in terms of their respective nationalities, "a German, largely classically trained experimental band *vis-à-vis* the archetypal American pop group."[23]

*Autobahn* was the first Kraftwerk album that established the group as a conceptual band or as a *Gesamtkunstwerk* (total artwork), similar to other pop groups who strove for a uniform image, like the Beach Boys, Kiss, or the Ramones. In his memoir *I Was a Robot*, Kraftwerk drummer Wolfgang Flür remembered how at the time of *Autobahn*, the band deliberately chose an "austere, extremely German image," cut their hair, and bought matching 1950s-style suits.[24] Ralf Hütter told his bandmates to refrain from moving around on stage, which would eventually lead to the robotic image of the *Man Machine* album. Like another *Gesamtkunstwerk* artist, Andy Warhol, Hütter made deliberately provocative statements in interviews to perfect Kraftwerk's image:

> We cannot deny we are from Germany, because the German mentality, which is more advanced, will always be part of our behavior. We create out of the German language, the mother language, which is very mechanical, we use as the basic structure for our music. Also the machines, from the industries of Germany.[25]

Some of these comments might suggest that Kraftwerk were toying with Nazi imagery, but Hütter has said elsewhere: "Our roots were in the culture that was stopped by Hitler; the school of Bauhaus, German Expressionism."[26] Incidentally, Ralf Hütter has made sweeping generalizations about German identity mostly in his interviews in English, furthered by his limited command of the language and by his interest in marketing the band internationally and by displaying a subtle humor that was also present in Kraftwerk's music. In contrast, in his interviews in German, Hütter has tended to speak less about Germany and has presented more balanced ideas.[27]

*Autobahn* did not take the *Gesamtkunstwerk* all the way—side two of the album, with its experimental, instrumental tracks, sounded much more like earlier Kraftwerk recordings. The album closed with the ambiguous "Morgenspaziergang" ("Morning Stroll"), which combined electronic bleeps with a simple melody played on a recorder to indicate a conflict between tradition and modernity that became part of Kraftwerk's appeal. *Autobahn* was a monumental success for the band. An edited version of the title track made it to number twenty-five on the Billboard charts, and the album eventually reached number five in the United States. In the wake of this success, Kraftwerk also became more popular in Great Britain and in Germany. The band immediately tried to replicate their success with the album *Radio Activ-*

*ity* (1975), which was based on both the concept of the radio (introduced by the car radio on "Autobahn") and the concept of radioactivity. The duality of the radio and radioactivity destabilized the notion of the *Gesamtkunstwerk*, as did the lyrics in both German and English. Subsequently, the album failed to make a dent in the German and US charts, although it did make a surprising appearance at the top spot in France. The band, usually very careful in crafting their image, took some missteps by featuring a short-wave radio developed by Joseph Goebbels on the cover and by seemingly endorsing nuclear energy on the title track ("radioactivity is in the air for you and me"). They also circulated a promotional picture taken at a nuclear power plant at a time when West Germany's environmentalist movement was gaining strength. To clarify their position, Kraftwerk changed the lyrics to "stop radioactivity" in a later remix of their song and referenced nuclear disasters in Harrisburg, Sellafield, Hiroshima, and Chernobyl. Conflicts over Kraftwerk's seemingly obvious messages (which could just as easily be retracted) revealed how unstable their German identity actually was.

In 1975, Kraftwerk toured the United States for three months and returned to Germany with a new European outlook to begin recording *Trans Europe Express* (1977), the first of a number of albums that were released as German and English editions, and the second that was about means of transportation (after cars and trains, Kraftwerk would turn to bicycles for *Tour de France Soundtracks*). The title track "Trans Europe Express," with its memorable fourteen-note melody, had many parallels to "Autobahn" and was the electronic simulation of a train ride, through tunnels and over mountains. In this context, John T. Littlejohn has argued: "By changing its lyrics, language, and form in a bid for commercial success, Kraftwerk turned its back on its national identity."[28] Yet, while Kraftwerk strove to become a European and eventually a global band, references to "Franz Schubert" (song title) and Fritz Lang (on "Metropolis"), their overall appearance as "very business-like, with the group being very tidy and technically precise with their machines,"[29] and their thick German accents contributed to their appeal as exoticized Germans in a similar way as that of another, more contemporary German band, Rammstein. As Florian Schneider pointed out, Kraftwerk were not singers "like Rod Stewart," and their linguistic heritage complemented their original sound: "Our music is derived from the feeling of our language. Our method of speaking is interrupted, hard-edged if you want; a lot of consonants and noises."[30] Kraftwerk's habitus, presented both visually and aurally, revealed a deep-seated conflict between German and European identities, between the national and the global.

The uneasy hybridity Kraftwerk created in striving to be both German and European was matched by the uneasy hybridity of the man-machine. The group had introduced the theme of "living" machines in their songs about cars, trains, and radios, and on later songs they would sing in a similar way about other technological inventions, namely telephones, computers, pocket calculators, and bicycles. These machines could be "servant and lord at the same time," as they pointed out on _Radio Activity_'s "The Voice of Energy." Two songs from _Trans Europe Express_ connected the "man machine" concept with the doppelgänger motif of German Romanticism. "Hall of Mirrors" described a narcissistic artist falling in love with and eventually becoming his looking glass image; "Showroom Dummies" depicted the band as inanimate dolls that come alive, break through the (looking) glass, and go dancing in a club. For Ralf Hütter, the ultimate "man machine" must have been the synthesizer, which he called an "acoustic mirror"[31] and which could make anybody sound like Franz Schubert.

Consequently, Kraftwerk's next album was called _The Man Machine_ (1978). It continued the themes introduced on earlier albums on the title track, on "The Model" (a number one hit in Great Britain in 1982), and on "The Robots," on which they declared: "We're functioning automatic / and we are dancing mechanic / we are the robots." Kraftwerk had further refined their synthesizer sound, had listened to African American musicians like James Brown and George Clinton, and now created intentionally danceable and internationally viable music. Visually, the new robot image was supported by the red-and-black album cover by Karl Klefisch, which, influenced by the 1920s poster art of El Lissitzky, depicted the band members gazing eastward and wearing red (instead of brown) shirts, so that the connection was with Soviet communism, not National Socialism. Ralf Hütter explained that the word "robot" referred to the Russian word _работник_ (_rabotnik_), which literally means "worker." Kraftwerk consequently were not so much artists as musical workers: "We work a lot. We all meet in the morning at the Kling Klang studio and we stay there throughout the day. We improvise and create new pieces. The very clean atmosphere of the city still stimulates us."[32] Kraftwerk added another visual element to their _Gesamtkunstwerk_ with the mannequins they had made of themselves in 1978 (actual robots would follow in 1991). The mannequins replaced the band onstage for the song "The Robots" and for some press conferences, so that Kraftwerk could poke fun at the formulaic questions of reporters. For a concert in Italy, the band bought the dummies front row tickets and, according to Ralf Hütter, "they were quite pleased with our performance."[33]

After the German concept of *Autobahn* and the European concept of *Trans Europe Express*, *The Man Machine* was a global album, but Kraftwerk were still playing with stereotypes of Germans as robotic automatons. The album cover displayed the title in English, French, and Russian, but on the back the band proudly proclaimed in capital letters that *The Man Machine* was "produced in Germany." Kraftwerk continued their globalized strategy on *Computer World* (1981), which was rhythmically more intense than its predecessors and was released in German, English, French, and Japanese editions. Nonetheless, Ralf Hütter maintained: "We have a Teutonic rhythm, really Germanic."[34] The vocoder voice of the title track discussed surveillance in the time of unnamed terrorism (possibly influenced by the fear of attacks by the Red Army Faction): "Interpol and Deutsche Bank, FBI and Scotland Yard / crime, travel, communication, entertainment / computer world." These lyrics were about globalization but, more particularly, German participation in globalization. Another song on *Computer World*, "Computer Love," foreshadowed the age of cybersex and online dating. As Florian Schneider quipped: "We love our machines. We have an erotic relationship with them."[35] In interviews, Ralf Hütter claimed that using synthesizers was a more contemporary way of music-making since "the guitar is an instrument from the Middle Ages."[36] Hütter emphasized his post-rock attitude by making fun of the "gymnastic exercise" of a drum solo and claiming that rock music was a "fascist art form," whereas Kraftwerk were making *elektronische Volksmusik* ("electronic folk music").[37]

Ralf Hütter's rejection of virtuoso musicianship pointed to Kraftwerk's complex gender politics. On the one hand, the group's mastery of technology was traditionally male and stood in contrast to Can's and Neu!'s deliberately dilettante approaches. On the other hand, as David Buckley notes:

It was Kraftwerk—suited like posh bank managers, barely moving on stage, dealing with any sexual themes (if they arose at all) in a totally detached manner—who were the real slayers of cock rock, not the punks. This was music with no guitars at all, no indebtedness to the blues, no appeal to any of the basic motivations behind so much pop music as to who to love and, essentially, no frontman for the audience to identify with. This was [ . . . ] a complete theoretical annihilation of most of the precedents and tenets on which modern rock music was based.[38]

Kraftwerk's disembodied and asexual stage presence and music inherently questioned heterosexist rock traditions. In a US context, this queering of rock simply appeared "gay." For instance, in the "Sprockets" skits that aired on American comedy show *Saturday Night Live* between 1989 and 1997, Mike Myers as Dieter played up to US stereotypes of Germans through his effeminate behavior, black turtleneck sweater, wire-rimmed glasses, and jerky dance moves, which were accompanied by Kraftwerk's "Electric Café," played at 45 instead of 33 RPM for comic effect.

After *Computer World*, Kraftwerk's work pace slowed down significantly, but the group continued their transnational politics. They released a twelve-inch single about cycling in 1983. "Tour de France" featured French lyrics and an album cover in red, white, and blue, the colors of the French flag (and, incidentally, the American flag). Kraftwerk made another album, *Electric Cafe* (originally titled *Technopop*) in 1986. Instead of releasing a greatest hits album, Kraftwerk remixed some of their own songs, resulting in the album *The Mix* (1991). Becoming more and more reclusive, the group toured very infrequently, rarely gave interviews, and only released a jingle for the world exposition "Expo 2000," which took place in Hanover, Germany, and was a financial debacle. Kraftwerk also extended their bicycle concept over an entire album, the critically acclaimed *Tour de France Soundtracks*, in 2003. Florian Schneider quit the group in 2008, but Ralf Hütter has successfully continued the Kraftwerk franchise.

Although Kraftwerk were so self-referential and self-contained that they turned down offers to collaborate with Michael Jackson and David Bowie, their impact on contemporary music was significant. Tim Barr has claimed that Kraftwerk is the most important band since the Beatles, because "you don't have to have ever listened to a single Kraftwerk record for their music to have affected you."[39] Kraftwerk directly influenced British "New Romantic" pop groups like Human League, Depeche Mode, and OMD, Yellow Magic Orchestra from Japan, as well as West German bands of the 1980s like Einstürzende Neubauten and DAF. Perhaps even more importantly, Kraftwerk had an influence on disco groups like Chic, on techno DJs like Derrick May and Juan Atkins, and on early hip-hop pioneers.[40] Afrika

Bambaataa's "Planet Rock" (1982) used samples of two Kraftwerk compositions ("Numbers" and "Trans Europe Express"), and Run DMC's Jam
Master Jay stated: "These guys proved to me you don't have to be where I'm
from to get the music. That beat came from Germany all the way to the
'hoods of New York City."[41]

Kraftwerk's international success had been brought about by their focus
on a reterritorialized German identity. The complexity of this identity mate-
rialized not just in an uneasy man-machine hybrid but also in a deliberate
clash between ironically invoked German stereotypes and European and
global directions. Kraftwerk's Germanness stood in marked contrast to Can's
cosmopolitanism, but what connected both groups was their intent to break
with a nationalist past that had become impossible to defend. A third major
krautrock group, Neu!, combined both Kraftwerk's and Can's strategies and
articulated a postnational identity by more explicitly engaging a critique of
consumer capitalism.

## Neu!

An offshoot of Kraftwerk, Neu! (German for "new") consisted of two musicians, Michael Rother and Klaus Dinger.[42] Rother was born 1950 in Hamburg, moved to Munich at age four, lived in Karachi, Pakistan, from ages nine
to twelve, and then settled in Düsseldorf. Rother began his musical career
playing electric guitar in beat bands and copying Eric Clapton and Jimi
Hendrix. Klaus Dinger was born in 1946 and grew up in a working-class
district of Düsseldorf. The self-proclaimed "total artist" was trained as a carpenter and studied architecture at an art school. As a drummer, he also began
his musical career playing Anglo-American beat and rock'n'roll with the No
and the Smash and later turned to free jazz. Dinger and Rother met as newly
recruited members of Kraftwerk. Dinger played drums on the song "Vom
Himmel hoch" from Kraftwerk's 1970 debut album. Rother was added to
the live lineup of the band, and Ralf Hütter left the group temporarily. As a
trio with Florian Schneider, who played heavily processed flute, Dinger and
Rother appeared as Kraftwerk for live shows and TV appearances, and in
songs like "Rückstoß-Gondoliere" began to develop their own unique
sound, which was much more groove-based and rock-improvisational than
that of any later incarnation of Kraftwerk. When Ralf Hütter rejoined the
group, Dinger and Rother left to form Neu!.

Neu! was, from the outset, primarily a studio band and, with only a guitarist and a drummer, relied on multitracking and electronic effects for their
sound. Konrad "Conny" Plank (1940–87) was not an official member of
Neu!, but, as their producer, he had a significant impact on their music and
was also responsible for production credits of other major krautrock bands
like Kraftwerk, Guru Guru, and Can. His approach was, like that of Michael
Rother and Klaus Dinger, quite antithetical to most 1970s rock in its minimalism and refusal of unnecessary studio gimmickry and bombast. Plank has
described Neu! as a rare example of a "meeting of foreign substance and
domestic imprint" in German rock music.[43] For Plank, Klaus Dinger in particular was a "strong-minded guy who doesn't easily let something foreign
pollute his brain."[44] Influenced by the industrial landscape of Düsseldorf,
Neu!'s sound was, in Dinger's words, "more straight, chic, stylish" than that
of *kosmische* Berlin School musicians like Tangerine Dream or Klaus
Schulze.[45] Often mainly consisting of different layers of electric guitar and
drums and lacking a verse-chorus structure, vocals, or even harmonic
changes, Neu! deliberately departed from blues scales and timbres that were
common in Anglo-American and African American music. Klaus Dinger
recalled: "I wanted to create my own image. I wore Levis too when I was
sixteen, but after a while it was all too American for me. We had to find
something in our own back yard."[46] In a similar vein, Michael Rother has
talked about striving for "freedom from this cultural dominance in which
we had grown up and the Anglo-American music and culture,"[47] which
involved an "intellectual process of forgetting" in order to create new
sounds.[48] In some interviews, Rother has even used the term *Stunde Null* to
describe the gestation of a new musical identity with Neu!.

Both Klaus Dinger and Michael Rother contributed in different ways to
Neu!'s radical reinvention of musical sound. Dinger became most famous for
his unique style of drumming, a straight metronomic 4/4 beat without
unnecessary flourishes, known generally as *motorik* because of its machine-
like quality but referred to by Dinger himself as *lange Gerade* ("long straight
line") for its similarity to driving on a straight, endless road (Dinger later also,
more obscurely, used the term "Apache beat"). The long-term influence of
Dinger's economic approach to rhythm, at a time when fifteen-minute drum
solos had become a common practice at rock shows, is immeasurable. Punk
rock godfather Iggy Pop recalled how Dinger's drumming "allowed your
thoughts to flow, allowed your emotions to come from within and occupy

the creative parts of your mind, it allowed beauty. To get there the guy has somehow found a way to free himself from the tyranny of stupid blues, rock, of all connections that I'd ever heard."[49] Brian Eno, who began his career with Roxy Music and later became a hugely influential solo musician and producer, simply stated: "There were three great beats in the seventies: Fela Kuti's Afrobeat, James Brown's funk and Klaus Dinger's Neu! beat."[50]

While Dinger's drumming was clearly turning heads, Rother's guitar sound was equally important to Neu!'s sound. Rother's layers of electric guitar, consisting of short repetitive melodic lines and using effects like phase shifters, wah-wah, and distortion informed his "approach to a music that was different from British and American music, that wasn't based on blues."[51] Rother was influenced by the repetitive and meditative aspects of the Pakistani and Indian music he remembered from his childhood, as well as the European classical music that his mother, a concert pianist, had played. Rother's focus on repetition and minimalism complemented Dinger's motorik drumming: "The first thing I did was to slow down my fingers: no more running around on the guitar neck at high speed. Then, consequently, the ideas of pop music and blues—their melodic and harmonic song structures— were scrapped from my musical vocabulary. All of this left me with the basic elements of music. One string, one idea, move straight ahead, explore dynamics."[52] Rother's minimalism was unparalleled—other krautrock guitarists like Michael Karoli (Can) and Manuel Göttsching (Ash Ra Tempel) also embraced electronic effects and non-Western music and moved away from blues patterns, but they were not as radically minimalist as Rother.

Although Rother and Dinger created a sound that consciously broke with Anglo-American and African American traditions, they were reluctant to embrace this sound as German. In this regard, Neu! formed an interesting middle ground between Can and Kraftwerk. Whereas Can looked beyond Germany's borders for musical influences, Kraftwerk emphasized their seemingly distinct German heritage in their songs about robots and the autobahn. Comparing his own approach to Kraftwerk's musical concept, Rother stated: "For me the term *German* didn't mean anything. It wasn't connected to a specific German idea. [ . . . ] My own influences come from all over the world."[53] Klaus Dinger noted: "I am not a big fan of Germany [ . . . ], very critical, my point of view, toward my home country."[54] He also identified his drumming as "more African or more machine-style."[55] Through these statements, Dinger situated himself between the embrace of the über-German

Fig. 1. The cover of the first Neu! album. (Courtesy of Grönland Records.)

robotic identity of Kraftwerk and the programmatic internationalism of Can.[56] In doing so, he deliberately hybridized the two major contradictory impulses at work in the creation of a new German identity after World War II, poking fun at any notion of a fixed Germanness and embracing the inclusion of non-German aspects that created his transnational identity.

Neu!'s eponymous first album was recorded in only four nights in December of 1971 and released the following year. Its minimalist album artwork, designed by Klaus Dinger, already set the tone. Consisting simply of bright red lettering on a white background spelling out the word "Neu!"—a common term in German advertising enticing customers by drawing attention to a product's novelty—the artwork was in stark contrast to typical 1970s rock album design and packaging. As Julian Cope observed: "At a time of Roger Dean's Yes sleeves and their ilk cluttered full of Space junk, mythical animals and members of ugly groups cast as supermen in some prehistoric void, Neu! artwork was speedfreak clean."[57] Dinger was clearly inspired by the covers for Kraftwerk's first two albums from 1971 and 1972, displaying that group's logo and a traffic cone, in orange on the self-titled debut and in green with an overlaid "2" on the second album. Similarly, Neu! used the exact same image on *Neu! 2* (1973) as they had on their first LP with the sole difference being a spray-painted neon pink "2" added to gray lettering on a white background. The irony of still labeling this product "new" became even more pointed on *Neu! 75* (1975), with the band-album name in white lettering on a black background (the "75" did not appear on the original album sleeve, making it literally a black-and-white reproduction of the first album cover). As with the music, the recycling of an old idea on the album covers and titles created an intentional conflict with the label "Neu!" and indirectly commented on Germany's always-unfinished substitution of National Socialism with consumer capitalism. Instead of presenting a fixed and resolved new national identity, Neu! left their Germanness decidedly unstable.

The musical concept of Neu!'s debut album was simple but compelling, alternating experimental, meditative pieces with rhythmically driven tracks featuring a steady beat and deceptively easy guitar figures and bass runs. All instruments were played by Rother and Dinger. The first song, "Hallogallo," defined the concept of the band perfectly—introducing Dinger's motorik beat and Rother's electric guitar playing variations on a simple E major chord, augmented through reverb and echoplex or backward playing. As Julian Cope noticed: "There is no melody. There is no vocal. There is nothing to tell you where you are in this seamless corridor with no end. If Neu! had split right after the opening track of their first LP they would still have changed rock'n'roll."[58] If the absence of a bass guitar, vocals, or traditional song structures was already a post-rock statement, the second track on the album took it even further. "Sonderangebot" ("Special Offer"—one of the many ironic references to advertising in Neu!'s music) consisted entirely of Dinger playing a cymbal through a phase shifter. The third and last song on side one of *Neu!*, "Weissensee," was the only one on the album that had more than one chord. Rother recalled: "I deliberated for a long time about that first harmonic change and whether it was necessary."[59]

Side two of Neu!'s first album continued the radical minimalism. The suite of three songs was titled "Jahresübersicht" ("Annual Review") and, like many later songs of the group, made coded references to Dinger's breakup with his girlfriend. It opened with the serene "Im Glück" ("Blissful"), which featured a guitar drone and the sound of Dinger and his girlfriend rowing a boat. The suite then turned to the rougher tones of "Negativland" with more "found sounds" (a jackhammer drill, applause from a Kraftwerk show), heavy use of flanger and distortion on the guitar, and a much processed Japanese banjo (or *shamisen*) as bass, producing an overall acoustic impression that would be the blueprint for post-punk groups like Joy Division and Public Image Limited. The album ended with Dinger's stricken, breathy, and incomprehensible vocals on "Lieber Honig," the title of which was a literal translation of "Dear Honey" into German. This was one of several Neu! song titles that poked fun at the Americanization of the German language by "translating" English words into German. These "translations" made fun of the attempts of many German and other European bands to submit to the dominance of the English language in popular music, as they reversed the process of translation and "Germanized" English phrases but also clearly "messed up" this process with newly coined terms or phrases that did not make semantic sense. Other examples of these "messy" translations were "Isi" and "Dänzing," which were phonetic approximations of the English words "easy" and "dancing."

Neu!'s debut album sold thirty-five thousand copies in West Germany upon its release, which, given its departure from conventional rock music structures, was quite successful. For the follow-up *Neu! 2* (recorded in January 1973 and released the same year), Dinger and Rother self-consciously produced a "sophomore slump" and devoted the entire album to the recycling of old songs, partly because their record company refused to pay any more money after side one had been recorded. Although many eclectic instruments were listed in the liner notes—among them bandoneón, turntable, violin, zither, and Farfisa piano—the sound of the album was anything but "new." Side one opened with the eleven-minute, aptly titled "Für immer" ("Forever") featuring another single-chord guitar riff and a relentless motorik beat seeming to go on indefinitely, followed by "Spitzenqualität" ("Top Quality," yet another reference to advertising) with more relentless drumming, this time with heavy reverb and decreased tempo. "Gedenkminute" ("Moment of Silence") included the sounds of church bells, wind effects, and a processed female voice and contained more references to Klaus Dinger's former girlfriend. Finally, "Lila Engel" ("Lilac Angel") revitalized the motorik beat, this time with a droning fuzz guitar and percussive singing.

If side one of *Neu! 2* was merely rehashing ideas from the first album, side two took the concept of recycling to the extreme. It consisted of variations of the previously recorded double A single "Neuschnee/Super," played at 16,

78, and 33 RPM speeds, with built-in skips, pops, and tape delays. "Neuschnee"
("Fresh Snow"—possibly a tongue-in-cheek reference to the German
expression *Schnee von gestern* or "snow of yesterday," the equivalent of "yesterday's news") was itself a derivative of "Hallogallo," and only the driving
rock track "Super" was a breath of fresh air. Yet, in conceptual terms, Neu!
not only invented the technique of the remix that would become so common in hip-hop many years later, they also reinforced their critique of Germany's postwar capitalist culture and the commodification of the counterculture. If advertising was lulling consumers into a false sense of novelty, so
could Neu!.

Although *Neu! 2* was another moderate commercial success, Dinger and
Rother discontinued the group until December of 1974 when they began
recording *Neu! 75*. Unlike its predecessor, Neu!'s third album actually did
explore new sounds, on side one with some melodic and ambient pieces on
which Rother played synthesizers and piano, on side two with some abrasive
jamming with fuzz guitar and vocals by Dinger that anticipated the advent
of punk rock. Side one consisted of three tracks with progressively slower
tempi, from the motorik beat of "Isi" to the slow guitar grooves and distant
thunder of "Seeland" to the glacial tones, crashing waves, and whispered gibberish of "Leb wohl" ("Farewell"). The more melodic and commercially
appealing sounds on side one of *Neu! 75* might have seemed to betray the
social commentary of the first two albums, but this could not be said of side
two, for which Neu! added Hans Lampe and Klaus's brother Thomas Dinger
on drums and percussion. They picked up the pace dramatically with the
incendiary "Hero," which had Klaus Dinger shouting over a driving beat:
"Fuck your business, fuck the press, fuck the bourgeoisie." "E-Musik"
(another ironic title, using the German term for "serious" music, which is
generally reserved for European classical pieces) contained another motorik
and phase-shifted beat, processed guitar, some more tape experiments, wind
sounds, slowed-down vocals, and backwards guitar. Finally, "After Eight"
took the same approach as "Hero" but with different, mostly incomprehensible lyrics.

Having dabbled in post-rock, remixes, ambient, and punk years before
they became popular genres and techniques, and having served their own
sonic version of a critique of West Germany's consumer capitalism after
World War II, Neu!, without ever blowing up commercially, had exhausted
their creative potential. The band broke up and only reformed once more in

the studio between 1985 and 1986 to record another album that was shelved for many years, and released by Klaus Dinger in Japan as *Neu! 4* in 1995 without Michael Rother's approval. After Dinger's death, Rother edited and released it as *Neu! 86* in 2010. The fact that there is no definitive version of this album (merely a Dinger version and a Rother version) can also be interpreted in terms of Germany's unfinished and oftentimes divided identity even after reunification. Musically, Neu!'s fourth album had less impact than their first three releases, containing synthesizer-driven funk and pop grooves, some motorik beats, some tape experiments and some recycling of melodies, a processed German national anthem, and snippets of German-language TV commercials.

Despite their relatively minor sales, Neu!'s impact on popular music was impressive. David Bowie's collaboration with Brian Eno on his Berlin Trilogy owed much to Neu!, in particular on the seminal album *"Heroes"*, presumably named after the song from *Neu! 75*. In the late 1970s and early 1980s, the SoHo contingent of the "no wave" scene in New York City also drew heavily on the sounds of the German group (especially the guitar playing of Rhys Chatham and Glenn Branca).[60] Before they hit the mainstream, post-punk bands like the Cure and U2 borrowed sounds from Neu!, and artists like Sonic Youth, Primal Scream, and LCD Soundsystem paid tribute to Michael Rother and Klaus Dinger on the 2009 release *Brand Neu!*. The combination of guitar and drums without a steady bass player has been revitalized by a number of indie rock bands such as the Yeah Yeah Yeahs, the White Stripes, No Age, and the Black Keys. Other influences of Neu! could be heard on the recordings of Stereolab, Radiohead, Tortoise, and a number of electronica artists. The Neu! albums, unavailable for a long time, have been successfully rereleased by German rock star Herbert Grönemeyer's Grönland Records in 2001 and again as a comprehensive vinyl box set in 2010. Ironically, by abandoning Anglo-American and African American musical structures and exposing the cracks and fissures of West Germany's economic miracle, Neu! managed to gain a belated transnational appeal, and to infuse globalized pop with their own brand of musical sound.

## After Neu!

Some of the music Michael Rother and Klaus Dinger produced outside Neu! was much more commercially successful than anything they had done together, but arguably none of it had the same historical significance. While Rother and Dinger continued some of their exploration of new musical territory and their critique of Americanized West German consumer capitalism in their later work, their former deterritorialized approach and transnational impact was replaced by a reterritorialized emphasis on location and locality. During their later careers, Rother's and Dinger's conflicting ideas, part of what made up the hybrid that was Neu!, became more apparent. Rother left for Forst, a small village in Lower Saxony, and increasingly turned to melodic and commercially viable guitar-driven ambient music, whereas Dinger stayed in Düsseldorf and made the city's urban landscape itself the subject of his stylish, synthesizer-driven pop music.

When Rother moved to a four-house farm in Bevern in 1973 to join Hans-Joachim Roedelius and Dieter Moebius of the experimental electronic group Cluster, he was following a trend of other krautrock musicians who left big cities to record in the rural parts of the northern German countryside: Faust, a group from Hamburg, had chosen communal life and work in their studio in nearby Wümme. Synthesizer guru Klaus Schulze, part of the Berlin School of electronic music, settled in another small town in Lower Saxony, Hambühren. Cluster had taken a similar path. Hans-Joachim Roedelius and Dieter Moebius had founded Kluster in 1969 in Berlin, later changed their name to Cluster and released the two krautrock albums *Cluster '71* (1971) and *Cluster II* (1972). Leaving the Berlin School with its emphasis on cosmic psychedelics behind, they moved to Forst and recorded the album *Zuckerzeit* ("Sugar Era," 1974), which listed Rother as producer. For this album, Cluster shortened their songs, employed cheap analog rhythm machines and drum boxes, and focused on pop minimalism, which showed their affinity to Neu!. In line with *Zuckerzeit*'s self-reflexive pop music, the album cover was styled like icing on a cake.

This trend continued on the two albums Rother recorded with the two Cluster musicians under the name Harmonia. For this group, Rother played electric guitar, keyboards, and electronic drums; Hans-Joachim Roedelius contributed keyboard melodies; and Dieter Moebius was responsible for synthetic bleeps and unusual sounds. Their first album, *Musik von Harmonia* (1974), featured another pop art cover, this time a comic book image of a light blue detergent bottle advertising, simply, "Music by Harmonia," with the musicians listed as ingredients (the cover played with the similarity of the words "ammonia" and "Harmonia"). Like Neu! before them, Harmonia were poking fun at consumer culture, but this time from the vantage point of the rural countryside; with the song title "Sehr kosmisch" ("Very Cosmic," which in German sounds similar to *sehr komisch* or "very funny"), they were mocking the "serious" big-city musicians of the Berlin School. Apart from two live tracks, the album was recorded in the band's low-fidelity home studio, which was depicted on the inside of the gatefold album cover. With Harmonia, Rother continued and in some ways perfected the exercises in electric guitar minimalism he had begun with Neu!. Corresponding with the humble provincialism of Harmonia's instrumental pop, the first album sold a meager 4,000 copies upon its release.

Harmonia's second album, *Deluxe* (1976), did not do much better than their first, although it was packaged with a glossy cover containing gold lettering and an orange sky with a bright sun. It was recorded in a professional studio, sounded rhythmically tight (thanks to the contribution of Guru Guru drummer Mani Neumeier), and even had vocals on two songs. If German audiences were not listening, some other people were. Brian Eno, a devoted Harmonia fan, joined the group onstage in Hamburg in 1974 and recorded the improvised ambient vignettes of *Tracks and Traces* two years later during an eleven-day visit to Forst with the group.[61] Rother left the group, which went on to record a number of critically acclaimed albums as Cluster in the years that followed. Despite Harmonia's retreat to the pastoral and the hermitic, all three Harmonia albums were successfully reissued three decades after they were recorded, and the band regrouped for appearances between 2007 and 2009.

The first three solo albums Rother recorded after leaving Harmonia with the assistance of Can drummer Jaki Liebezeit, which contained simple multitracked guitar melodies, proved to be his commercial breakthrough. *Flammende Herzen* ("Flaming Hearts," 1977), *Sterntaler* ("Star Money," 1978), and *Katzenmusik* ("Caterwaul," 1979) each sold 150,000 copies in West Germany but had less long-term impact than the albums Rother made with Harmonia and Neu!. Rother's fame began to wane in the 1980s. Nonetheless, he has continued to record and perform live, most recently on his 2010 "Hallogallo" tour.

Whereas Rother found a pastoral home for his increasingly meditative music in the rural community of Forst, Klaus Dinger moved in a different direction. Taking Neu!'s ironic play with advertising slogans a step further, Dinger chose the urban landscape of Düsseldorf as a trope of *Lokalpatriotismus*—

the local patriotism that, after World War II, remained the only acceptable form of patriotism in Germany. Düsseldorf, design and fashion capital of Germany, a city of extreme class differences "horribly destroyed and spoiled by industrialization,"[62] produced a number of significant musicians in the 1970s (among them Kraftwerk and Wolfgang Riechmann), all of whom depicted the "curse of progress."[63] Yet, no other group was as specific in localizing this agenda as Klaus Dinger's La Düsseldorf, named after a photo business and performing in "White Overalls" (also a song title) to appear as working class but also "chic." With this group, which also featured the two drummers from *Neu! 75*, Thomas Dinger and Hans Lampe, Klaus Dinger abandoned the transnationally appealing globalism of Neu!, with their mostly instrumental songs and only the vaguest references to specific places (both "Seeland" and "Weissensee" could refer to multiple locations), and turned to the city in which he grew up and spent most of his life.

The cover of La Düsseldorf's first, self-titled album used a night shot of the city's airport terminal on the cover and featured two songs, "Düsseldorf" and "La Düsseldorf," in which Dinger repeated the city's name like a mantra. The lyrics referenced Düsseldorf's main industries (Mannesmann and Rheinmetall); name-dropped Königsallee, the city's upscale shopping street; and addressed fashion, prostitution, crime, and commerce. In some ways similar to Kraftwerk's "Computer World" but with lyrics that addressed more specific localities, La Düsseldorf's songs could be construed as critiques of capitalism, but because the critiques were so inexplicit, they could also be seen as celebrating the city's industries, with chants of working-class soccer fans added to the mix. Side two of La Düsseldorf's debut album featured the instrumental synth pop of "Silver Cloud," a minor hit in West Germany, and added some globalism with the multilingual "Time" with lyrics in English, French, German, and Italian. Musically, La Düsseldorf's first album continued some of Neu!'s ideas—the motorik beat, this time played by the two new drummers, the absence of the bass guitar, the simple harmonies—but the emphasis was now fully on the keyboards and synthesizers, played by Dinger under his pseudonym Nikolaus van Rhein and paving the way for the *Neue Deutsche Welle* (NDW) bands of the 1980s.

*La Düsseldorf* was a moderate commercial success and was followed by *Viva* (1978). The album cover recycled ideas from Neu! by reducing the artwork to a spray-painted logo. Side one presented an eclectic mix of accessible songs including the symphonic instrumental "Rheinita" (another radio hit in West Germany), its title celebrating the river Rhine that runs through Düsseldorf, and the social commentary of "Geld" ("Money"). Side two prefigured Klaus Dinger's later work with the twenty-minute monotonous groove of "Cha Cha Cha 2000," containing Dinger's *sprechgesang* of semi-ironic futuristic slogans about "futur d'amour" where "the wars have all gone [ . . . ] and we care for the weak and share with the poor." *Viva* sold a staggering 150,000 copies in West Germany. After one more album, *Individuellos* (1980), and a final maxi single, "Ich liebe dich/Koksknödel" (1983), La Düsseldorf broke up amidst bitter fights between the band members over royalty payments. Dinger, who admitted to have taken over one thousand LSD trips, released a number of quickly assembled albums under monikers like Neondian and La!Neu? before succumbing to heart failure in 2008. The most memorable song of Dinger's later years was probably "America," with its comparison of US imperialism and the Nazi SS. While lacking the ambiguity that had made Dinger's work with Neu! and La Düsseldorf so compelling, it came full circle with his long-time resistance against Americanization.

La Düsseldorf's legacy proved to be quite substantial. Arguably the most important popular music movement in Germany outside krautrock, the *Neue Deutsche Welle* swept the country between 1979 and 1983. The city of Düsseldorf became a major hub of NDW activity with bands like Rheingold, Fehlfarben, die Krupps, and DAF, all of which were clearly influenced by La Düsseldorf's new wave globalism.[64] The group's impact on musicians outside Germany was not as pronounced, but the first two La Düsseldorf albums have been internationally rereleased.

As three of the best-known bands associated with krautrock, Can, Kraftwerk, and Neu! made music that was connected to the articulation of an unstable German identity after World War II and the student demonstrations of 1968. These groups had conflicted relationships to both classical music and rock and strove to take control over their production. Can, Kraftwerk, and Neu! deemphasized the lead guitar and lead vocals of 1970s "cock rock" and incorporated electronic instruments like drum machines and synthesizers into their music. The hybridization of man and machine was made more explicit through Kraftwerk's robot personae but was also present in Can's and Neu!'s music through editing and mixing, which were vital for the sound of both groups.

While Kraftwerk drew on European classical music, emphasized melody, and used German lyrics to create a semi-ironic Teutonic identity that played with stereotypes of Germans as robotic automatons, Can distanced themselves from Germany's past by drawing on world music, employing non-German singers, and using the English language for song lyrics and even the band's name.[65] Finally, Neu!'s music directly addressed unfinished German identity and consumer capitalism through their minimalism and references to advertising. Klaus Dinger and Michael Rother continued their exploration of "new" musical territory in their separate careers with Harmonia and La Düsseldorf, but both turned to a more localized understanding of reterritorialized identity—Rother in the pastoral environment of northern Germany's countryside, Dinger in the urban landscape of one of Germany's most industrialized cities.

Michael Rother and Klaus Dinger's articulation of an unfinished German identity through musical expression was certainly subtle—after all, much of their music was instrumental and only rarely made direct references to the nation-state—but it was this subtlety that so aptly described German identity as always incomplete. While Can opted for a musical internationalism, Kraftwerk dared to confront the ghosts of the past by bringing them back to life, explicitly addressing and parodying German national identity in a postmodern context. All three groups, Can, Kraftwerk, and Neu!, by invoking a musical *Stunde Null*, acknowledged the complexities involved in being German in a globalized world.

# 2 Community and Conflict

## The Communes of Amon Düül,
## Faust, and Ton Steine Scherben

Although krautrock was far from being a unified movement, the quest for developing alternative national and personal identities sometimes took on similar forms. It is remarkable how many bands chose communal living in an attempt to break out of hierarchical and nationalist structures. Communes, of course, were not unique to Germany in the 1970s and arguably had a more significant history in North America than in Europe. The similarities between alternative living and music-making as an expression of counter-cultural desires in West Germany and the United States do in fact point to globalized or at least transnational developments. Yet the way communal living was applied to the specific historical and musical circumstances in West Germany is apparent in the works of some of the most recognized krautrock groups, and it served as a deterritorializing mechanism in the context of Americanization and globalization.

The krautrock groups whose communal lifestyle heavily impacted their music included Embryo, Guru Guru, Xhol Caravan, and even Cluster and Harmonia. The three groups best suited to articulate some of the conflicts between personal and national identity formations were also three of the most important German bands of the 1970s: Amon Düül (I and II), Faust, and Ton Steine Scherben.[1] Amon Düül began as a countercultural commune with ties to Kommune 1 and morphed into a professional band that musically stayed close to Anglo-American psychedelic rock but also toyed with problematic notions of Germany. Faust, initially with support from their record company, worked to create a sound that dramatically broke with Anglo-American rock traditions and only became popular outside their home country. Finally, Ton Steine Scherben purposefully employed German lyrics but stayed very close to blues-rock structures in their music. Their connection to the squatter movement and radical New Left politics eventually weakened and made way for an expression of personal identity, in particular singer Rio Reiser's homosexuality, which clashed with their fans' expectations. All three groups emphasized a tribalism that situated them at the heart of krautrock's contested network of spatial and sonic identities.

## Communes

Communes can generally be defined as systems in which "people of predominantly equal status shape their production sphere and everyday praxis together in conscious dissociation of other forms of socialization"[2] and as "residentially-based groups whose members pool most or all of their assets and income and share a belief system or at least a commitment to important core concepts."[3] Ron Roberts names three elements that distinguish modern communalists from other utopists: first, a rejection of hierarchical structures; second, a non-Marxist line of thinking that views the current organization of society as being too large in scale; and third, a consciously antibureaucratic approach.[4] One could add that despite these ideals many modern communal societies reproduce gender and class hierarchies as well as bureaucracies of larger society.

Communal living has a long history, not just in North America and Germany but worldwide. As a utopian ideal, communal living was already advocated by Plato in his *Republic*, and religious, spiritual, and political communes have included European monasteries, the Paris Commune of 1871, the socialist Kibbutz in Israel, anarchist communes in Spain, collective farms in Japan, and Auroville in south India.[5] With the Shakers, the Amana Colonies, the Hutterites, and the Oneida Perfectionists, utopian communalism has had a particularly rich history in the United States. According to Robert Sutton, "utopian communalism developed as an unbroken motif in American history. It was a persistent, unbroken expression of what some Americans, and some Europeans, thought the United States ought to be."[6] The mushrooming of communes in the 1960s drew on all of these traditions: "In a period of a few years communal fever gripped the youth of the [ . . . ] developed world."[7] These were not exclusively hippie communes but also included political radicals, artists, and religious groups (especially Christian and Buddhist denominations). The majority of these oftentimes short-lived communes were "young, white, and of middle-class background."[8] Many American communards were inspired by *Walden Two*, B. F. Skinner's utopian novel from 1948 that reimagined the self-reliance of Henry David Thoreau's *Walden* within a community setting. Many attempts were made to put Skinner's utopia into practice, the best-known probably being the Twin Oaks community in Louisa, Virginia, founded in 1967 and still in existence.

Communal living was common among many of the San Francisco bands of the 1960s, including Jefferson Airplane and Janis Joplin's group Big Brother and the Holding Company. The most famous of these band communes was undoubtedly the Grateful Dead's house on 710 Ashbury Street, widely known as a model for collective music-making and drug consumption.[9] Bandleader Jerry Garcia and other members of the Grateful Dead had been part of the Merry Pranksters, a group of early sixties communards experimenting with LSD. Although the actual commune only lasted from 1966 to 1968, "for the rest of its life the Grateful Dead scene was heavily communal, both for the band (which had little turnover in personnel) and for the prime audience, the Deadheads who followed the band from concert to concert as something of a neotribal rolling community."[10] To some extent, other groups like Phish have continued this model to the present day.

Germany's rural communes of the Weimar Republic had included nationalist, anarchist, communist, and Zionist projects. The communes that formed in West Germany in the 1960s and 1970s, estimated at about one hundred to two hundred in number, were part of a transnational student movement that involved transatlantic cooperation and collaboration.[11] As in the United States, the media focused on drugs and sexual experimentation, but the reality in many communes was much more mundane. Contemporary communes in Germany often primarily focus on sustainability and ecology, an example being the Niederkaufingen commune in Hessia, which was founded in 1986.

To understand the history of the communal krautrock bands, the single most important group is Kommune 1, founded on January 12, 1967, in Berlin and consisting initially of nine adults and one child. K1, as they were also called, promoted giving up private property and, according to member Fritz Teufel, wanted to "live together, share finances, and have discussions."[12] Giving up familial relations, traditional views on morality, and monogamous relationships were also part of the program.[13] K1 bemoaned what they viewed as the recreational socialism of the student movement and instead

called for restructuring one's entire life practices. The group became internationally famous for their Situationists-inspired fun activism with the "pudding assassination" of US vice president Hubert Humphrey during his visit
to West Germany in 1967. The aborted attempt to attack the politician with
smoke bombs and a mixture of flour, yogurt, and pudding was even covered
by the *New York Times*.

Kommune 1's politics of satire and provocation also involved throwing
hundreds of copies of Mao Tse-tung's *Little Red Book* from the Gedächt-
niskirche, a famous church in Berlin that was bombed in World War II and
kept as a monument. Media attention grew with a popular photograph that
depicted the communards naked from behind, standing spread-eagled against
a wall, and with member Rainer Langhans's well-publicized relationship
with fashion model Uschi Obermaier from Munich, who had also briefly
joined Amon Düül. Langhans and Obermaier became a well-known countercultural couple in Germany and possibly inspired John Lennon and Yoko
Ono in their celebration of the private as the political.

The politics of Kommune 1 remained a bit murky. Fritz Teufel was
accused of treason and spent a few months in prison in 1967, and Rote
Armee Fraktion (RAF) members Andreas Baader and Gudrun Ensslin were
friends of the group before they became militant, but leftist political groups
like SDS (Sozialistischer Deutscher Studentenbund) criticized K1 for their
hedonism.[14] Living in several different apartments in West Berlin, the commune lasted until 1969 when it fell apart, among other reasons because of
founding member Rainer Kunzelmann's heroin addiction. In German popular culture, Kommune 1 remained one of the most recognized models of
communal living.

## Amon Düül

The musicians' commune Amon Düül shared some members with Kommune 1 but was based in Munich, not Berlin. They consciously chose a name
that was neither English nor German. Instead, it referred to an Egyptian
deity and a Turkish word of unknown origin.[15] Most members of the group
came from privileged families, and they initially lived in the posh Prinzre-
gentenstraße, which was predominantly inhabited by doctors and lawyers.
According to founding member Renate Knaup, it was a "huge flat with
seven rooms. [ . . . ] It was a house where Hitler once gave a speech from the

Fig. 2. Members of the original Amon Düül commune. (Courtesy of Eurock Archives.)

balcony. In front was a taxicab rank with all these drivers hanging around all day."[16] In order to undermine the upper-class environment, the communards shared the rooms with many visitors and took lots of drugs. Ingrid Schober reported that Amon Düül's rooms had white walls with posters, no curtains on the windows, and were empty except for vinyl records and mattresses on the floor.[17] According to Peter Leopold, another early member, "we wanted to radically break with all those bourgeois structures and said we'd rather live with eight people in a truck or an apartment."[18] The two children that were raised in the commune were largely left to their own devices, and alternative foodways coexisted with heavy drug consumption.

The original members of Amon Düül participated in many demonstrations and played on college campuses. The first major gig of the group was at the Essen Song Days. In their letter of application they had introduced themselves to producer and festival organizer Rolf-Ulrich Kaiser in the following way: "We are eleven adults and two children, and we have decided to do everything together, including music!"[19] Eight adults and one child actually appeared at the concert; the rest had split and founded the musically more proficient Amon Düül II. The *Kölnische Rundschau* reported:

The musicians were young men with artfully combed or shoulder-length hair in fanciful clothes and equally unconventional-looking girls in floor-length dresses. Oblivious to their surroundings, they worked their instruments—except for one blonde female musician who occasionally had to stop playing to keep the communards' band's toddler from falling off the stage or to hold a microphone down to the little blond boy so he could crow into it.[20]

While the newspaper article tried to make fun of the musicianship of the group, Christian Burchard of fellow krautrock band Embryo gave a more positive account of the anticommercial, participatory idealism of early Amon Düül: "It was about living together. Those who couldn't play well or didn't know how to play an instrument were still encouraged to join in the music. They were given bongos or a Moroccan drum or taught a few chords on the guitar so they could still enrich the sound."[21]

The musical amateurism of Amon Düül I was preserved in a string of releases that were all recorded in one ten-hour session, enhanced with minimal overdubs. *Psychedelic Underground* (1969) consisted almost entirely of relentless one-chord guitar strumming and percussion, "a perversely repetitive, primitive and self-indulgent drone all but dissolving in its own fuzz."[22] Sound quality and musicianship may have been lacking on *Psychedelic Underground*, but the album still found an audience. The musical primitivism was not so far from seminal American groups like the Velvet Underground or the Stooges, and one song title supposedly inspired British DJ John Peel to popularize the term krautrock ("Mama Düül und ihre Sauerkrautband spielt auf"—"Mama Düül is Playing with her Sauerkraut Band"). LSD—an important, if problematic, element of the counterculture—was continuously invoked on *Psychedelic Underground*. Three song titles paid tribute to the fictional "Garden Sandosa," a reference to LSD-25 producer Sandoz ushering in a new Eden, and a surrealist German-language fairy tale, printed on the inside of the gatefold cover, made yet another reference to the drug by ending with "and if you don't believe it, you will be given a lump of sugar by Mama Düül." Amon Düül I would eventually release one more LP and another double album culled from the same ten-hour session that produced *Psychedelic Underground* (*Collapsing Singvögel rückwärts*, 1969, and *Disaster*, 1971), as well as *Paradieswärts Düül* (1970) with German folk influences reminiscent of other largely acoustic krautrock groups like Witthüser & Westrupp.

In their communal music-making and their rejection of consumer capitalism, Amon Düül I had been radical, but music was not a priority for most members of the group. They merged with West Berlin's Kommune I and more or less disappeared from the public eye, while Amon Düül II with its professionalized psychedelic blues rock took over. Over the years, the group would have many personnel changes, but the main members were Chris Karrer (born 1947; guitar, violin), Renate Knaup (born 1948; vocals), John Weinzierl (born 1949; guitar), Peter Leopold (bon 1945; drums), Falk Rogner (born 1943; keyboards), and Lothar Meid (born 1942; bass guitar). Renate Knaup recalled why they separated and formed their own group: "There were [ . . . ] certain rules you had to obey and if you broke any you had to go in front of this tribunal and explain your actions to these fuckers! Even when I wanted to buy a new pair of stockings I had to ask the 'cashier' for money. This is why we split from Amon Düül I; they were too involved with this political shit."[23] Although the newly formed Amon Düül II were less interested in overt political statements, they continued to espouse what Barry Shank has called the "political force of musical beauty" through sonic experimentation and still lived as a commune.

Like most members of Kommune I and the militant Rote Armee Fraktion, the musicians of Amon Düül II came from wealthy families, and many even went to the same boarding school. They initially lived in Herrsching, just outside Munich, but had to move out in 1970 when their power was shut off, rats invaded the kitchen, and the trash kept piling up outside. These failures did not deter the group's communal spirit, and, with members of the High-Fish commune, they managed to rent a three-story castle at Kronwinkl 12, about forty miles outside of Munich. The communards enjoyed wearing long plush coats and had grown their hair out. Olaf Kübler, producer and manager of Amon Düül II, described the daily insanity at the Kronwinkl 12 commune, which had deteriorated from an alternative family to a group of egotistical rock stars:

Kronwinkl had three stories. In the basement was the 540-square-foot nursing home kitchen with a giant stove where you could fry 3,000 eggs at the same time. Sometimes this stove was on for days when one of the stoned freaks had forgotten to turn it off. Then the entire house was heated like an incubator from top to bottom. It's a miracle that the place never burned down. John Weinzierl lived on the first floor in the sunroom. John was the best looking guy in the group at the time. The other Düül guitarist Chris Karrer lived on the second floor in a cathedral-like room where he smoked all the time. He was always talking about Düül's creativity. Peter Leopold, the group's drummer, lived right next door to Chris Karrer. Whenever Peter got angry, he took his Winchester out of the cupboard and shot at the wall Chris was sitting behind! If he hadn't been a drummer, he probably would have become a terrorist. Singer Renate Knaup-Krötenschwanz resided on the third floor with her lover Falk Rogner, Düül's keyboarder and graphic designer. Falk was responsible for most of Düül's lyrics and album artwork. The third floor looked like a mixture of Dracula's mansion and 1920s Hollywood, because all the good furniture had been brought to a pawnshop when money was in short supply. In addition, some girls, radicals, and RAF members occasionally stayed in the many empty rooms at Kronwinkl.[24]

Less a commune than a rock star dwelling, Kronwinkl 12 reflected the ambiguous political commitment of Amon Düül II, the individualization of the members, and a sense of impending doom. Another inhabitant of the house, Wolfgang Krischke, appeared on the cover of *Yeti* as the Grim Reaper. He died shortly after, freezing to death outside the castle while tripping on acid. The connections to RAF members like Andreas Baader led to numerous run-ins with the police. After visiting the commune, journalist Werner Burkhardt mockingly asked the readers of *Brigitte* to enter for a drawing with one day with Amon Düül II as the first prize and two days with the group as the second prize.[25]

Musically, Amon Düül II presented an eclectic mix of Anglo- and African American blues rock, free jazz, Arabic, Indian, and Chinese music on lengthy and complex suites on their earlier LPs but gradually drifted into fairly standard rock territory from 1972 on. According to Falk Rogner, they wanted "to start out with a blank slate and create new sound structures, to amaze people and put them in touch with universal sound and make them forget about their mundane habits. You could call it futuristic music."[26] By emphasizing a musical beginning (after World War II) and moving toward universal sound structures, Amon Düül II were very much in line with other krautrock groups. Chris Karrer stressed: "We were very anti-German. We did not want to be German, we wanted to be multicultural."[27] In a different interview, Karrer noted: "I always had to play violin. I hated this instrument. Then I rediscovered the violin through my engagement with Indian music."[28] Although Amon Düül II certainly incorporated musical influences from around the world, they also retained a strong and conflicted relationship to their home country, culminating in the 1975 release *Made in Germany*. Renate Knaup's operatic singing drew on German traditions, as did Chris Karrer's violin playing (he was sometimes referred to as *Karajani der Teufelsgeiger*, "Karajani the violin virtuoso," in reference to Italian violinist Niccolò Paganini and Austrian conductor Herbert von Karajan). Liberty's press release for the group's first album, *Phallus Dei* (1969), even proclaimed: "Amon Düül II regard themselves as a German band and foster the German element in their musical expression."[29]

Amon Düül II's complex and conflicted relationship with national identity and internationalization became particularly pronounced in their simultaneous rejection and embrace of Anglo-American musical traditions. John Weinzierl noted: "Basically, we didn't want to cultivate the four-minute pop songs that the Americans and Brits had made. We wanted to make music but not this standard Anglophone shit."[30] Yet the early live performance of the band was called "Transparent Magic Vacuum Show" (in English) and used a similar light show as American psychedelic rock bands. British bass player and later Hawkwind member Dave Anderson joined the group for their most important album, *Yeti*, and the hours of listening to British and American rock music in the commune left more traces on Amon Düül II's albums than most of the Indian or Arabic music they had been exposed to. German director Wim Wenders, a friend of the group, even called them "Germany's Jefferson Airplane,"[31] and while Renate Knaup could claim some German opera as an influence on her singing and added *Krötenschwanz* ("toad's tail") to her last name, her phrasings were indeed quite similar to those of Grace Slick. The surreal lyrics, generally sung in English with a Bavarian accent, were pretty common psychedelic rock fare as well, as was the emphasis on studio effects, non-Western influences, and complex song structures. Even the communal hippie lifestyle echoed the Grateful Dead in everything but Jerry Garcia's leadership.

After playing at Munich discotheque PN every Monday for six months and gathering a devoted following, Amon Düül II recorded their debut record, provocatively titled *Phallus Dei* ("God's Penis"), in 1969. In the press release for the album, which had an ominous cover depicting a leafless tree with crows at twilight, the band still emphasized a communal structure as its core concept: "Collective living, while considering individual needs as much as possible, is what this group sees as the only way of existing outside conventional society (in an economic or artistic sense)."[32] Quickly recorded and assembled and containing only five songs, the album reflected communal living in its live feel, particularly on the twenty-minute title track, a psychedelic rock suite that covered the entire second side. Julian Cope called the music on the album "a swirling meltdown of Teutonic San Francisco *Kosmische* psychedelia with absolutely no commercial restraints."[33] The sound was propelled by two drummers (Peter Leopold and Dieter Serfas), as well as various kinds of Tibetan, Cuban, Turkish, and North African percussion. Vocals served primarily as instruments, and some of the melodic and harmonic structures on guitar, organ, and violin were reminiscent of Indian classical music. At the same time, these musical structures and the timbral and instrumental delivery were firmly rooted in European, African American, and Anglo-American traditions, in particular blues rock. The result was a deterritorialized musical hybrid, challenging essentialized Germanness through its cosmopolitanism. The connection to Germany was most evident in the only song with significant lyrics, "Dem Guten, Schönen, Wahren" ("Dedicated to the Good, the Beautiful, and the True"). Also known as "Child Murderer's Song" and recalling traditions of German murder ballads, as well as Bertolt Brecht's "Mac the Knife," it told the story of a child rapist and killer with verses from the perspective of the rapist and a chorus sung by the "just society." However, Amon Düül II would not use German lyrics again until their 1972 release *Wolf City*.

After their relatively successful first album, Amon Düül II returned to the studio to record their magnum opus, the 1970 double album *Yeti*. The cover showed a motif common on old German woodcuts, the aforementioned Krischke as the Grim Reaper in a lake of fire (an image also used for the book cover of Julian Cope's *Krautrocksampler*). Much more heavily produced than the first album and separated into one LP of compositions and one LP of improvised pieces, *Yeti* signaled a move away from communal politics and toward professional musicianship and international rock stardom. A bit premature, the press release for the album proclaimed: "Amon Düül II has left the communal experiment behind. Their main emphasis is on the music."[34]

The press release also quoted the band saying: "You won't achieve anything with demonstrations."[35] Turning away from explicit social commentary and focusing on music that was still made communally proved to be the formula for the group's most significant work—long and riff-heavy psychedelic rock suites with elements of progressive rock as well as folk rock reminiscent of the British Canterbury scene, all the while referencing German fairy tales ("The Return of Rübezahl"), LSD ("Sandoz in the Rain"), and Indian and other non-Western influences. On *Yeti*, Amon Düül II moved from kraut-rock with its limited reach to a unique transnational blend of music that catapulted them briefly into the same league as groups like Led Zeppelin and King Crimson. Lester Bangs, who had panned *Psychedelic Underground* as "undoubtedly the worst record out this year,"[36] called *Yeti* "one of the finest recordings of psychedelic music in all of human history."[37] British music magazine *Melody Maker* wrote: "Amon Düül II is the first German group whose music can be regarded as a contribution on its own to international pop culture."[38] Amon Düül II's success in Britain and France gave manager Peter Kaiser a sense of pride, "because you suddenly felt that the Teutonic elements of our past had something positive."[39] Yet the German *Sounds* bemoaned "the arrogance of the [German] audience, who unfortunately still don't want to realize that the times are gone when you had to cross the Atlantic to hear good music."[40] The contradictions between being commu-nal and being pop stars, being German and rejecting Germanness were evi-dent both in *Yeti*'s music and in the discourse around it.

One important element in the development of Amon Düül II's music from *Phallus Dei* to *Yeti* was Renate Knaup's voice. Having sung mostly backup vocals on the first album (with the exception of "Henriette Kröten-schwanz"), Knaup had to fight for her role as lead vocalist: "This was always a man's band and if any of them could have sung properly they would never have chosen me, a girl, to be their vocalist."[41] By becoming one of the very few prominent female members of a heavily male-dominated German rock scene, Renate Knaup proved that women's voices could help krautrock to become internationally viable (something Florian Fricke of Popol Vuh real-ized in the early 1970s as well by employing Djong Yun and later also Renate Knaup as vocalists). One song on *Yeti* that prominently featured Knaup's vocals was "Archangel's Thunderbird," which she had composed from a Ger-man hymn she used to sing in her local church choir. Transforming a Ger-man hymn into a psychedelic rock song exemplified Amon Düül II's multifaceted and transnational musical identity. With *Yeti*, Knaup became the most heavily featured singer in Amon Düül II and provided some of the most important contributions to the group.

As Amon Düül II were gearing up for yet another major release in 1971, conflicts in the Kronwinkl 12 commune increased, because individual members were playing music in their own rooms and only met each other outside the house. Peter Leopold recalled: "As we jammed together less and less, we gradually lost our musical common ground. You can't create chaos retroactively."[42] As a consequence, the band underwent many personnel changes. Bass player Lothar Meid, who came from the group Embryo, was the first musician who chose not to live with the band but in a separate apartment with his wife and children. With Meid, Amon Düül II produced another double album, *Tanz der Lemminge* (also released under the translated title *Dance of the Lemmings*). Although the commune was coming to an end, the group issued another political manifesto for the album's press release. Under the title "What We Were, What We Want," they promoted "new forms of communication,"[43] talked about their experience of oppression in the boarding school environment and how they had moved from commune to *Wohngemeinschaft* (roughly translated as "living community," this term refers to sharing an apartment or house with roommates). The band explicitly rejected capitalism, alcohol, and the police state and declared: "To articulate a fundamental critique of the current system, it was necessary to provide a countercultural model through music."[44] The music and lyrics on the album were just as complex as those on the predecessor *Yeti* and included the soundtrack for the movie *Chamsin*.[45] Reflecting the fragmentation of the formerly communal band, three individual members were in charge of the other sides: Chris Karrer for the acoustic sounds of the first side, John Weinzierl for the progressive rock jam on the second side, and Falk Rogner for electronic experiments on the third side that were reminiscent of the *kosmische Musik* of Tangerine Dream and Klaus Schulze. Musically, *Tanz der Lemminge* continued *Yeti*'s bold experimentation and eclecticism, and critics and fans received the album well. For instance, Lester Bangs noted the transnational dimension of the music: "This is one time that somebody far from these shores has something to teach us (and fry our brains in the process) about 'our' music and the music of the universe."[46]

The Kronwinkl 12 commune, already shaken by a fire during an Amon Düül gig in Cologne in March of 1971 that destroyed all the band's equipment and killed four audience members, moved out of their residence toward the end of the same year. As a send-off to communal living, their 1972 LP *Carnival in Babylon* contained a song dedicated to "Kronwinkl 12," and in the liner notes Amon Düül II gave "thanks to all the paranoid people who meanwhile have moved out." In line with the renunciation of communal living, the album introduced a new sound, fairly standard rock music with conventional song structures. As another sign of communal dissent, Amon Düül II recorded two more albums with different, rivaling formations in 1972, *Utopia* and *Wolf City*, the latter their most successful straightforward rock album. Some tension between world music and Germanic influences remained on *Wolf City*. "Wie der Wind am Ende einer Strasse" ("Like the Wind at the End of a Road") had a romantic German title but featured sitar and tabla, and on "Deutsch-Nepal," guest vocalist and actor Rolf Zacher recited German lyrics about a Nazi general dreaming of Nepal, a reference to Heinrich Himmler's fantasy of invading the Himalayas. Lothar Meid, who wrote "Deutsch-Nepal," noted that the song was inspired by his militarist father, his own interest in Nepal, and the connections he saw between hard rock and military marching bands.[47] Amon Düül II's self-stylization as Nazis particularly reinforced stereotypes held by their numerous British fans. One of the group's first appearances in England in 1972 was disrupted by a fan with a toy machine gun who yelled "Heil Hitler!" and was escorted out by British police.[48] Consequently, the cover of their 1974 *Live in London* release depicted "a gigantic German-helmeted Stormtrooper insect claw[ing] the London Post-Office tower from its foundations as flying-saucers lay the city to waste overhead."[49] This engagement of Nazi tropes was meant to be satirical but not clearly marked as such and could also be misconstrued. To some extent, toying with fascist symbols signaled the failure of the communal as an alternative to the national for the band.

For *Vive La Trance* (1973), *Hijack* (1974), and their greatest-hits collection *Lemmingmania* (1975), Amon Düül II largely refrained from further engaging German stereotypes and opted for standard rock songs with English lyrics (only "Da Guadaloup" from *Hijack* featured a distorted German national anthem). Yet for their ambitious 1975 project *Made in Germany*, the German stereotypes were back in full force. Probably inspired by the success of Kraftwerk's *Autobahn* and with the US market in mind, Amon Düül II conceived a rock opera with Germanic themes. On "Emigrant Song," they proclaimed: "The Krauts are coming to the U.S.A. / yodeling and shouting loud hurrah

/ they stand on top of Sierra Nevada." Lacking a coherent narrative, the songs name-dropped Wilhelm II, Ludwig II of Bavaria, Fritz Lang, Richard Wagner, Siegfried, Krupp steel, Mercedes, Immanuel Kant, and Adolf Hitler. In another reference to the United States, "Blue Grotto" lambasted the reinvention of Neuschwanstein Castle by Walt Disney: "Swan-stoned Ludwig / you missed your flight to Disneyland / where all your fantasies / come to a plastic end." "5.5.55" featured a mock interview with Hitler by a British radio DJ. Stylistically diverse, the music of *Made in Germany* consisted of European classical elements, rock, electronica, jazz, tango, musical theater, and a version of the shanty "La Paloma" retitled "La Krautoma." In a raving review for the German *Sounds*, Manfred Gillig wrote that the album was "American in character," adding: "Teutonic sounds that oftentimes indicate the negative quality of German productions are just the means to an end here: to show that despite all refinements and a well-practiced rock vocabulary they are still a German group. This should conquer America like Volkswagen has done before."[50] Yet *Made in Germany*, released as a double album in Germany, with the band dressed up as Ludwig, Wilhelm, and other German characters on the cover, and released as a single LP with Renate Knaup as Marlene Dietrich on the cover in the United States, failed to chart on either side of the Atlantic. Despite the intended irony, the explicit references to German themes did not work as a reterritorializing force. The band fell apart after the disappointment of *Made in Germany* but has seen various reunions over the years.

Amon Düül I and II are generally listed among the most important German bands of the 1970s and, like many other krautrock groups, were initially at least as successful in Great Britain and France as in Germany. Yet they have not seen the same surge in interest by a younger audience in Europe and the United States as Can, Neu!, or Faust. Because they did not break with Anglo-American rock traditions as clearly and dramatically as Faust or Kraftwerk, neither the monotonous, tripped-out jam sessions of Amon Düül I nor the musically complex progressive rock of Amon Düül II had the same long-term appeal as Can's instant compositions, Faust's avant-garde simplicity and tape experiments, or Neu!'s motorik new wave. The group's most important legacy, besides their musical accomplishments, was their embodiment of both promise and failure of the communal as a counter-model to the nationalist.

## Faust

If Amon Düül represented a short-lived hippie commune that developed into a professional rock band, the same could not be said of Faust, whose members rigorously maintained the same art commune for many years, and who, musically and conceptually, celebrated dilettantism and radically broke with the Anglo-American traditions that continued to inform Amon Düül II's recordings. The group initially received massive support from their record company Polydor. The label supplied the band's recording facilities and their communal residence in Wümme near Hamburg. Partly because of their uncompromising artistic vision, Faust were rejected both by critics and audiences in Germany but became quite successful in Great Britain and other European countries. The four albums the band produced between 1971 and 1973, while no major successes at the time, have proven to be some of the most influential records of the decade and have had an impact on countless American and British bands.

Like most other krautrock groups, Faust were concerned about breaking with the Nazi past, but they also more decidedly moved away from any American influences. Founding member Gunther Wüsthoff noted: "After World War II there was this big void. Death had put on the mask of a loyal official and our parents had become used to the rules and never asked any questions. And then Coca Cola and rock'n'roll came bursting into the void. And all of a sudden, we realized that we can choose NOT to do anything."[51] Hans-Joachim Irmler, another founding member of Faust, said: "We didn't want to do any beat or rock music—that was quite clear."[52] He also talked of setting the group apart from "the generation above us who had been Nazis and in large parts still stuck to a watered-down form of that ideology, while on the other hand, we didn't want to play the music of the imperialist USA, who after the war had been flooding the land with their culture."[53] As part of their artistic conceptualization, the band wanted to embrace a reterritorialized form of national identity. Jean-Hervé Péron, yet another Faust member, noted: "We were not happy being a deluded echo of what went on in the music scenes of England and the States."[54] He added: "We're German, we're not afraid of it, we're not ashamed of it, and we make different music."[55]

Faust's Germanness was apparent in their name choice, which was referencing both Johann Wolfgang von Goethe's famous character and the German word for "fist." Yet influences on the band were manifold and included American as well as German artists—the Fluxus and Dada movements, the Beach Boys, Karlheinz Stockhausen, and the Velvet Underground, among others. Parallels could also be drawn to *musique concrète*, the Beatles'"Revolution No. 9," and American artists explicitly in conflict with their own national identity: Captain Beefheart, Frank Zappa (who inspired the nickname of Faust's Werner "Zappi" Diermaier), the United States of America, and jazz musicians John Coltrane and Sun Ra (some of whose own influences had been non-Western). Promoting absurdity and playing with particularly British notions of German identity, the "Faust Manifesto," handed out at their 1973 UK tour, listed influences like Hitler, the Heisenberg principle, antimatter, relativity, cybernetics, and game theory.[56] The manifesto concluded by calling Faust's music "the sound of yourself listening," a description that clearly transcended national boundaries.[57]

The origins of Faust are well-documented. When Polydor was looking for a German version of the Beatles, the record company contacted Uwe Nettelbeck, former editor for *Konkret*, a leftist publication that had also counted Ulrike Meinhof among its contributors (Meinhof later became a wanted RAF terrorist). Nettelbeck assembled Faust from two existing groups to present to Polydor. Jean-Hervé Péron (bass), Rudolf Sosna (guitar), and Gunther Wüsthoff (saxophone) came from Nukleus; Werner Diermaier (drums), Arnulf Meifert (drums), and Hans-Joachim Irmler (keyboards) came from Campylognatus Citelli. Combining the sounds of the two groups was a bold move, since the Nukleus musicians were singer-songwriters with an emphasis on composition and lyrics, whereas Campylognatus Citelli's music developed out of improvisation and experimentation and emphasized rhythmic texture and ambience. Although the group met in Hamburg's Schanzenviertel, they were not necessarily a local band, since half of their members claimed non-German affiliations (Péron was French, Diermaier was Austrian, Sosna was part-Russian). Uwe Nettelbeck wanted Faust to be thought of as a rootless rock band and said they were avant-garde by accident:

> As far as content is concerned, we are realising the particular situation a German band is in by not having any roots in rock music but, on the other hand, knowing all the stuff because you neither speak English nor have any connections to anything in it. It's a second sort of reality. So we try to make an amalgam, from all the material which comes to us, to form

something which goes beyond quotations. The material should be altered, shouldn't stay the same, never, and this should be combined with sounds.[58]

The band's politics, then, were as unstable as their national and musical identities. Hans-Joachim Irmler explicitly rejected Germany's political rock scene as "gross"—"it bothered me that serious issues were obscenely presented with the music of the occupation"[59]—and instead saw Faust as creating "the sound and the heart of the revolution everybody was busy planning."[60] Unlike both Amon Düül II and Ton Steine Scherben, who addressed New Left politics much more explicitly but were musically firmly rooted in Anglo-American traditions, Faust turned the music itself into a political tool.

The only Faust song that could be considered political in a more overt way was their very first known recording, entitled "Lieber Herr Deutschland" ("Dear Mr. Germany") and later released on the anthology *71 Minutes*. The track was Faust's demo recording for Polydor. As a pun on the German word *Demo* (a homonym that could refer both to a demo recording and a political demonstration), it began with found sounds from a union rally. Continuing to abandon conventional song structures, the song turned to an abrasive instrumental passage. In yet another abrupt shift, the song then featured two voices on different channels reading instructions for a washing machine and mocking consumer capitalism: "The future-assured fully-automatic washing machine offers you everything that a future-assured fully-automatic washing machine can offer you—for example, a light panel so you can follow the wash programme precisely, and the fully-automatic washing powder input, so you don't have to think anymore."[61] The second half of the song collage consisted of a more abstract piece with unintelligible lyrics. Of all Faust recordings, "Lieber Herr Deutschland" had the most obvious political message. As a parody of nationalism and capitalism it had parallels in many of Frank Zappa's compositions. Like Zappa, Faust invoked politics more Dadaist than Marxist on their first known recording. These politics disappeared halfway through the song, when the emphasis clearly shifted from the linguistic to the musical. Understanding musical sound itself as political was what Faust would exhibit much more poignantly on the four LPs they produced between 1971 and 1973.

The record deal with Polydor that Uwe Nettelbeck managed to secure for Faust included the funding with which they were able to start an art commune. Polydor provided them with living quarters and a recording studio in a converted schoolhouse in Wümme, twenty-five miles outside Hamburg in the Lüneburg Heath. They were joined by Polydor's sound engineer Kurt Graupner, who had previously worked with European classical musicians. Andy Wilson has described the layout of the commune:

> A small control room, a kitchen and communal living area supported the studio space, and there were separate bedrooms for the band's accommodation. The building was in the shape of a flattened "H," with the studio at one end, living quarters at the other, and a kitchen and other amenities in between. It was wired to allow instruments to be played more or less anywhere, and the group would often record with members in different rooms, sometimes even lying alone on their beds as they improvised. Tape machines were running almost continually to capture every idea, any of which could subsequently be edited and mixed in with other material.[62]

Faust and Amon Düül shared the idea that music and personal life were inextricably linked, but Faust, with their commune-as-studio, further blurred the line between privacy and production. The actual recording studio, the school's former classroom, could be used day and night, and while the Beatles and the Beach Boys had pioneered treating the studio as an instrument, and Miles Davis had already composed in a cinematic "frame-by-frame" approach, Faust's complete merging of living, music-making, and recording was unheard of at the time. Unlike Amon Düül II's Kronwinkl 12 commune, where Anglo-American rock was blasted constantly, there were no radios or record players in Wümme, so Faust could eliminate outside influences from their own music-making, and the band was known to switch instruments regularly. In their attempt "to free sound from it's [sic] enslavement to given structures,"[63] as Hans-Joachim Irmler called it, Faust were greatly supported by sound engineer Kurt Graupner. He developed the "black boxes," a type of stereo synthesizer and multi-effect unit: "Made of perspex, they were about a meter long and had twenty controls, a patch bay, and pedals to control tone and pulse generators, a ring modulator, filtering; equalisation, distortion, reverb and delay, as well as allowing external processors to be connected inline."[64] These black boxes could be wired together, allowing each musician to control the overall sound of the group and to be an equal partner in the production process.

The black boxes and the commune-as-studio were examples of Faust's experimentation with sound and their politics of starting a revolution within, not outside, their music. Irmler noted that Faust wanted to "move somewhere together where everyone can live out his preferences, yet has to stand his ground against the other five—which sometimes led to real fights."[65] Uwe Nettelbeck remembered endless discussions in Wümme resulting from the participatory process of music-making and communal living.[66] In this regard Faust was quite similar to the communes of Amon Düül II and Ton Steine Scherben. In other commune-typical behavior, Faust consumed copious amounts of hashish, LSD, and alcohol (the latter in the form of cognac and fine wines, contrasting with Amon Düül II's rejection of alcohol as bourgeois), "all the while Péron looked after the dogs and wandered the grounds naked in sun, wind and rain."[67] Uwe Nettelbeck had to report back to Polydor regularly on the progress of the group's first album. He managed to keep the record company waiting for a year after Faust had signed the contract. The group had to assemble their debut album quickly, which, according to Werner Diermaier, was done in one night while tripping on LSD.[68] Released in 1971, the album, which did not have an actual title and has generally been referred to as *Faust*, *Faust I*, or *Clear*, must have perplexed the Polydor executives.

The packaging of Faust's first album consisted of a transparent sleeve and a transparent insert with the lyrics and other texts printed in red letters, containing a transparent vinyl disc. The only image on the sleeve was the x-ray of a clenched fist. The peculiar packaging could be interpreted in many different ways. The title, *Faust*, could have referred to the fist on the cover (which itself could be read as an inverted black power salute, among other things) or to Goethe's Faust selling his soul to the devil (just as the group had done by signing to a major record company). The transparent design could be read as reflecting the emptiness of postwar Germany, but also, in a broader sense, nihilism or Buddhism. The song lyrics in English and German, printed on the insert, resembled William S. Burroughs's cut-and-paste experiments. The critical engagement with Germany's Americanization after World War II was clearly part of the concept, as the other texts on the insert showed. Uwe Nettelbeck's quote "I like the Beach Boys!" acknowledged the influence of Brian Wilson's experimentation on *Pet Sounds* and the then-unfinished *Smile* album. The lyric sheet also contained a confusing story fragment, mostly in German, about a couple in Los Angeles and apparently meant as a surrealist parody of American crime novels and film noir motifs. One sentence read: "'Shall I show you my private part again?' she cooed in her deep, roughened, and intimate voice, while her fabulous breast pointed straight at him and seemed to want to dazzle him."

The engagement of a Dadaist or surrealist critique of Anglo-American influences continued in the actual music on the disc. There were only three "songs" on the album, all of them collages that blurred the lines between music, sound, and noise, and all of them radically breaking with blues rock conventions like pentatonic scales and tonic-subdominant-dominant progressions. *Faust* contained cacophony, distortion, silence—or at least very quiet passages—and was difficult to listen to. "Why Don't You Eat Carrots?" opened the album with snippets of the Rolling Stones' "Satisfaction" and the Beatles' "All You Need is Love" amidst grinding noise, leaving traditional rock music as represented by those two groups behind. The song featured a part by Ludwig van Beethoven, free jazz, strange voices with Dadaist lyrics, ship horns, and underwater sounds and blended into the other track on side one, "Meadow Meal," which incorporated yet another song, "Linus." On these tracks, Faust did not present discrete pieces of music, and they would continue this trend on their following LPs, in particular *The Faust Tapes*. Side two of *Faust* was one long piece of improvisation with the ambiguous title "Miss Fortune" (a variation of "misfortune"). It started as a wah-wah-heavy two-chord jam session before morphing into cacophonous sounds, pseudo-operatic vocals, off-key jazz rock, a quiet piano passage, electronically manipulated vocals, an organ playing the chords of the Kingsmen's 1955 hit "Louie Louie," and finally some spoken-word lyrics over gentle acoustic guitar strumming that culminated in an overtly political statement, "our wish to be free, to organize and analyze," but also the realization "that nobody knows if it really happened."

Polydor's March 1971 "Faust Press Release" inaccurately proclaimed that the group was "building as much on the immense tradition of German music as on the Anglo-Saxon traditions of current pop"[69]—in contrast to what the marketing machine had hoped for, Faust broke with German and American musical traditions alike. The reaction in Germany was muted and the album sold less than one thousand copies. A German TV documentary from 1971 dismissed their music as "ignorant" and "rock amateurism sold as the new sound."[70] Furthermore, a live appearance at the Musikhalle in Hamburg in the fall of 1971 turned into a disaster when the sound failed with all the major media representatives present. Incidentally, the first positive assessment of the group was by a British critic, Ian MacDonald. In a piece for the *New Musical Express* from 1972, MacDonald called Faust "the first genuine example of rock that Britain and America could not only never have conceived [ . . . ], but which they would, at present, find technologically impossible to emulate."[71] MacDonald also elaborated on how Faust's collages might have borne some similarities with those of Frank Zappa, but how the group had also managed to create a very unique sound: "Faust aren't, like Zappa, trying to piece together a jigsaw with the parts taken from different jigsaw sets; they're taking a single picture (which may be extremely unorthodox in its virgin state), chopping it into jigsaw pieces, and fitting it together again in a different way."[72] Hans-Joachim Irmler explained why British critics and fans, and eventually also American audiences, were interested in Faust long before they had any positive reaction in their home country: "We gave them the Teutonic because we were brutes, but we were also weird. That did not correspond with the image of Germans that the Brits had."[73] Faust's "weirdness" and their musical avant-garde politics provided an interesting comparison to Amon Düül's communal hippie spirit and eventual turn toward German stereotypes. Partly because of their "Germanness," both bands had early successes in Great Britain, but Faust were more deliberately challenging foreign notions of Germany than either formation of Amon Düül.

After the commercial failure of their debut, Faust toned down their radical aural politics for the LP *So Far* (1972). Individual tracks were more distinct and had somewhat more traditional song structures. The album began with the seven-and-a-half minute track "It's a Rainy Day Sunshine Girl." The song repeated a single chord and the absurd title ad nauseam while slowly building up a beat that could be described as "not so much 4/4 as 1/1."[74] Eventually, harmonica and a saxophone riff added some more texture to the track. Similar to songs by the Velvet Underground, the simplicity and low fidelity apparent on "It's a Rainy Day" foreshadowed punk rock's do-it-yourself approach. Jean-Hervé Péron noted: "I think that Faust [ . . . ] felt this ur-urge to stomp. This is an ancient and universal expression of togetherness, of belonging to the clan, joining in with the universe."[75] The communal primitivism espoused by Péron was in many ways similar to Can's embrace of world music as a means of creating an internationalized counter-model to German nationalism. Side one of *So Far* continued with the gentle acoustic guitar picking and synthesizer of "On the Way to Abamäe" before making way for the ten-minute "No Harm," morphing from an organ solo into a long, straightforward guitar-bass-drum groove with another absurd line repeated like a Dada mantra: "Daddy take the banana, tomorrow is Sunday!"

Side two of *So Far* showed the breadth of Faust's sound repertoire. It opened with the mellow guitar groove and staccato horns of the title track, followed by the atonal industrial sounds of "Mamie is Blue" that inspired an entire genre, electronic body music (EBM). The final medley of four shorter songs resembled Frank Zappa's work and featured pitch-manipulated voices mocking consumerism; polyrhythmic free jazz on saxophone, guitar, and piano; tape experiments; and campy bar-band rhythm and blues. The album was packaged in an entirely black sleeve, mirroring both the cover of the Velvet Underground's *White Light, White Heat* (1968) and the suprematism of Russian painter Kazimir Malevich's *Black Square* (1915). The "black box" cover also inverted the first album's translucent packaging. Inside the album cover were a series of prints by Edda Kochl, which illustrated each song in a surrealist or naive style, very much in line with the politics of the music.

Although not quite as profound a statement as the first album, Faust's *So Far* maintained a dedication to anticonsumerist, antinationalist, and avant-garde politics. The second album was much easier to listen to than the debut but also failed to impress German audiences and critics. In a scathing review, the German *Sounds* called *So Far* weak and amateurish: "After a crappy debut album and lots of support from their 'patrons' and their record company, they were surprisingly bold enough to produce a second, almost equally crappy LP."[76] Unfazed by this critique, Faust continued to record music in Wümme, including the album *Outside the Dream Syndicate* (1972) with violinist Tony Conrad, a minimalist composer who had worked with John Cale and La Monte Young and was experimenting with drones. Tony Conrad, entering the commune as an outsider, had a unique perspective on Wümme. According to Conrad, Faust "had been, to some substantial degree, incarcerated in this farmhouse for months, and they had their partners and sexual liaisons and different social complexities enacted on a long-term basis within this farmhouse. It was a microcosm, where everything seemed to have been evolving in some strange way over the course of months and months."[77] Faust's seclusion and their radical rejection of any outside influences contributed to a more consistent artistic vision than life in either the Amon Düül or the Ton Steine Scherben communes, but this seclusion also put Faust on the fringe of German society, which might have been why they were ignored completely in their home country at the time. Faust's reception was quite different outside Germany. Philippe Paringaux wrote in 1972 for French magazine *Rock & Folk* that it was precisely Faust's disregard for rock traditions that was their strength. For Paringaux, Faust "view rock as it's played in its lands of origin with a certain amount of detachment, eliminating to the best of their ability any attempts to reproduce a 'feeling' which cannot belong to them [ . . . ], taking no more from American or British rock than a state of mind."[78]

When Faust's second album also failed to produce any commercial success, Polydor unceremoniously dropped the band, but they were picked up by the British Virgin label. The band quickly assembled an album culled from fragments recorded in Wümme, which was released in 1973 under the title *The Faust Tapes*. As an innovative marketing strategy, the record was sold for forty-nine pence, the price of a single, selling at least fifty thousand copies, which got it on the British charts. Interestingly, the music on the album was less of a commercial compromise than *So Far* and returned to the avant-garde collage approach of Faust's debut. Initially only containing two long pieces, *The Faust Tapes* was broken up into twenty-six tracks for its *Wümme Years* reissue. Discrete songs were hidden within a mix of tape splicing, found sounds, and noisy textures. The music's experimental and fragmentary nature was already evident in titles like "Exercise—with Several Hands on a Piano" or "Untitled (All on Saxes)." More song-like tracks on the album included the sprawling, piano- and acoustic-guitar-driven "Flashback Caruso" and the hectic guitar-riff- and saxophone-heavy "J'ai Mal Aux Dents." Faust revealed their rejection of traditional semantics when they later changed the name of the latter to "Schempahl Buddha" because a fan had misunderstood the lyrics "*j'ai mal aux dents, j'ai mal aux pieds aussi*" ("I have a toothache, and my feet hurt too") as "Schempahl Buddha, ship on a better sea." The French recitation of "Chère Chambre" established Faust as more than just another German band singing in English. Finally, "Stretch Out Time" emphasized how Faust set out to deconstruct the concept of musical time—instead of adhering to a rigid (German) concept of time like Kraftwerk, they freed time through communal music-making.[79]

Faust's deconstruction of musical and nonmusical time as well as musical and nonmusical language and their continued references to emptiness were a conceptual variation of Can's, Kraftwerk's, and Neu!'s musical *Stunde Null*. As an art commune, Faust might have been even more explicitly avant-garde than most other krautrock groups, which again was reflected in the cover art of the *Faust Tapes*. The album has appeared with four different sleeves. Along with the mostly untitled tracks, this multiplicity continued the empty signification of the first two albums' transparent and opaque cover art. The original release featured the optical illusion of Bridget Riley's painting *Crest*, a black-and-white, diamond-shaped depiction of interfering waves in the op-art tradition, and, on the back cover, self-referential reviews of Faust's music from various publications.

After the release of *The Faust Tapes*, the group successfully toured in Britain. The deconstructive sound experiments Faust had undertaken in the studio continued on stage, where they performed almost in complete darkness. The only lights were the LEDs of the black boxes, a few color TV sets, and pinball machines with which they triggered sound effects. Hiding behind their electronic equipment, Faust in some ways paralleled Kraftwerk's anti-rock stage act. As Uwe Nettelbeck put it: "Basically, Faust is a machine, but everybody is sitting on the machine and trying to get freedom out of it."[80] Blurring the line between music and noise, Faust also used construction tools like jackhammers, cement mixers, sanders, and sheets of metal on stage, an idea later picked up by Einstürzende Neubauten and other industrial bands. In addition, Faust's questioning of rock authenticity was a first step toward what Kraftwerk later developed into their robot act. As Nettelbeck envisioned it in 1973: "We had the idea later, if we can do it, to project a film next to [guitarist Rudolf Sosna] on stage which shows him playing a guitar solo but he's standing still and not doing it."[81] Faust's deterritorialized anti-rock, ignored in their home country, turned heads when it crossed the border. The concerts in Britain received raving reviews in *New Musical Express* and *Melody Maker* in 1973. For instance, Ian MacDonald called the group "the most significant conceptual revolution in rock for ten years."[82]

The group's last major release, *Faust IV*, was recorded in Virgin's Manor Studios in Oxfordshire and included only a few leftovers from the Wümme years. The album returned to *So Far*'s more listenable, somewhat more song-oriented concept and featured another album cover signifying "nothing," this time with a series of empty staves. As on the three other original releases, no image of the band was included in the artwork, reinforcing Faust's Foucauldian deconstruction of the author. Faust's rejection of authenticity was particularly noteworthy at this time because during the breaks in the recording of *IV* pop auteur Mike Oldfield cut his first album *Tubular Bells* at Manor

Studios all by himself, a surprise hit for Virgin that far surpassed Faust's success and seemed like the antithesis of their work.

*Faust IV* opened with the twelve-minute one-chord monotony of "Krautrock," another Faust song whose harmonic simplicity was enriched by subtle changes in dynamics. The self-referential title was clearly ironic. As Hans-Joachim Irmler put it, Faust wanted to clarify that "we are not those 'krauts' that you think we are and who you hate so much but we also don't play that 'rock' that you want to force upon us. So we said, let's play a really heavy song and then we'll call it 'Krautrock.'"[83] "Krautrock" was followed by what some might read as another song subtly inverting German national identity, "The Sad Skinhead," a Teutonic reggae that featured the line "going places, smashing faces, what else could we do?" Yet the song was probably not meant as a comment on neo-Nazis, since at the time skinheads were oftentimes reggae and ska fans without any strong political leanings. Side one closed with the fairly conventional ballad "Jennifer" that abruptly shifted to white noise and ragtime piano at the end.

The experimental side of the group was also evident on side two of *Faust IV*, which contained the driving beat and electronic effects of "Just a Second," an extended version of one of the songs from *So Far*, "Picnic on a Frozen River," here with an added section with vocals entitled "Giggy Smile"; and a song written in 13/8 time and ending with the sounds of two clashing metronomes, "Läuft." The album closed with "Run," a song not named on the album cover, which contrasted gentle keyboard sounds with buzzing guitar, and the acoustic ballad "It's a Bit of a Pain," which could have passed for one of the Velvet Underground's mellower compositions were it not for a short reading from the Swedish translation of Germaine Greer's feminist book *The Female Eunuch* and the disruptive sounds of a heavily processed electric guitar.

With some success in Great Britain and France but still no major impact in Germany, the band fell apart after *Faust IV*. They had been working on a fifth album, which was only released in bits and pieces years later. The reception in Germany continued to be mostly negative. As late as 1984, Hermann Haring wrote for a major encyclopedia of West German rock music that Faust sounded like "talented amateurs who had smoked a joint." He bemoaned that they could not keep their timing and called them overall "unbearable."[84] Yet Faust's dilettantism had an unmistakable impact on British and American bands from the 1980s and 1990s, which included industrial bands like Throbbing Gristle and Nurse with Wound, post-rock groups like Tortoise, as well as many others, from Sonic Youth and Einstürzende Neubauten to Mercury Rev and My Bloody Valentine. Julian Cope was a major force in putting Faust back on the map of rock history. In his *Krautrocksampler*, he praised them as one of the most important German bands of the 1970s and quipped: "There is no band more mythical than Faust."[85]

The band itself reemerged in the 1990s in different incarnations and has released many albums, including a reissue of the original catalog. Rudolf Sosna passed away in 1997, but some other founding members have remained active, in particular Hans-Joachim Irmler, Jean-Hervé Péron, and Werner Diermaier. The radical deterritorialization in the art of the commune that was and to some extent still is Faust bears some similarities to other krautrock groups. Simon Reynolds has compared Faust's "fission" to Can's "fusion," and taken together, these two groups had a massive impact on nonmainstream rock music. Faust's cut-up and collage techniques, their Neu!-like tape-splicing and remixing, their deconstruction of musical time, and their blurring of the lines between music, sound, silence, and noise were revolutionary in a more implicit way than the communal politics of Amon Düül and Ton Steine Scherben, but their effect was possibly even greater.

## Ton Steine Scherben

Unlike Amon Düül and Faust, Ton Steine Scherben's commune had a very specific political agenda from the outset and expressed their reterritorialization through German-language lyrics. Musically, however, they were the most Anglo-American influenced of the three. Explicitly communal throughout their existence, the Scherben's left-wing politics and their connection to the squatter scene gradually made way for more introspective songs and a move to the northern German countryside. Singer Rio Reiser's identification as gay had an important part in this process. The legacy of Ton Steine Scherben is politically ambiguous, as they continue to be a voice for young leftist youth but have also been discovered by neo-Nazis. Unlike Amon Düül and Faust, the Scherben have hardly had any impact outside their home country because their main contribution was their German lyrics, not their Americanized music.

Ton Steine Scherben may have been the first rock band to unconditionally embrace German lyrics and radical New Left politics, but they quickly became part of a scene of likeminded bands that included Checkpoint Charlie, Franz K., Ihre Kinder, Hotzenplotz, Floh de Cologne, Lokomotive Kreuzberg, and Eulenspygel. By 1974, the German-language political rock scene had become so big that Olaf Reuther wrote in *Sounds* that it "hadn't merely caught up with its Anglo-American idols but had taken a more straightforward path that made more sense politically."[86] Whereas some of the other German-language political rock groups drew on indigenous folk music traditions, Ton Steine Scherben were steeped in Anglo-American and African American music, in particular blues scales and phrasings. Scherben drummer Wolfgang Seidel admitted: "We were fed on a steady diet of American music."[87] The embrace of what Hans-Joachim Irmler of Faust had called "the music of the occupation" was at odds with some of Ton Steine Scherben's politics. This trend continued with the politics of German punk that, influenced by developments in New York City and London, revived some of the Scherben's overt political messages.

Ton Steine Scherben evolved from Hoffman's Comic Teater, a West-Berlin theater group that had written what was arguably the very first rock opera, *Robinson 2000*, back in 1967. Founded in 1970 as VEB Ton Steine Scherben (VEB referring to *Volkseigene Betriebe*, the "people-owned enterprises" of East Germany), they later dropped the first part of their name. Literally translated as "Clay, Stones, Shards," the name of the group was a parody of the West German trade union *Bau-Steine-Erden* ("Construction, Stones, Soil") but also played with the ambiguity of the word *Ton* (meaning both "clay" and "sound"). Asked about the name of the group, Rio Reiser would later note that clay, stones, and shards was all that German archaeologist Heinrich Schliemann found when he excavated Troy.[88] Despite these German references, the word *Steine* was also a tribute to the Rolling Stones as a major early influence on the group. Regularly referred to as the German Stones, Ton Steine Scherben drew so heavily on the British band that, at least initially, only their German lyrics distinguished them from other Anglophile groups.

Like the Rolling Stones, Ton Steine Scherben created their musical alchemy through the collaboration of a singer, Ralph Möbius (born 1950), and a guitarist, Ralph Peter Steitz (born 1950). Rechristened Rio Reiser[89] and R. P. S. Lanrue, they became the core members of the group, along with bass player Kai Sichtermann (born 1951). Wolfgang Seidel, the Scherben's first drummer, left in 1971, and the group did not find a steady replacement until 1974 with Klaus "Funky" Götzner. Other important early members

were manager and part-time vocalist Nikel Pallat and flautist Jörg Schlotterer. From the beginning, the band had strong connections to West Berlin's
squatter scene. Starting in 1971, they lived in their own commune at the
"T-Ufer," 32 Tempelhofer Ufer, in the working-class district of Kreuzberg.
They collectively moved to rural Fresenhagen in 1975. As Rio Reiser put it,
living with the band was an "absolute necessity."[90]

Rio Reiser evoked the group's theater background when he described
the T-Ufer commune's enactment of alternative lifestyles, where roughly
twelve men and women lived in two connecting apartments:

> Someone—I don't remember who—had decided a long time ago to
> unite these twelve people in this particular time and place.—There was
> no initiation ritual. Whoever arrived, arrived. Whoever stayed, stayed.
> Whoever left, left. The kitchens of the two apartments were connected
> via the back stairs, and the apartments became the stage for an open-
> ended play. Each actor in this play was his own writer and his own direc-
> tor. And his own audience. Whoever walked through the front door either
> left never to come back or returned to keep the plot going. If all of the
> actors took their roles seriously it would have never gotten boring.[91]

The T-Ufer was much more open to the outside world than Faust's commune in Wümme. Similar to Amon Düül II's Kronwinkl 12, people with
terrorist connections, some with warrants, occasionally showed up (these
included Anne Reiche, Jörg Schlotterer, and Holger Meins). Less elitist than
Kronwinkl 12, the T-Ufer commune welcomed young dropouts and derelicts to keep what Rio Reiser called a "proletarian balance."[92] By 1974, about
twenty people were living in the commune, in addition to an unknown
number of "friends, lovers, and familiar as well as unfamiliar visitors."[93]

The commune's utopian socialist approach also applied to Ton Steine
Scherben's means of production. They founded Germany's very first independent label, David Volksmund Produktion (in a reference to David of
David and Goliath and the word *Volksmund*, which roughly translates to
"voice of the people"). Ton Steine Scherben's album covers were simple and
homemade; the records had a fixed price and were distributed through leftist bookstores. T-Ufer's phone number was printed on the first LP cover, and
the Scherben were booked regularly for concerts organized by high schools
or young worker organizations for a minimal fee. They also engaged in

political dialog with the audience after each show. In contrast to Amon Düül II and Faust with their major record deals, Ton Steine Scherben had an explicit and rather unambiguous political message. It was only later that musical expression would replace sloganeering and add more complexity to what politics might actually mean for the band. Yet they were most successful with their earlier, clear-cut politics and firm anticorporate stance that presented a viable alternative to rock's capitalist business practices.

Ton Steine Scherben's first single was the programmatic "Macht kaputt, was euch kaputt macht" ("Destroy What Destroys You"), consisting of three chords and featuring a poignant guitar riff.[94] The song had initially been written for Hoffmann's Comic Teater with lyrics by Norbert Krause and was inspired by Bob Dylan's "Subterranean Homesick Blues." As an anarchist outcry against the capitalist system (it listed mass media, consumer goods, the military, and factory work as oppressive), the theater piece "Macht kaputt" was not without its performative qualities, but it had a very immediate impact. For instance, when the group played the song at a 1970 festival on the northern German island of Fehmarn (which also featured Jimi Hendrix's final gig), the audience, frustrated by the poor organization of the event and encouraged by Rio Reiser, set the festival grounds on fire. The fact that some of the fans interpreted their early political material literally showed both Ton Steine Scherben's significance and their risk of being misread.

Ton Steine Scherben's debut album, *Warum geht es mir so dreckig?* ("Why Do I Feel So Rotten?"), was released in 1971. One side was recorded in a makeshift studio in a factory in Kreuzberg and the other side live with an audience. Primarily addressing young workers and the underclass, oftentimes by using the second person, the lyrics consisted of straightforward messages and slogans. The critique of consumer capitalism and the German justice system was expressed in "Der Kampf geht weiter" ("The Struggle Continues"), written in support of the RAF terrorists, and another song in which employers were compared to "Slave Traders" ("Sklavenhändler"). Yet musically Ton Steine Scherben's electric-guitar-driven blues rock was much more in line with US capitalism than German communism, with the exception of Bertolt Brecht and Hanns Eisler's "Einheitsfrontlied" ("United Front Song"), which was tacked to the end of "Macht kaputt, was euch kaputt macht." As the cover of the album proclaimed, Ton Steine Scherben were the *Agitrockband Berlin*, with *Agitrock* equaling "agitprop + acid rock." It is remarkable that using Anglo-American rock music for a decidedly anticapitalist cause

did not appear to be a contradiction for either the musicians or the fans of
Ton Steine Scherben at the time.

In 1972, Ton Steine Scherben released their second and commercially most
successful album, the double LP *Keine Macht für Niemand* ("No Power for
Nobody"). The grammatical errors of the title (it used a double negative and
*niemand* instead of *niemanden*), combined with its anarchism, signaled the
continuation of proletarian and anticapitalist communal politics. In the booklet to the album, the group announced: "We have stopped working for a boss
and we live together. In Berlin. We have no party affiliation. Our philosophy
is: Do what you want." The booklet also featured the humorous Bible pun
"Mao, Mao, why have you forsaken us?" and reiterated theater metaphors to
describe the performance of daily living: "We are standing on the stage. It is
we who act. Everything is reality. There is no audience." The packaging consisted of a folded piece of cardboard in which the vinyl disc was wrapped (a
design by Rio Reiser's father Herbert Möbius), with the title printed like a
graffiti slogan. The original album also came with a plastic-covered metal
catapult, which could have been interpreted as condoning violence but was
clearly ironic, as Wolfgang Seidel noted: "Exactly at the time when a part of
the formerly anti-authoritarian left called for armed resistance and began
using real guns, the Scherben came out with a kid's toy."[95]

Musically more expansive than Ton Steine Scherben's first album, *Keine
Macht für Niemand* presented a combination of pentatonic blues rock and
more experimental songs with agitprop lyrics. "Wir müssen hier raus" ("We
Have to Get Out of Here") introduced Rio Reiser's brash and unadorned
vocals alongside a shuffle rhythm played by an overdriven electric guitar, and
"Feierabend" ("Quitting Time") with its standard blues changes envisioned
breaking out of conformist work and life structures. The anti-military, anti-
police song "Die letzte Schlacht gewinnen wir" ("We Will Win the Last
Battle") featured a rock guitar riff and the chorus "the red front and the
black front, that's us!" in a somewhat confusing embrace of both communism and anarchism. Ton Steine Scherben's politics also remained a bit
murky on "Paul Panzers Blues," the revenge fantasy of an oppressed worker
beating up his boss, revealing his secret desire to become a consumer. It was
sung (or rather yelled) by Nikel Pallat, the Scherben's manager, and set to a
slow blues replete with guitar and harmonica solos. Pallat had made head-
lines when, in a preconceived "happening," he used an axe to split a desk in
a TV studio in the presence of *kosmische Musik* producer Rolf-Ulrich Kaiser

in 1971. The destructive act happened after Pallat had talked about TV as an "instrument of oppression" and had accused Kaiser of supporting "capitalist pigs." As in much of Ton Steine Scherben's seemingly simple sloganeering, the group was aware of its performative qualities. Wolfgang Seidel mentioned that the people in the TV studio did not feel seriously threatened and understood the theatrical character of Pallat's action.[96] In a similar way, "Paul Panzers Blues" could be read as performing in character.

The politics of Ton Steine Scherben and their sound became much more expansive on the following tracks, which featured longer instrumental passages and more melodic singing and rhythmic complexity. The lyrics repeatedly referenced Christianity, for instance on "Schritt für Schritt ins Paradies" ("Step by Step into Paradise"). In "Der Traum ist aus" ("The Dream Is Over"), Rio Reiser quoted Luke 2:14. The song featured Jörg Schlotterer's Jethro Tull-inspired flute solo as well as piano phrases from Christmas pieces by Carl Orff and Georg Friedrich Händel. Two other songs with chanted vocals and boogie-woogie piano introduced the fictional character "Mensch Meier." In the first song, Meier violently opposed the inflated ticket prices of West Berlin's public transportation service BVG. The second song with Meier, the squatter anthem "Rauch Haus Song," reflected the group's interest in protesting urban renewal and the gentrification of West Berlin. Ton Steine Scherben had been directly involved in the occupation of two sites in Kreuzberg. In the first instance, Reiser encouraged the crowd to take over a vacant building after a concert in July of 1971 that also featured Ash Ra Tempel and Agitation Free. The other occupied building was the "Rauch-Haus," which inspired the song by the same name. The Martha-Maria-Haus of the defunct Bethanien Hospital in West Berlin was occupied by squatters in December of 1971 and renamed after Georg von Rauch, a militant anarchist who had been killed by a police officer. The occupation of the building, chronicled in the song, was successful, and the inhabitants of the house have survived various confrontations with the police and an arson attack as late as 2011.

*Keine Macht für Niemand* ended with two songs that proved that Ton Steine Scherben's political spectrum was actually quite broad. Rio Reiser wrote the anarchist mantra of the title track, a simple rock song with a prominent bass riff and a saxophone solo, for the RAF, who rejected it as irrelevant for the anti-imperialist struggle. In contrast, the last track "Komm schlaf bei mir" ("Come Sleep with Me") was the band's first love song and featured glockenspiel and acoustic guitar. According to Rio Reiser, who did not officially come out as gay until the mid-1970s, the song was secretly directed at a man. Despite of or maybe because of its overt but somewhat inconsistent politics, *Keine Macht für Niemand* became widely regarded as one of the most important German rock albums of the 1970s. As Hartmut El Kurdi wrote: "There were really only two options at leftist student parties [in the 1970s]: Stones or Scherben. [ . . . ] The advantage of the Scherben songs was that you could understand the lyrics and that they set the terms for a specifically German lifestyle."[97] With its reterritorialized lyrics and music that was mostly indistinguishable from groups like the Rolling Stones, the double album has remained popular in German alternative circles through the 1980s, 1990s, and beyond but is virtually unknown outside Germany.

Ton Steine Scherben's eclectic politics included Marxism, anarchism, Christianity, and rock star hedonism. They had issued the programmatic text "Music is a Weapon" in 1970, and Rio Reiser regularly read from Mao's *Little Red Book* onstage, which he liked to carry around with him. At many of their shows, a banner displayed Georg Büchner's famous quote *"Friede den Hütten! Krieg den Palästen!"* ("Peace to the shacks! War on the palaces!"). The group also supported the politically charged American proto-punk band MC5 on their 1972 tour of Germany. The Scherben clearly sided with the squatter scene and participated in demonstrations and protests. Despite their earlier rejection of political parties and much to the chagrin of some of their fans, they eventually campaigned for the Social Democratic Party and the Green Party, and in the 1990s Rio Reiser supported the former East German Communist Party, which had re-formed as the Party of Democratic Socialism (PDS).

To some extent, what connected Rio Reiser's different belief systems and ideologies was a romantic embrace of the disempowered. In this, he echoed one of his idols, German author Karl May (1842–1912), famous for his depictions of the American Old West and his noble savage hero Winnetou. Rio Reiser declared: "Just like Karl May allowed the 'I' in his novels to be strong but good and with a love for humanity, we wanted to turn the 'we' into the oppressed, persecuted, and exploited good that would eventually win. Four billion Old Winnetous!"[98] Reiser's fascination with the controversial German writer went so far that he named one part of Ton Steine Scherben's Fresenhagen estate "Winnetou's Garages," and that each album, beginning with *Keine Macht für Niemand*, contained one song named after a Karl May novel ("Menschenjäger," "Durch die Wüste," "Der Fremde aus Indien,"

"Ardistan"). Identifying with a romanticized ideal of Native Americans was fairly common among countercultural groups, and the krautrock band Gila recorded an entire album entitled *Bury My Heart at Wounded Knee* in 1973. Yet by embracing Karl May, Rio Reiser took the countercultural identification with the racial other a step further, since Winnetou was so obviously fabricated that he could almost be labeled "camp."

Retrospectively, one might view not only Rio Reiser's obsession with Karl May but even some of his New Left politics as "campy." As Reiser was coming to terms with his gay identity, his performance became politically motivated through various other forms of acting "queer." In March of 1974, Ton Steine Scherben caused a controversy by throwing glitter at fans, wearing satin on stage, and performing 1950s rock'n'roll under the name Holly and the Hollyheads, and in 1976 they were verbally attacked for selling out after hiring female backup singers.[99] The Scherben's short stint with glam rock was clearly motivated by gender politics. As Wolfgang Seidel noted: "What we were doing was not just politically from the wrong shore of the Atlantic, but sexually from the wrong shore too."[100] The Scherben's Americanization was not new, but some fans viewed the band as traitors because, by playing 1950s rock'n'roll, they were more overtly referencing music of the occupation. More importantly, the group's campy performances exposed the homophobia of the German counterculture. Rio Reiser explained that he wanted to show that "there should be an end to the privilege of leftist men to wear sackcloth and ashes, parkas and beards, and that the leftist man should pay at least as much attention to his looks as the worker he courts or even the woman he courts."[101] To some extent mirroring the playful sexual ambiguity of British rock stars like Marc Bolan, David Bowie, and Elton John, Rio Reiser's queer performance was a bold statement and continued to inform his work until his untimely death in 1995.

The T-Ufer's urban commune that had provided the environment in which the early Ton Steine Scherben lived and worked began to strain in the mid-1970s. Since the T-Ufer was in the midst of a bustling city, visitors were constantly coming and going, making it difficult to focus on the music. On June 1, 1975, Ton Steine Scherben moved to Fresenhagen, a small town close to the Danish border in northern Germany, where they had bought a dilapidated farmhouse for fifty thousand Deutsche Mark. As guitarist R. P. S. Lanrue remembered: "The reason for leaving Berlin was the desire to have more privacy."[102] Living as an alternative family with initially sixteen people

Fig. 3. Ton Steine Scherben, around 1975. (Courtesy of Gert Möbius.)

and various animals, and growing tomatoes, radish, and hemp, Ton Steine Scherben began recording another double album. It was released under the title *Wenn die Nacht am tiefsten* ("When It's Darkest Night") in 1975. The album cover was the first to include an image of the band (and affiliated commune members, a total of eighteen people with first name, age, and occupation). In the liner notes, the Scherben collectively wrote: "Two years ago we were just five people, now we are sixteen, from age fourteen to thirty-three." Among the new Scherben members were a few women, including percussionist Britta Neander, who later founded the all-female group Carambolage.

Despite taking its title from a Ho Chi Minh quote ("when it's darkest night, day is close at hand"), the music on *Wenn die Nacht am tiefsten* was much less overtly political than on Ton Steine Scherben's first two albums, trading the second-person narratives of earlier days for the introspective first person. More broadly utopian than agitprop, songs on the album addressed a similar low-class perspective and the same political convictions as previous efforts but with a decidedly more positive outlook (compare, for instance, the first album's frustrated "Ich will nicht werden, was mein Alter ist"—"I Don't Want to Become What My Old Man Is"—with the breezy "Samstag nachmittag"—"Saturday Afternoon"—from *Wenn die Nacht am tiefsten*, in which Rio Reiser proclaimed "I see paradise in a vase of flowers"). Christian themes resurfaced on "Durch die Wüste" ("Through the Desert") and "Land in Sicht" ("Land, Ho!"), and Nikel Pallat revived the Paul Panzer character for the sarcastically titled "Guten Morgen" ("Good Morning"), a song about working-class drudgery. The double album also contained one of the Scherben's most straightforward love songs, the piano ballad "Halt dich an deiner Liebe fest" ("Hold On to Your Love"), signaling Rio Reiser's turn to romantic love songs in his later career. Musically, *Wenn die Nacht am tiefsten* was expansive, reflecting the new communal spirit with lighter but complex instrumental and vocal arrangements (such as the canon on "Komm an Bord," "Get on Board"). The Scherben added flourishes like the jazz saxophone on "Samstag nachmittag," the funk bass on "Durch die Wüste," and the drum solo on "Nimm den Hammer" ("Take the Hammer"). The band also used some unusual time signatures (10/4, 5/4, and 12/8). Yet they continued to draw predominantly on African American musical traditions and were improvisational in a more conventional sense than Can or Faust.

The second phase of Ton Steine Scherben's communal project initially came with some difficulties, partly because of the abrupt move from an urban to a rural environment that some members were not prepared for. After six months, only half of the original sixteen communards remained in Fresenhagen. For those who stayed, some of the idealist conceptions with which they had started the project were challenged by the social realities of the commune. Jörg Schlotterer remembered:

> When we left for Fresenhagen, we had ideas like: we don't need a leader, everything belongs to everybody—the house, money, debt, books, clothes, drugs. It also meant you were partly responsible for the house and the grounds and the company, DAVID VOLKSMUND PRODUKTION. Soon those ideas turned out to be illusory. Hierarchical structures became more rigid, which seemed inevitable. Pope and king, spiritual and worldly power, ministers and the people. The tendency of people to claim private property was also unavoidable. Chores were not divided equally either. Very soon we were caught in the very lifestyle we had set out to change.[103]

The internal struggles of the Fresenhagen commune were worsened by financial hardships. Because of their nonprofit politics, the Scherben were broke by the end of the 1970s, despite having sold three hundred thousand albums and playing countless shows. The Fresenhagen commune continued to exist, but it took six years before Ton Steine Scherben released another album.

Ton Steine Scherben's communal ideas had moved from the explicitly political with ties to the urban squatter movement to the internal with a focus on musical experimentation in a rural environment. Rio Reiser's politics focused even more on the personal in later years and combined a quest for the spiritual with an expression of his homosexual identity. Biblical references appeared in many later Scherben songs, and Tarot influenced their fourth album *IV* (1981), initially untitled and with essentially the same all-black cover as Faust's *So Far*. Each of the double LP's impressionistic and introverted songs reflected a card that a band member had drawn. Musically, Ton Steine Scherben became less experimental in later years and settled for standard contemporary rock, as could also be evidenced on their final album, simply entitled *Scherben* (1983).

Rio Reiser embraced his homosexuality much more openly in his later work. Ton Steine Scherben collaborated with two gay theater troupes, Brühwarm ("Lukewarm") and Transplantis, and Reiser's lyrics on songs like "Morgenlicht" ("Morning Light") and "Verboten" ("Forbidden") were unapologetically gay. This even continued after Reiser, to the dismay of some of his earlier fans, signed a lucrative major record deal with Sony. On his pop hit "König von Deutschland" ("King of Germany," 1986), he celebrated mainstream queerness by declaring himself "Rio the first, Sissi the second" (the latter referring to Austrian empress Elisabeth). Reiser released five solo albums and died in 1995 at age forty-one of a circulatory collapse. He was still living in the Fresenhagen commune at the time of his death.

Ton Steine Scherben's legacy could most easily be found in German-language rock, which they had pioneered, and in punk. Rio Reiser managed to bend the German language to suit Anglo-American rock music in a way that allowed both political and romantic concerns to be expressed without shame. Blixa Bargeld of Einstürzende Neubauten noted: "Ton Steine Scherben were much more than just a political rock band. They were the essence of German rock music *per se*, definitely the only or at least the best translators of the idea of rock music into German."[104] Apart from German-language lyrics, Ton Steine Scherben's other major legacy was their anticapitalist economic approach, which found its continuation in the independent punk labels that were mushrooming in the 1980s both inside and outside Germany.

One of the most bizarre turns in the posthumous career of Ton Steine Scherben has been their growing popularity among right-wing youth in Germany.[105] As it turned out, the ambiguous lyrics of songs like "Schritt für Schritt ins Paradies" and "Allein machen sie dich ein" ("If You're Alone They'll Do You In") could easily be turned into neo-Nazi anthems. Although clearly not meant to be understood as nationalist fantasies, Ton Steine Scherben's songs, with their emphasis on the German language and their romanticization of political power gained from being radical outsiders, spoke to the concerns of German low-class youth from both ends of the political spectrum. How neo-Nazis have been able to mediate the contradiction of Aryan ideology with Rio Reiser's sexual orientation and the Americanized rock'n'roll of Ton Steine Scherben remains an open question.

Communal living presented an alternative to a German national identity tainted by the Nazi past, yet it was also rife with conflict. Amon Düül I and II, Faust, and Ton Steine Scherben expressed different kinds of tribalist community and left a rich legacy for punk, psychedelic rock, and other genres.

Paradoxically, the two more overtly political groups, the left-leaning Amon
Düül and the expressively anticapitalist Ton Steine Scherben, were more
openly drawing on traditional (American) rock structures than the art commune that was Faust. The latter's *Stunde Null* reinvention of sound paralleled
the minimalism of Can and Neu! (in opposition to Amon Düül II's more
ornate approach). What connected all these groups were their deterritorialization and reterritorialization of national identity, core krautrock concerns
that also extended to redefining spirituality.

# 3 New Age of Earth

## The kosmische Musik of Tangerine Dream, Ash Ra Tempel, Klaus Schulze, and Popol Vuh

Experimenting with alternative spiritualities was an important element of the counterculture both in the United States and in Western Europe, and 1970s rock music reflected a search for meaning in the lives of many famous musicians—George Harrison embracing Eastern mysticism (and taking the Beatles to visit the Maharishi Mahesh Yogi), Bob Dylan turning from Judaism to evangelical Christianity, Cat Stevens becoming Muslim and being reborn as Yusuf Islam, to name just a few of the most famous examples. Yet for the alternative spiritualities that emerged in krautrock, transforming national identity became a more integral part of conversion narratives than for British and American rock musicians. After all, Catholic and Protestant churches in Germany had collaborated with the Nazis. It is in this context that the world music tribalism and neopaganism of Can and Amon Düül and the unconventional Christianity of Ton Steine Scherben came to fruition. Alternative spiritualities emerged even more prominently in the kosmische Musik that Rolf-Ulrich Kaiser imagined and promoted with the krautrock groups Tangerine Dream, Ash Ra Tempel, and Popol Vuh.

*Kosmische Musik* ("cosmic music") was Rolf-Ulrich Kaiser's vision of deterritorialized, postnational cosmological identity, which involved the consumption of psychedelic drugs and the invention of new sounds, in particular through the use of the synthesizer. Although Kaiser's artists eventually abandoned him because of personal differences, they maintained elements of his vision in their music (in a different turn, Klaus Schulze's music expressed a return of the national with an affinity to classical German composers). It was Manuel Göttsching of Ash Ra Tempel who named his 1975 recording of pretrance electronica *New Age of Earth*, picking up a term that could apply to Can's fascination with Aleister Crowley and Ton Steine Scherben's Tarot album alike. Yet even more so, New Age seemed to be the philosophical grounds on which kosmische Musik was operating and which Florian Fricke would push further with Popol Vuh's embrace of a redefined Christianity, while simultaneously abandoning the synthesizer that had informed the sonic quality of cosmic spirituality.

## New Age Spirituality

The term New Age can be traced back to the late nineteenth century but would enter public discussion more widely in the 1980s and 1990s, quite a few years after Manuel Göttsching's landmark album.[1] While New Age movements were and are heterogeneous, the current use of the term can be situated in a particular post-1960s religious history in the United States.[2] New Age's detraditionalized spirituality is not just a rejection but also "a product of established orders of modernity."[3] Influences range from major world religions to pagan teachings, in particular Celtic, Druidic, and Native American spiritualities, leading some scholars to speak of a neopagan movement. The most important tenet of New Age thinking appears to be the overcoming of the ego and the celebration and sanctification of the self.[4] The commodification of New Age spirituality and the emergence of pro-capitalist New Age yuppies have led to some controversies. For instance, the New Age appropriation of Native American spirituality disregards that the latter is generally focused on community, not the self.[5]

New Age and kosmische Musik shared some important ideas, like the focus on "positive thinking" and "planetary healing," and Rolf-Ulrich Kaiser's connection with Timothy Leary got him in touch with one of the major proponents (or "gurus") of both LSD and New Age. Yet kosmische Musik's embrace of the synthesizer as a technologically advanced machine was in stark contrast to New Age's back-to-nature technophobia. As Stuart Rose points out: "Participants in the New Age seek a stronger spiritual basis to their lives as a reaction to what they see as a technocratic, dehumanized, and meaningless existence which has been the result of social and cultural change started by the Industrial Revolution and which is still continuing to evolve."[6] Was the synthesizer as the ultimate "man-machine" disrupting or propelling the cosmic consciousness of musicians like Klaus Schulze or Tangerine Dream's Edgar Froese? To understand kosmische Musik's engagement with technology it is vital to trace the history of the synthesizer and its connections to identity formation.

## The Synthesizer and kosmische Musik

The history of the synthesizer is embedded in twentieth-century discourses of technology. In popular music, these discourses involved and continue to involve dichotomies like acoustic/electric and analog/digital. As Paul Théberge astutely pointed out in his study of music and technology, "technological invention is [ . . . ] not only a response to musicians' needs but also a driving force with which musicians must contend."[7] Musicians like Florian Fricke, Klaus Schulze, and Edgar Froese experimented with synthesizer technology in the early 1970s and sought to use the instrument not simply to reproduce sounds of traditional instruments but to create new, unheard sounds. To some degree, by doing this they had to let themselves be run by the machines, since early synthesizers were notoriously complex, unreliable, and impossible to control. New Age proponents like George Gurdjieff might have warned of what they saw as the dangers of automated processes: "All the people you see, all the people you know, all the people you may get to know, are machines, actual machines working solely under the power of external influences."[8] The *kosmische* musicians, however, were challenging this simplistic view by deconstructing the man/machine dichotomy.

The synthesizer as the ultimate "man-machine" or "cyborg," a hybrid of the organic and the artificial, might be the most persistent trope in krautrock's history and does not just pertain to the *kosmische* bands but also to many other musicians discussed in this book. To some extent, the cyborg trope exceeds a narrow German context and applies to larger philosophical issues. As Gilles Deleuze and Félix Guattari noted in *Anti-Oedipus*, "producing-machines, desiring-machines everywhere, schizophrenic machines, all of species life: the self and the non-self, outside and inside, no longer have any meaning whatsoever."[9] Donna Haraway saw a utopian and oppositional potential in the cyborg, in particular in regards to gender: "We are all chimeras, theorized and fabricated hybrids of machine and organism; in short, we are all cyborgs."[10] Through their engagement with synthesizers, krautrock musicians found an artistic expression for the larger social phenomena discussed by these theorists.

In terms of popular music history, the synthesizer may be the single most important technological innovation of the twentieth century. Synthesizer technology had wide-ranging effects, arguably even superseding the development of the electric guitar. As Trevor Pinch and Frank Trocco have noted:

> The synthesizer is the only innovation that can stand alongside the electric guitar as a great new instrument of the age of electricity. Both led to new forms of music, and both had massive popular appeal. In the long run the synthesizer may turn out to be the more radical innovation, because, rather than applying electricity to a pre-existing instrument, it uses a genuinely new source of sound—electronics.[11]

The electric guitar became firmly associated with a British and US context through companies like Fender and Gibson and performers like Chuck Berry, Jimi Hendrix, and Jimmy Page. Synthesizer technology, on the other hand, involved American and European inventors like Robert Moog and Peter Zinovieff of EMS as well as further developments by Japanese companies, and performers have constituted an even more transnational group, effectively spanning the entire globe.

Precursors of the synthesizer included the telharmonium (1906) and the theremin (1919), the latter a device controlled by hand movements and made popular in the second half of the twentieth century on soundtracks to movies like *Spellbound*, *The Day the Earth Stood Still*, and *The Thing*. The theremin also appeared on the Beach Boys' hit "Good Vibrations" (1966). Another precursor of the synthesizer was the Hammond organ. Initially developed in the 1930s as an electronic imitation of a church organ, it was quickly picked up by secular musicians. The Hammond B-3 became a staple in popular music, most famously played perhaps by Booker T. Jones of Booker T. & the MG's and Jon Lord of Deep Purple. Other electronic keyboards like the Rhodes and Wurlitzer pianos followed. As yet another precursor to the synthesizer, the Mellotron was developed in England in the early 1960s, reproducing prerecorded instrumental sounds with a tempered keyboard and making a famous appearance on the Beatles' "Strawberry Fields Forever" (1967). In 1964, Robert Moog invented the first modular synthesizer, an expensive and complicated machine. The popular dissemination of synthesizer technology followed in 1970 with the lower-priced and portable Minimoog. Companies like ARP and EMS also began mass-producing synthesizers. Technological developments of the 1970s led to the distribution of polyphonic synthesizers that could play more than one note at a time, microprocessor-controlled synthesizers like the Prophet 5, sequencers, and samplers that took the use of prerecorded sounds to another level. European disco music popularized many of these new technologies, an example being Giorgio Moroder's production of Donna Summer's 1978 hit "I Feel Love," which featured a driving sequencer. Finally, digital synthesizers by Casio, Korg, and Yamaha entered the sound of mainstream popular music in the 1980s. By the 1990s, genres like techno, house, and hip-hop fully relied on the new technologies.

In the late 1960s, when krautrock musicians began dabbling with the Moog synthesizer, hardly anybody could have predicted the later developments of the instrument. As Paul Théberge notes: "During the late 1960s, the 'industry' consisted of little more than informal networks of individual engineers and independent dealers working directly with a small number of musicians and enthusiasts."[12] Kosmische Musik's early synthesizer experiments were embedded in a transnational web of "serious" music that reached from Karlheinz Stockhausen (Germany) to John Cage (United States) and *musique concrète* (France). Wendy Carlos had released the first commercial Moog recording *Switched on Bach* in 1968. Massively popular, the album had the appeal of a novelty record of European classical music. George Harrison had also bought a Moog and released his one-off experiments with modular synthesizers as *Electronic Music* in 1969. What was different about kosmische Musik's use of synthesizers was the connection to space and Rolf-Ulrich Kaiser's fully formed New Age philosophy.

Certainly krautrock musicians were not alone in their fascination with outer space. As Ken McLeod has pointed out: "Rock and roll developed roughly contemporaneously with the era of space exploration and the concomitant boom in science fiction. [ . . . ] Indeed, the association of space and alien themes with rock'n'roll rebellion is found throughout rock's history and has had an impact on nearly all its stylistic manifestations."[13] This development linked space-themed rockabilly with David Bowie's invention of Ziggy Stardust. Yet kosmische Musik cannot be easily placed within this history, since its musical structure was decidedly anti-rock. Rather, it drew on "serious" electronic compositions like those of György Ligeti. It should be noted that in actuality there is no sound in space, since only vibrating air or water molecules can transmit sound waves. Therefore, a quiet, atmospheric, relaxed, or eerie quality is not an accurate reproduction of cosmic sound but only how humans imagine it. Kosmische Musik took this idea to the extreme by creating keyboard- and synthesizer-heavy, ambient, "spacey" soundscapes that only occasionally involved spoken-word vocals and were mostly instrumental. Kosmische Musik countered notions that synthesizers were cold, soulless machines and ranged from the postnational, cosmic, and future-oriented (Tangerine Dream) to the nationalistic, classical, and past-oriented (Klaus Schulze's Richard Wahnfried).

In many ways, kosmische Musik disrupted rock music's conventional narratives. Punk rock has generally been credited for breaking with the classical music leanings and garish kitsch fantasy of groups like Yes and King Crimson, but, like punk rockers, Rolf-Ulrich Kaiser's musicians were often decidedly amateurish in their embrace of the cosmos and refrained from populating their aural landscapes with gnomes and wizards. Moreover, their gender politics were more diffuse than those of progressive rock. Anglo-American rock music had been largely defined by what Steve Waksman has labeled the *technophallus*, the electric guitar played by white men to emulate what they perceived as the potency of black men through both the shape and volume of the instrument.[14] Contrarily, keyboard players in rock, like Elton John, were able to add queer elements by drawing on the history of nineteenth-century parlor pianos being played by the woman in the home. This was true for the synthesizer as well. While Keith Emerson tried to turn his seventeen-square-foot-550-pound "Monster Moog" into yet another technophallus, the aforementioned Wendy Carlos more effectively drew on the transformative qualities of the instrument, which clearly connected with Donna Haraway's notion of the cyborg. At a time when Christine Jorgensen was one of the very few publicly known transgender individuals, Carlos, born as Walter, had undergone hormone treatment and was cross-dressing in early 1968, living as a woman in May 1969, and had her sex-change operation in 1972: "Part of her new identity became bound up with the machine. The transformative power of the synthesizer may have allowed her not only to conjure up a new musical meaning but also helped her to identify as a newly gendered person."[15] The ability of the synthesizer to transform gender also worked to transform national identity for musicians like Tangerine Dream, Popol Vuh, and Klaus Schulze, the latter of whom would perform in an anti-rock gesture by sitting on a shag carpet with his back to the audience, surrounded by his equipment, at the same time technophile and nonphallic, German and cosmic.

## Rolf-Ulrich Kaiser

Much of the notion of kosmische Musik was shaped and directed by one man, Rolf-Ulrich Kaiser. Kaiser was born in Buckow near Berlin in 1943, studied German literature, philosophy, and theater, and became a journalist for print media and radio. He also published a number of books about popular music, some with the major publishing house Econ and some with his own publishing company. His early interest in folk music manifested itself in his first major publication, *Das Songbuch* ("The Song Book"), from 1967, a collection of essays, interviews, lyrics, and portraits of musicians like Joan Baez and Bob Dylan but also of folk singers from West and East Germany, Spain, and the Soviet Union. Kaiser's account of the American counterculture was sympathetic and unapologetic, discussing protests against the Vietnam War and nuclear weapons as well as criticizing consumerism. Kaiser became actively involved in the burgeoning counterculture in West Germany when he organized the International Essen Song Days in 1968. The Song Days established Kaiser as a main player in the West German rock scene. For Kaiser, the only use of mainstream pop was to support the establishment by numbing the senses, whereas the International Essen Song Days represented a "musical happening that opens up other levels of experience by psychedelically expanding consciousness."[16]

This description already hinted at Rolf-Ulrich Kaiser's interest in mind-altering drugs, which would dramatically influence his shifting politics and eventually lead to the disintegration of his business endeavors. Two of Kaiser's major publications showed this development—as well as his growing involvement with German bands. In his *Buch der neuen Pop-Musik* ("Book of the New Pop Music," 1969), Kaiser praised Anglo-American musicians like the Beatles, the Rolling Stones, Bob Dylan, and Frank Zappa and criticized German schlager and the latest developments in jazz. Kaiser briefly discussed Tangerine Dream and Amon Düül, calling the latter "so progressive that Anglo-American bands can't keep up with them."[17] Drawing on Herbert Marcuse and Theodor Adorno, Kaiser developed the notion of an anticonsumerist underground that required "complete autonomy of the producers and the bands' engagement of the political and social context in which they operate."[18] Three years later, in his book *Rock-Zeit* ("Time of Rock"), Kaiser bemoaned what he saw as the commercialization of rock music and mass media's appropriation of the counterculture. In his reevaluation, the Beatles, the Rolling Stones, and Bob Dylan, praised earlier, received some harsh words: John Lennon "profited from class struggle and sold it in his songs as an illusion,"[19] and the Stones "cover their eyes and ears, so that they don't become aware of societal structures."[20] The only Anglo-American bands that escaped Kaiser's criticism were the Grateful Dead and the Incredible String Band. Kaiser discussed the new German groups in a very positive light and offered scattered thoughts on various aspects of pop music like sexuality, sound production, and "race."

The most striking change in Rolf-Ulrich Kaiser's thinking was his open endorsement of mind-altering drugs. He extensively quoted Timothy Leary, "the great guru of our consciousness,"[21] and argued that people who take LSD and marijuana "listen in a more delicate way, respond in a more sensitive way, dress in a more fantastic way, live more peacefully, and care about each other."[22] In a utopian vision that connected communal living, psychedelic drug use, his feelings for his girlfriend and collaborator Gille Lettmann, and the notion of cosmic identity, Kaiser now promoted "true" music that had turned inward to express New Age sentiments:

> Truth is not just expressed through words or content that can be described with words. It is so much more. Truth is the serenity in the eyes of someone who has experienced many trips, the peacefulness on the faces of a group of people who quietly live as a family somewhere in the country, the fairy tales from the East and ours which we remember, the knowledge of the vast cosmos in which we feel secure, or the gentleness in the gestures of two lovers.[23]

By this time Kaiser had become a major player in the West German music industry. In 1970, Kaiser and schlager producer Peter Meisel had founded Ohr records, with distribution through Metronome. Ohr ("Ear") would become one of the major krautrock labels, employing the skilled producers Konrad "Conny" Plank and Dieter Dierks and issuing thirty-two LPs in the three years of its existence. Their motto "*Macht das Ohr auf!*" ("Open Your Ears!") was a clever pun on a slogan of West Germany's major tabloid *Bild*, much hated by the New Left, who called for German reunification with "*Macht das Tor auf!*" ("Open up the Gate!"—in reference to Berlin's Brandenburg Gate on the border between East and West Germany). The first five Ohr releases shared Reinhard Hippen's cover art of dismembered doll parts but were musically very eclectic. They ranged from the political cabaret of

Floh de Cologne's *Fließbandbabys Beat-Show* ("Assembly-Line Baby's Beat Show") to the German folk music of Bernd Witthüser's *Lieder von Vampiren, Nonnen und Toten* ("Songs of Vampires, Nuns, and the Dead"), and from the experimental rock of Tangerine Dream's *Electronic Meditation* and Limbus 4's *Mandalas* to the jazz rock of Embryo's *Opal*. Expanding their business endeavors, Kaiser and Meisel also founded the label Pilz ("Mushroom") in 1971, with distribution through the chemical company BASF. It was in this context that Nikel Pallat of Ton Steine Scherben severely criticized Kaiser's capitalist practices on TV and split a table with an axe. In reality, Ohr and Pilz did not yield a profit because Kaiser was taking on too many bands, the majority of which had little commercial potential.

Around 1972, Kaiser's embrace of mind-altering drugs, in particular LSD, led to a dramatic shift in his personal life and his business politics. With his girlfriend and collaborator Gerlinde "Gille" Lettmann (born 1950), a textile designer from Cologne, and under the influence of Timothy Leary (1920–96), Kaiser increasingly began to push only music that fit his idea of *kosmisch*. Kaiser would eventually meet Leary in his Swiss exile after the former Harvard psychology professor had escaped from a California prison where he was serving time for drug possession. In between, Leary had spent some time in Algeria with the Black Panthers. Kaiser was fascinated by Leary's philosophy of higher consciousness triggered by LSD, which Leary saw as bringing humans in contact with extraterrestrial life.[24] Kaiser's increasingly erratic behavior forced Ohr employees Bruno Wendel and Günter Körber to leave and launch Brain, soon to become the top label for German music (in 1976, Körber also founded the equally successful Sky Records). Meisel ended his collaboration with Kaiser in 1973, resulting in the demise of Ohr. Kaiser and Lettmann founded the short-lived label Kosmische Kuriere ("Cosmic Couriers"), invoking Timothy Leary's name for LSD dealers, and later rechristened Kosmische Musik before folding in 1975.

The term *kosmische Musik* was coined by Tangerine Dream's Edgar Froese to describe his own synthesizer soundscapes, but in Kaiser's appropriation it could equally apply to Ash Ra Tempel's blues jams. In his liner notes for the sampler *Kosmische Musik* with tracks by Klaus Schulze, Tangerine Dream, and Popol Vuh, still for the Ohr label, Kaiser mused:

> Music is a medium of the cosmos. Both are based on electronic waves, on the vibrations of DNA information. Those vibrations become audible

when you feel the music. [ . . . ] All music about the cosmic journey is cosmic music: the Grateful Dead, the Incredible String Band. Therefore, the term *kosmische Musik* more narrowly relates to the specific direction of musicians who, as a medium, realize life's molecular processes directly through their instrument of electronic vibrations. The music of cells is a song of flashes organically superimposed over each other, whose moments are eternities and whose eternities are moments.[25]

Kaiser and Gille Lettmann sent out pages upon pages of similar prose as promotion materials for their releases. Lettmann also designed multicolored, "cosmic" clothes for the musicians, an idea that never really took off, and only Kaiser and Lettmann wore them. Kaiser severed ties with *Sounds*, the major countercultural music publication in Germany, after it had published CIA images of Timothy Leary (which had previously been printed in an issue of the American *Rolling Stone*). The relationship with the magazine had been strained for years. Finally, lawsuits filed by Edgar Froese and Klaus Schulze in 1973 allowed them to leave Kaiser's label, but they did not receive any payments from the financially strapped manager. Allegedly Kaiser had coerced the musicians to take LSD, leading Klaus Schulze to quip: "I can't play when I'm tripping."[26] Despite the lawsuit, Schulze remained thankful for what Kaiser had done for him. Froese was less forgiving, eventually rejecting the term *kosmische Musik* that he himself had invented. In 1975 he stated: "*Kosmisch* is just *komisch* [funny] to me today. [ . . . ] The label *kosmisch* that Kaiser gave us three years ago . . . [ . . . ] I've never had a 'cosmic' feeling. What does that even mean?"[27]

Kaiser's disintegration and eventual disappearance should detract neither from the way his alternative spirituality clearly resonated in postwar West Germany nor from the accomplishments of various musicians under his supervision between 1970 and 1975. In addition to jumpstarting the careers of Tangerine Dream, Ash Ra Tempel, Klaus Schulze, and Popol Vuh, all of which are discussed more fully below, Kaiser brought together some of his most seasoned musicians for collaborations on a number of quirky krautrock releases—Sergius Golowin's *Lord Krishna of Goloka*, Walter Wegmüller's *Tarot*, and five albums released under the name Cosmic Jokers. Both Golowin (1930–2006) and Wegmüller (born 1937) were Swiss mystics and friends of Timothy Leary, and it was through them that Kaiser met Leary and got to record him for his collaboration with Ash Ra Tempel on *Seven Up* (1973).

One could argue that the influence was quite one-directional, as neither Kaiser, Golowin, nor Wegmüller were mentioned in Leary's autobiography *Flashbacks*. Golowin, author of *The World of Tarot* and the *Gypsy Dreambook*, recorded meditative recitations for the LP *Lord Krishna of Goloka* (1973). Drawing on a Hindu deity worked within the context of Kaiser's New Age eclecticism, as did the occultism of Walter Wegmüller's double album *Tarot* (also 1973). Like Ton Steine Scherben's *IV*, it contained one song for each card of the game, but also a full Tarot deck painted by the artist himself. As Golowin had done before, Wegmüller contributed spoken words to an album that also had purely instrumental passages. Both Golowin's and Wegmüller's releases were manifestations of the breadth of alternative spiritualities espoused by Kaiser's New Age philosophy.

The five Cosmic Jokers albums of Kaiser and Lettmann were all culled from jam sessions in 1973 with musicians like Klaus Schulze and Manuel Göttsching, who had also contributed to the albums by Golowin and Wegmüller. They were released in 1974, allegedly without the musicians' consent. Coming "in a coherent package, a ridiculous and crass marriage of the spiritual and the supermarket,"[28] they included the self-titled *Cosmic Jokers* as well as *Galactic Supermarket, Sci Fi Party, Planeten Sit-In*, and the sampler *Gilles Zeitschiff*. For the latter, Lettmann provided vocal overdubs to previously released music tracks. In the liner notes, she recounted her and Kaiser's meeting with Timothy Leary and the recording of both the Golowin and the Wegmüller LPs in LSD-fueled prose, ending with the statement: "TIME is the new dimension. In it grows the cosmic music. TIME contains three big experiences. They make you fly to the Queen of Sunshine. Love is in TIME. Flight in Joy."[29] Many of the Cosmic Jokers LPs, which had matching covers with space-inspired imagery, ended up in the bargain bins of record stores but were sold for astronomical prices on eBay a few decades later. Although not endorsed by all participating musicians, the Cosmic Jokers project managed to connect the psychedelic rock and synthesizer soundscapes of kosmische Musik with a more explicitly articulated New Age philosophy.

Kaiser and Lettmann's ideas of kosmische Musik allowed musicians like Tangerine Dream and Ash Ra Tempel to develop music that broke with Anglo-American rock traditions by embracing some form of deterritorialized, cosmic New Age thinking. Even in their most eccentric publications, Kaiser and Lettmann occasionally positioned themselves in interesting ways as both inside and outside of German history. In one of their final publica-

Fig. 4. Gille Lettmann promoting *kosmische Musik*. (Courtesy of Eurock Archives.)

tions, a 1975 press release with the title "Star Sounds: Discover the Galaxy Sound of Cosmic Music," they described the musicians on their label as children of "the most fantastic composer of all times, Ludwig van Beethoven (Germany, Terra),"[30] and cited other famous Germans like Wernher von Braun, Albert Einstein, and Bettina von Brentano as influences but also name-checked Leonardo da Vinci, Tutankhamun, Cagliostro, *Star Trek*, and UFOs. Kaiser and Lettmann stated: "Cosmic composers know no rules. They master all styles. Rock, folk, classical, synthesizer."[31] They also explained their vision of "sci fi" as "science fiction without horror," a positivist version of the

genre quite unlike the dystopian visions of George Orwell or Aldous Hux-
ley, "full of adventures, full of joy."[32] While musicians like Klaus Schulze and
Edgar Froese did not necessarily agree with this representation of their
music, their recordings both before and after they worked for the Ohr and
the Kosmische Musik labels did not seem at odds with Kaiser and Lettmann's vision of a cosmic consciousness.

By 1975, Lettmann and Kaiser had taken on the new names *Sternenmäd-
chen* ("Star Girl") and *Meson Cristallis* and, according to some sources, had
both been diagnosed with schizophrenia. They disappeared from public
view, presumably living with Lettmann's mother in Cologne until 1990.
After the death of Lettmann's mother, they were evicted, and books with
personal dedications to Kaiser surfaced at a flea market in Cologne. Nothing
is known of their whereabouts or whether they are still alive.[33] It should be
noted that while Kaiser has been vilified and ridiculed in the German media,
he remains a hugely important figure in the history of krautrock. As Julian
Cope put it: "Kaiser should be forgiven and even made a hero for his mis-
guided but Visionary zeal, for he (temporarily) forced music beyond the
Canopy of Earth and far far out into the Stars."[34]

## Tangerine Dream

Out of all the bands that worked with Kaiser, Tangerine Dream most clearly
departed from conventional Anglo-American musical structures with their
synthesizer-driven anti-rock. As a result, their instrumental kosmische Musik,
at least initially much more successful outside than inside Germany, was
perceived as paradigmatically German: "Their cult status, won in the 1970s,
was based more or less on their *difference*, their funny-foreignerdom, their
Germanness as on their music."[35] Although Tangerine Dream were one of
the krautrock groups that broke with rock traditions most dramatically, they
had close affinities with Pink Floyd and derived their name from the "tangerine trees" of the Beatles' LSD-inspired "Lucy in the Sky with Diamonds."
These contradictions established them as possibly the most important German group to seek postnational cosmic spirituality through fully embracing
the synthesizer as their instrument of choice.

Over the years, Tangerine Dream changed personnel frequently, but one
permanent member was Edgar Froese. Born in 1944 in Tilsit (East Prussia),
Froese studied painting and sculpture at the Berlin Academy of Arts and,

influenced by British and American music, began playing with beat band the
Ones. In 1965, Froese met Salvador Dalí in northern Spain and was hired
two years later to play the music at the inauguration of Dalí's Christ Statue,
a sculpture made of rain barrels, bicycles, and metal pieces. According to
Froese, "this was the biggest change I ever had in music. By seeing the way
he was talking and thinking, I found that *everything* was possible. I thought
that I would do the same thing as he did in painting, in music."[36] With his
newly founded group Tangerine Dream, Froese pursued this ambitious goal
in West Berlin, a fertile ground for new electronic and psychedelic musicians. The city was not only home to the Zodiak Arts Lab, which provided a
space where visual artists, theater students, and musicians could experiment,
but also to electronic music expert Thomas Kessler, who instructed aspiring
musicians in his publicly funded, semiprofessional studio.

The Berlin that Tangerine Dream, Ash Ra Tempel, and Klaus Schulze
thrived in, performers that were later dubbed the "Berlin School of Electronics," was only tangentially connected with the prewar Berlin David
Bowie would be looking for in the three years he spent in the city. In the
highly charged political atmosphere of 1968, wet soil was put on Tangerine
Dream's amplifiers at a campus gig in Berlin by protesters who thought they
were not "political" enough, and the leftist publication *Pardon* dismissed the
band's "Kosmo Kitsch."[37] One could claim that the real politics of the Berlin
groups, like those of many krautrock outfits, could be found in the music
itself, which radically broke with rock instrumentation and harmonic and
rhythmic structures. As Klaus Schulze remembered: "When we began to
make music in the underground scene in Berlin, we were striving for a style
that had nothing in common with British or American pop music of the
time."[38] Froese added some historical specificity, explaining the turn to the
cosmic with the particular spatiality of West Berlin, an island-city surrounded
by East Germany: "Berlin was different from other [German] cities, in particular because it was isolated. [ . . . ] Since it was difficult to cross borders, a
sound developed that moved upwards: Kosmische Musik."[39] The turn to the
cosmic also explained Froese's reluctance to think of himself as a German
artist: "We as a band are absolutely cosmo-political [sic]. I'm not at all interested in being called a 'German musician.'"[40] In a different interview, Froese
was a bit more open about acknowledging his national background while
still maintaining his cosmopolitan identity: "I did not have country or rock-

abilly or rock'n'roll roots. [ . . . ] I was born and raised in this country [Germany]. Therefore I am German, but I always felt more like an Earthling."[41]

The first incarnation of Tangerine Dream consisted of Froese, Klaus Schulze, and Konrad Schnitzler. With some guest musicians, they recorded *Electronic Meditation* in 1970, advertised by Kaiser's press release as "sci-fi rock" and "acoustic LSD." Despite its title, the album was not very meditative, containing experimental music and free jazz, found sounds, and disorienting electronic effects. It included both highly abstract pieces, like the first track "Genesis" with its cello and guitar drones from which drum rolls and flute glissandos slowly emerged, as well as more regular structures, like "Ashes to Ashes" with its steady 4/4 beat and blues guitar and organ soloing. The musicians played conventional instruments but also used sounds like the electronically manipulated cracking of a whip and the crackle of burning paper. The liner notes compared the effect of the music on the listener to a psychedelic drug experience: "In the era of electronic experimental music, everything's possible. When you unfold this record cover, you'll see a dissected burning brain. When you hear the record, a dissected human life will pass in front of you. One of billions." The experimental quality of the music on *Electronic Meditation*, compared by Schulze to punk rock in its attempt to violently break with traditions,[42] was still quite different from what would later emerge as kosmische Musik. In its destabilizing of the man/machine dichotomy, Tangerine Dream's first album was similar to what would become a common theme in other formations of krautrock, from Can to Kraftwerk and Neu!—in Froese's words, "many surprises, positive ones as well, resulted from the fact that we just couldn't control the instruments."[43]

By the time Tangerine Dream's second album, *Alpha Centauri* (1971), was released, Schulze and Schnitzler had quit the band, and Froese had recruited new musicians for what now became much more clearly his personal vision of kosmische Musik. Influenced by electronic composers like György Ligeti, John Cage, and Karlheinz Stockhausen, and after he had listened to King Crimson's *In the Wake of Poseidon* at 16 RPM, Froese decided to abstain from conventional guitar solos in order to create what he declared a "musical film in slow motion."[44] Cosmic notions dominated the album, which was dedicated to "all people who feel obliged to space." The album cover and the song titles all referred to outer space, and the music, consisting mostly of flute, organ, and reverbed drums, took on an atmospheric, "spacey" sound as well. Froese argued that *Alpha Centauri* had "a foreground, middleground, and background; it's three-dimensional and does not cling to the loudspeakers but escapes and becomes spatial."[45] The emphasis on cosmic spatiality was a new development. On *Electronic Meditation* the only vocals had been Edgar Froese reading from the back of a ferry ticket from Calais to Dover, played backwards. In contrast, the second album's side-long title track "Alpha Centauri" moved the concept of spatiality from the mundane to the cosmic, ending with a prayer-like recitation in German: "The spirit of love fills the cosmos, and he who joins the universe knows every sound. The spirit rises and its enemies scatter, and those who hate it flee its sight. Send out your spirit, and life begins. Come, spirit, fill the hearts of your people and ignite the fire of eternal life in every one of them." While this kosmische Musik manifesto borrowed heavily from Christian theology, the non-traditional spirituality of the cosmic consciousness at work here might be more aptly described as New Age thinking.

Having established the main idea of kosmische Musik, Froese took a left turn with the hard-rocking single "Ultima Thule" shortly after the release of *Alpha Centauri*. The single had a steady rhythm and employed a Mellotron as well as a guitar riff very similar to "Fly and Collision of Comas Sola" from *Alpha Centauri*, but at full volume, making a comparison with Pink Floyd's heavier early songs inevitable. In 1972, Tangerine Dream returned with the glacial sounds of double album *Zeit* ("Time"), which was devoid of any rock elements. The group had now basically become three keyboard players, Froese, Peter Baumann, and Christopher Franke, a lineup that lasted until 1977.[46] *Zeit* was called a "largo in four movements" and served as Tangerine Dream's most radical offering, messing with conventional notions of (musical) time on its four side-long ambient tracks, which were almost free of any conventional rhythm or melody and instead focused on slow harmonic shifts and dynamic swells. As Julian Cope observed: "Its remarkable unchanging unfolding near-static barely-shifting vegetable organic-ness takes over the room and permeates the whole house."[47] Continuing some of *Alpha Centauri*'s cosmic themes by featuring a total solar eclipse on the cover, *Zeit* added "time" (or "timelessness") to "space" and veered away from rock textures even more radically than its predecessor or any Tangerine Dream album that would follow. The deconstruction of time and the full embrace of synthetic sounds (with the exception of four cellos on the first track) and quasi-religious cosmic ideas were a dramatic break with the German past, both musically and ideologically.

On *Atem* ("Breath," 1973), Tangerine Dream continued *Zeit's* sonic philosophy but reintroduced the organic and, with Froese's infant son on the cover, returned to planet Earth and the birth of humanity. In addition to synthesizer soundscapes, the album opened with breathing sounds, featured animal noises recorded in a zoo, and some ape-like human yelling. Sonically not as rigorous as its predecessor, the album returned to krautrock's hybridization of organic and artificial. *Atem* caught the attention of influential British DJ John Peel, who helped Tangerine Dream secure a record deal with Virgin Records.[48] The first album for Virgin was *Phaedra* (1974), which was inspired by Greek mythology and established Tangerine Dream's melodic, sequencer-driven trance sound that made it to number fifteen on the British charts and was enthusiastically received in France (but did not sell well in their home country). Turning their New Age sonics into a lucrative business, Tangerine Dream emphasized the spiritual connotation of their music by playing in a number of churches. The group performed in front of hundreds of thousands in England and France, and they were the first German band to play at London's Royal Albert Hall in 1975. The same year, Froese admitted a loss of spontaneity in Tangerine Dream's music that came with the preprogramming of synthesizers: "You have to have more control over things today. We used to work more intuitively in the past."[49] Tangerine Dream climbed new commercial heights with soundtracks for Hollywood movies like *The Sorcerer*, *The Keep*, and *Risky Business*, but arguably their music had become what Jim DeRogatis has called "snooze-inducing synthesizer instrumentals" and "bland New Age."[50] Having perfected the synthesizer version of kosmische Musik, the group lost the experimental dimension of their deterritorialized spirituality.

### Ash Ra Tempel

Whereas Tangerine Dream went on to become the most popular group of the many that Kaiser recruited for the Ohr label, Ash Ra Tempel was the band that most fully realized his vision of kosmische Musik. They did so by including both "earthy" blues rock and "spacey" synthesizer soundscapes in their repertoire and by endorsing the use of mind-altering drugs. Syncretic spirituality was already hinted at in the name of the group: "Ash," referring to the ephemeral, the physical, and to death; "Ra," referring to rebirth and growth in the form of the Egyptian sun god; and the German word for "temple," referring to a place of worship that could apply to various religious and spiritual groups.[51] As the driving force behind the group, Manuel Göttsching (born 1952) even continued pointing to the spiritual dimensions of his music after parting ways with Kaiser when he entitled his 1975 album *New Age of Earth*, which he recorded under the name Ashra.

Ash Ra Tempel's original lineup consisted of Göttsching on electric guitar, Hartmut Enke on bass guitar, and Klaus Schulze, who had just left Tangerine Dream, on drums. Enke and Göttsching had started out as the Steeplechase Blues Band, playing psychedelic blues rock in the style of Jimi Hendrix and Cream. Although they explored other musical territory with Ash Ra Tempel, Göttsching in particular often returned to African American and Anglo-American musical patterns like blues scales and bent-note guitar solos. It is therefore only partly true when the guitarist stated in an interview that Ash Ra Tempel were "trying to withstand the Anglo-American invasion. They were creating their own typically German style by turning their backs on common song structures."[52] Rather, it was the combination of blues-based psychedelic rock and serene ambient drones that characterized the band's music. On their first four albums they demonstrated their ability to do both, generally through two lengthy pieces, a hard-rocking, electric-guitar-driven A side and a slower-paced B side dominated by synthesizers.

Ash Ra Tempel's 1971 debut had a multi-fold-out cover. It displayed a pharaoh's head, a Mayan pyramid, four religious symbols (crescent, cross, Buddha, pentagram), and it reprinted the opening lines of Allen Ginsberg's "Howl" in English and German. The group was thus introduced as a countercultural force drawing on alternative spiritualities in a transnational context. Side one, "Amboss" ("Anvil"), began with slowly swelling guitar drones, eventually turning into a psychedelic rock jam featuring a lengthy guitar solo with effects like feedback, distortion, wah-wah, and phase-shifting over free jazz drum patterns and bass phrases. Here, Ash Ra Tempel resembled both Jimi Hendrix's improvisations and those of another Ohr group, Guru Guru. While drawing on Anglo-American rock, the side-long piece contained no lyrics or clearly recognizable song structure. It consisted of movements attributed to human emotions, ranging from meditative and quiet to aggressive and panic-stricken, and ultimately back to a rebirth. The song referenced an anvil as both a bone in the middle ear that produces sound as well as the rhythmic quality associated with the ancient tool. Side two, "Traummaschine" ("Dream Machine"), was instrumental as well, but much more restrained and contemplative. It contained mostly long guitar and synthesizer drones by Göttsching and Schulze and some subdued percussion, emphasizing the cosmic over the human "machine."

Ash Ra Tempel's first album with its two-faced representation of cosmic consciousness was the model for their following albums, which generally featured psychedelic rock with electric guitar, electric bass, and drums on side one and ambient synthesizers on side two. The inclusion of vocals mostly worked to make the connection to hallucinogenic drugs more explicit. On *Schwingungen* ("Vibrations," 1972), which introduced the new drummer Wolfgang Müller and had guest musicians on saxophone and bongos, Manfred Brück (credited as "John L.") sang about his "lysergic-daydream." On Ash Ra Tempel's collaboration with Timothy Leary, *Seven Up* (1972), named after a soda bottle spiked with LSD and consumed during the recording, as well as Leary's seven stages of consciousness and being "up" or "high," the Harvard professor was one of four vocalists, mimicking black vocal inflections on the twelve-bar blues segment "Right Hand Lover." For *Join Inn* (1973), recorded during the production of Walter Wegmüller's *Tarot* with Schulze on drums and synthesizers, Göttsching's girlfriend Rosi Müller, a fashion model from Berlin, contributed childlike spoken-word vocals in German. The lyrics were thinly veiled drug references with lines like "let yourself fall into the infinite" and "take me with you, far, far away." Müller was also the vocalist on the follow-up *Starring Rosi* (1973), which featured song-like structures and shorter tracks. At this point, both Enke and Schulze had quit the band, leaving Göttsching as the only founding member in the lineup.

In the wake of Kaiser's gradual disappearance, Göttsching's work became less focused on psychedelic drugs as a gateway to cosmic spirituality and more on the tranquil, meditative side of his music. Göttsching turned to distortion-free guitar and synthesizer experiments that resulted in a string of highly influential records, released under his own name or as "Ashra." *Inventions for Electric Guitar* (1974), the soundtrack *Le Berceau de Cristal* (recorded 1975 but not released until 1993), and especially *New Age of Earth* (1975) established the ambient sound that has been copied on innumerable CDs for the New Age market. Consisting mostly of keyboards and synthesizer sounds, the album that coincided with the beginning of the term's contemporary usage opened with the deliberately repetitive but melodic "Sunrain," which had a more pronounced rhythm than the meditative tracks that followed. "Ocean of Tenderness," "Deep Distance," and the side-long "Nightdust" were slow, "pleasant" keyboard pieces with some heavily reverbed guitar playing. Both by its name and by what could be perceived as its transcendental sound, *New Age of Earth* was a fully developed expression of alternative spirituality.

After three more LPs of ambient guitar, Göttsching went on to produce an album that has been regularly cited as the blueprint for electronic music genres like techno and house, the chess-themed, instrumental *E2-E4*, recorded in 1981 and released three years later. According to Göttsching, "it took me exactly one hour, no overdubs, no editing. The only alteration I had to make was to cut the piece into two parts for the LP format."[53] The album contained only one track with an incessant drum machine beat, a sequenced keyboard playing two chords, and, for its second half, some electric guitar soloing. It was almost one hour long and had only subtle melodic variations. This electronic minimalism updated ideas of Kraftwerk, Can, and Neu! and aligned the New Age spirituality of kosmische Musik with their notions of the cyborg.

Ash Ra Tempel's alternative spirituality incorporated much of Tangerine Dream's cosmic consciousness of synthesizer ambience but also prominently featured blues guitar jams more akin to British and American psychedelic rock groups. Göttsching dropped overt references to mind-altering drugs in his later works, which turned to meditative New Age music and proto-techno. Whereas both Tangerine Dream and Ash Ra Tempel combined the postnational with the cosmic, Schulze, who participated in both groups, would eventually return to the national as an inspiration for his solo career.

## Klaus Schulze

Klaus Schulze was the drummer on Tangerine Dream's *Electronic Meditation* and Ash Ra Tempel's debut album, but the most important part of his career began when he turned to synthesizers in 1972. He eventually fell out with Kaiser and released ten albums of keyboard music in seven years that, while grounded in kosmische Musik, also marked a significant turn toward a reterritorialized German nationalism. Culminating with *X* (1978), Schulze's affinity with European classical music nonetheless maintained some connections to British and American rock music and was another example of a musician who succeeded internationally before gaining recognition in Germany. The spirituality of Schulze's synthesizer sounds was more implicit than explicit but always present, making national identity a more central theme than in the deeply religiously motivated music of Popol Vuh, discussed below.

Schulze was born in 1947 and studied experimental composition at the Technical University of Berlin. Despite his formal musical training, Schulze would later soft-pedal any influence by modern composers like Terry Riley, John Cage, and Karlheinz Stockhausen, pointing out that Stockhausen's music was unlistenable, that only a very small fraction was actually electronic, and that Jimi Hendrix was his real inspiration.[54] In his early career as a drummer for Psy Free (1967–69), Tangerine Dream (1969–70), and Ash Ra Tempel (1970–71), there was indeed little evidence of any formal training, and in his later synthesizer work the strongest influence appeared to be the title track from Pink Floyd's *A Saucerful of Secrets* (1968). Schulze's solo works were more improvised than composed, but they continuously evoked German classical music. As Schulze acknowledged in the liner notes to *X*: "I had soon become tired of rock music." Overall, the conflict between "popular" and "serious" music, between "German" and "foreign" influences, was at the heart of Schulze's musical philosophy.

Working in his own studio since 1971, Schulze initially did not have access to synthesizers. His first solo album *Irrlicht* ("Will-o'-the-Wisp") was subtitled a "quadrophonic symphony for orchestra and electronic machines" and contained sounds of an electronically manipulated orchestra playing D minor for ten minutes, as well as guitar, zither, human voices, and a Teisco organ. The blend of technological inventions and references to European classical music (the "symphony" consisted of three "movements") set the tone for much of Schulze's solo career. The follow-up *Cyborg* (1973), a double album, featured more organ drone experiments and ambient pulse music and used the same orchestra, this time played backwards. As the album title suggested, Schulze saw himself as a man-machine playing a hybrid of acoustic and electronic music. In 1972, he had said: "My technology is a living machine for me, an extension of my natural organs—like an artificial limb."[55] Almost a decade later, in 1981, Schulze would reiterate his point about the agency of machines, which clearly echoed Kraftwerk's notions about cyborg hybridity: "You know, I have had this computer for only a short time and am only just starting to get to know it and it's starting to get to know me."[56]

Schulze began using synthesizers in 1973 when he bought a Moog from PopolVuh's Florian Fricke. He went on to acquire a huge arsenal in the years that followed, including a Minimoog and various ARP and EMS synthesizers as well as sequencers. The sound Schulze developed can most aptly be described by the name of one of his songs, as "floating"—cosmic synthesizer and sequencer melodies free of traditional rock structures, lengthy pieces made up of mostly minor chords but, unlike most music classified as New Age, always containing some contrasting, "ugly" sounds (an example is the harsh noise that abruptly ends *Timewind*'s first side). Eventually, Schulze employed a more rhythmically driven synthesizer sound through sequencers and a real-life drummer, Harald Großkopf. Schulze's playing relied on technological knowledge but was nonaggressive and not as phallocentric as most rock music. Although much of this could be said about Pink Floyd's music as well, they mostly stuck to traditional song structures to maintain their commercial appeal and, while incorporating Schulze-like passages, compromised the experimental quality of their music with traditional pop vocals and shorter, more conventional songs.[57]

Unlike Tangerine Dream, Schulze countered his growing international popularity (particularly in Great Britain and France) in the 1970s with explicit references to European "high art." On *Blackdance* (1974), Schulze underscored his classical ambitions by incorporating arias by Giuseppe Verdi (sung by Ernst Walter Siemon) and envisioning one of the tracks as a ballet piece. *Timewind* (1975) was dedicated to Richard Wagner and used a more harmonic sound and string synthesizers on its two pieces, the improvised "Bayreuth Return" and the composed "Wahnfried 1883" (both were references to Wagner). In addition to the music, Schulze's albums laid claim to European art with Urs Amann's signature covers, which were heavily influenced by the surrealist paintings of Salvador Dalí. Despite his move from Berlin to the quiet Hambühren in the northern German countryside in 1975, Schulze produced music that was even more transnationally focused in the years that followed: he contributed to three progressive rock albums for the project Go with international stars like Stomu Yamashta, Steve Winwood, and Al Di Meola; his own *Moondawn* (1976) began with the Lord's Prayer recited in Arabic; his two *Body Love* albums (1977) were from a soundtrack for a hardcore porn movie by Lasse Braun, an Italian director who took on a Swedish pseudonym; and on the cover of *Mirage* (1977) he called the synthesizer "the universal music machine." Musically, there was no major difference, whether Schulze's music was meant to commemorate the death of his brother (on *Mirage*) or to orchestrate sex scenes (on *Body Love*).

Schulze's fascination with Germany's past returned with his tenth solo album, aptly named *X* (1978). The double LP was presented as Schulze's magnum opus and was his first major success in his home country. As the extensive liner notes suggested, *X* consisted of "six musical biographies." The all-instrumental tracks were named after German philosopher Friedrich Nietzsche, Austrian poet Georg Trakl, American science-fiction writer Frank Herbert, German composer Friedemann Bach, King Ludwig II of Bavaria, and German author Heinrich von Kleist. Throwing Frank Herbert into the mix, whose name sounded German but who was actually American, was Schulze's way of pointing to other influences in his work, yet the return of the national appeared to be the album's main focus. *X* featured strings on many tracks, but "Ludwig" stood out as the attempt to create the ultimate hybridization of the organic and the synthetic: cyborg music in which strings and synthesizers became indistinguishable. The booklet contained some of Schulze's musical scores as well as an essay by KD Müller, who promoted Schulze as a "'classical' composer and musician, even if his understanding of classical music diverges from conventional ideas." According to Müller, Schulze's improvisational and entertaining qualities actually harkened back to the "Old Masters," supposedly bestowing on him the credibility of composers such as Beethoven and Bach.

Schulze remained a prolific and successful musician in the following decades, although other European synthesizer players like Jean-Michel Jarre and Vangelis perfected the commercial aspects of his music. Schulze's classical aspirations resurfaced with the prominently featured cello on *Dune* (1979) and *Trancefer* (1980), the opera *Totentag* ("Day of the Dead"), and *Klaus Schulze Goes Classic*, an album of compositions by Johannes Brahms, Ludwig van Beethoven, and Franz Schubert (both in 1994).[58] Despite having success in faraway places like the United States, Hong Kong, and Australia, Schulze defied internationalism by promoting German bands on his Innovative Communications label,[59] running a local synthesizer school, and even openly espousing anti-American sentiments.[60] Schulze never fully realized his return to the national, which in his interviews sometimes overshadowed the spiritual aspects of his music. His mostly instrumental pieces were yet another version of kosmische Musik, and his influence can be heard in ambient and trance music, which is generally more transnational than nationalist. Schulze himself has undermined his hyperbolic self-representation as a classical composer by saying: "I am still no keyboard player. In comparison, say, to Oscar

Peterson, I am an amateur. Because my craft is not playing the keyboard, but finding and combining sounds, building and using a structure to create emotions with sounds."[61] It was in the latter that the spirituality of Schulze's music was expressed most profoundly.

## Popol Vuh

In contrast to Klaus Schulze's neonationalist politics, Popol Vuh linked their evocation of cosmic spirituality most explicitly with religious ideas. Yet embracing this spirituality as the main motivation behind their music also involved abandoning the instrument that had been the driving force behind kosmische Musik: the synthesizer. This return to the "organic" was a deliberate deviation from the cyborg aesthetics of Tangerine Dream, Ash Ra Tempel, and Klaus Schulze. In the second half of the 1970s, Popol Vuh entered the discourse about German national identity from another angle when they scored a number of films for the director Werner Herzog.[62]

Popol Vuh were mainly the product of one individual, Florian Fricke. Founded in 1970 with Frank Fiedler and Holger Trülsch, the group underwent many personnel changes over the years with Fricke being the only constant member. He was born in 1944 in Lindau (Bavaria), studied piano and composition, and, beginning in 1967, worked as a music and film critic for the major German newspaper *Süddeutsche Zeitung*. In 1969, Fricke, who came from an upper-class background, acquired a Moog synthesizer. At the time, he was one of only two people in Germany who owned this expensive and complex instrument.[63] For Fricke, playing the Moog meant "searching for the sound that manifests human desire itself."[64] Similar to Edgar Froese and Klaus Schulze, Fricke's early work employed the synthesizer to produce otherworldly, cosmic sounds that were tied to emotional and spiritual experiences.

Popol Vuh took their name from the Mayan book of creation, and religion and spirituality were important themes for the band from the beginning. In an early interview, Fricke explained the name of the group by stressing their attempts to tap into the unconscious and to establish a connection to indigenous peoples without necessarily appropriating "other" cultures: "Through our music, we express a form of meditation that derives from our culture, not from India or any other culture."[65] What Fricke referred to as "our culture" was represented on the inside of the gatefold cover for the

Fig. 5. Popol Vuh. (Courtesy of Eurock Archives.)

first Popol Vuh album, *Affenstunde* (1970, literally "Monkey Hour"), which showed a Bavarian lake. Despite the professed focus on German identity, the album featured non-Western percussion (in particular tabla, hand drums from India) on top of bubbly and ominous Moog sounds and has been referred to as "raga rock" by critics, or as "Shaman music" by Fricke himself.

The eclectic influences from both in- and outside Germany continued on Popol Vuh's second and last album to feature the Moog synthesizer, *In den Gärten Pharaos* (1971, "In Pharaoh's Gardens"). It had a distinctive orange cover, which featured an exotic bird sitting on a flower, and referenced ancient Egypt in the title (as Ash Ra Tempel's debut album had done). Yet in the press release for the album, Popol Vuh also noted their appreciation of German influences, from poetry to philosophy and classical music, while also acknowledging Germany's fascist history. The spiritual conflict between German and international influences was expressed musically through a mix of synthetic and organic sounds. In addition to various kinds of keyboards, PopolVuh played congas and Turkish percussion instruments. Side one featured the Moog synthesizer, but the attempt was to move away from synthetic sounds and recreate a soprano voice singing an aria, which according to PopolVuh member Frank Fiedler involved a painstaking process of applying complex filters to the synthesized sound.[66] Side two was recorded with the organ of a rural Bavarian church and consisted of one sustained chord with only slight variations and some percussion.

In a 1972 interview, Fricke still embraced the synthesizer but also began to declare religious convictions more openly, mostly through a decidedly anticapitalist, anticonsumerist form of Christianity.[67] Fricke's conversion to a nondenominational Christianity led to a thorough restructuring of Popol Vuh's sound for *Hosianna Mantra* (1972). In halting English, Fricke explained why he had abandoned the Moog synthesizer (which he had sold to Klaus Schulze) in favor of mostly acoustic instruments and voice: "In the course of the years music has become more and more a form of prayer for me. Today it seems to be more beautiful and honest to cleanse oneself without technical aids, to introspect and then with simple, human music, touch the inner man."[68] One might wonder if Fricke did not consider recording in a studio and using microphones "technical aids," but turning away from the synthesizer, the instrument that had defined the sound of cosmic spirituality, was a significant sonic and ideological move. Instead, PopolVuh's sound was now much more melodic and dominated by traditional European and Indian instruments (piano, guitar, oboe, harpsichord, English horn, tambura, and sitar), played by Fricke and ConnyVeit. The only nonacoustic instrument on the album was an electric guitar, which Veit used to play blues licks over Fricke's classical piano phrases. Another new feature was the voice of Korean soprano Djong Yun, daughter of avant-garde composer Isang Yun. In an interview, Fricke citedYun's vocals as the reason to leave synthesizers behind, since he found the voice he had been trying to create on the Moog.[69]

The transnational quality of Popol Vuh's music was enriched by a new spirituality, which crossed religious borders on *Hosianna Mantra*. The title cleverly emphasized nondenominational faith by combining Christian and Hindu concepts, and the lyrics were taken from Jewish philosopher Martin Buber. However, despite the religious diversity of PopolVuh's music, Fricke described it as essentially Christian: "I have realized that to meet God within the culture in which you were raised is the purest endeavor. If I meet an

Indian God, it involves a lot of mediated mystery that I have not experienced from inside, from my roots. Therefore [ . . . ] I don't want to make Eastern music but Christian music."[70] What Fricke posited as Christian was always open to other influences, both musically and spiritually, and it was this hybridity that connected Popol Vuh's turn to traditional forms with the alternative spiritualities of New Age kosmische Musik. As Fricke noted himself: "In my own understanding, *Hosianna Mantra* is Christian music, but you can't call it church music—except if you understand your own body as a church and your ears as the portal."[71]

Popol Vuh continued their acoustic, meditative music on *Seligpreisung* ("The Beatitudes," 1973), on which Fricke sang lyrics taken from the Gospel of Matthew, and on two albums with Djong Yun reciting texts from the Old Testament's "Song of Solomon" about sacred love (*Einsjäger und Siebenjäger*, 1974, and *Das Hohelied Salomos*, 1975). These albums featured Daniel Fichelscher of Amon Düül on electric guitar and blended blues with Eastern scales, occasionally also incorporating sitar and non-Western percussion. For *Letzte Tage letzte Nächte* ("Final Days, Final Nights," 1976), Renate Knaup, another Amon Düül member, joined the group. *Sei still wisse ICH BIN* ("Be still, and know that I am God," 1981) was yet another Bible-inspired project and featured the choir of the Bavarian State Opera. The album was produced by Klaus Schulze and accompanied by a film shot in the Sinai desert with the Messiah played by a female actor wearing a beard.[72]

In developing their artistic vision of nondenominational Christian spirituality, Popol Vuh took Kaiser's vision of kosmische Musik to another level, paradoxically by abandoning the synthesizer, which had defined cosmic spirituality in their earlier works as well as those of Tangerine Dream and Ash Ra Tempel. New Age spirituality, Christian or otherwise, was the defining characteristic of all the cosmic bands. With the exception of some of Klaus Schulze's solo works, kosmische Musik was another attempt to redefine German national identity, this time in terms of transcendence (which in Ash Ra Tempel's early music was explicitly linked with drug consumption). Krautrock groups like Kraftwerk, Can, and Neu! talked to the machines and addressed the nation-state more directly. Bands like Amon Düül, Faust, and Ton Steine Scherben sought new ways of living through communes. All the while, Tangerine Dream, Ash Ra Tempel, and Popol Vuh gazed at the stars.

# 4  Ecstatic Heritage

## Popol Vuh's Soundtracks for Werner Herzog

If krautrock was the attempt to define a new, different German identity in the wake of World War II, similar claims can be made about the New German Cinema. In the late 1960s, directors like Rainer Werner Fassbinder, Wim Wenders, and Volker Schlöndorff began making films that revolved around the same issues krautrock groups engaged with: discourses of Americanization, a reterritorialization of the national by reimagining and reinventing the German past, and a movement across borders that challenged any form of fixed German national identity. It should come as no surprise that popular music featured prominently in the New German Cinema, but none of the directors who gained international acclaim in the 1970s integrated music into the artistic vision of his or her films as fully as Werner Herzog did, in particular in his collaborations with Popol Vuh.[1]

Popol Vuh contributed music to twelve Werner Herzog films, most notably four feature films that starred Klaus Kinski in the leading role: *Aguirre* (1972), *Nosferatu* (1979), *Fitzcarraldo* (1982), and *Cobra Verde* (1987). Other important scores, also discussed here, accompanied the documentaries *The Great Ecstasy of Woodcarver Steiner* (1974) and *The Dark Glow of the Mountains* (1985) as well as the feature film *Heart of Glass* (1976).[2] Unlike Popol Vuh's other 1970s output, their soundtracks for Herzog's films emphasized organ more than guitar, replaced Djong Yun's vocals with otherworldly choirs, and saw a return of the synthesizer. In conjunction with Herzog's images, Popol Vuh's manifestation of the cosmic-as-spiritual took on additional meanings, aurally accompanying and enriching notions of Western civilization's decline and the failings of colonialism, the ecstatic experience of nature as culture, and the reimagining of the national as the universal. While the narratives of

Herzog's films often involved problematic elements of neocolonialism and the conquest of nature, the aestheticization of the films in *both* sound and vision emphasized conflicts between human and artificial, nature and culture, self and other. The major characters in Herzog's feature films all grappled with insanity and ended up failing. Their unstableness extended to the aural and visual realizations of their narratives.

In analyzing the soundtracks to Herzog's films, it is important to not only consider the music but also other kinds of sounds as well as silences. The emerging field of sound studies provides a theoretical framework for this approach. As Kara Keeling and Josh Kun have noted, sound studies is "an interdisciplinary umbrella for scholars, writers, architects, engineers, and sound-makers of all stripes" and "has grown into a field hospitable to anyone interested in exploring sound's social meanings, cultural histories, technological evolutions, political impacts and spatial mappings, to name only a few of the many directions being explored through this new attention to critical aurality and the practices and performances of listening."[3] Following Keeling and Kun's direction, I focus on a broad range of sonic details in my analysis of the soundtracks to Herzog's films.

## Werner Herzog and the New German Cinema

Werner Herzog emerged as one of the directors associated with the New German Cinema (*Neuer Deutscher Film*).[4] Inspired by the French *Nouvelle Vague*, a number of directors, including Alexander Kluge and Edgar Reitz, declared the death of the old and the birth of a new German cinema in the Oberhausen Manifesto of 1962. The diverse movement did not really take off until the late 1960s. It featured younger West German directors like Wim Wenders, Margarethe von Trotta, and Rainer Werner Fassbinder, most of whom were born during the Third Reich and World War II. In their films, they tackled political and societal issues ignored by the popular German cinema of the immediate postwar period. The films were generally only viewed by an elite art crowd and relied on public funding, in particular through television networks. A major breakthrough was Volker Schlöndorff's film version of Günter Grass's novel *The Tin Drum* (*Die Blechtrommel*, 1979), which won an Academy Award for best foreign film. However, the early 1980s saw a decline of the New German Cinema with the death of major contributor Rainer Werner Fassbinder in 1982 and the election of a conservative government the same year, which discontinued much of the public funding.

Herzog, born 1942 in Munich, did not necessarily see many similarities between his own films and those of others labeled as New German Cinema. Yet just like many of the musicians categorized as krautrock who did not fully identify with the term, Herzog referred to overcoming the Nazi past and warding off the influx of American popular culture as common points of reference: "What was very clear to my generation was that by the early 1960s we German filmmakers desperately needed to grow up and take our destiny into our own hands, and this is exactly what we did. It is this which united German filmmakers in the late 1960s, not the films themselves, and certainly not the themes of our work."[5] For instance, unlike the works of other German filmmakers, most of Herzog's productions were not strictly coded as German, and the majority were filmed and took place outside of Germany. Like many krautrock groups with similar transnational leanings, Herzog achieved more success in France, Italy, and the United States than in his home country: "I have always had to struggle—film after film—to get audiences' attention in Germany."[6] Herzog had begun making films by explicitly moving away from Hollywood conventions. Importantly, just like some krautrock groups that had abandoned Anglo-American and African American musical structures, developing a seemingly distinctive German style brought Herzog success outside his home country.

In the United States, Herzog has been received as an *auteur* and a major director.[7] After moving to California and making the popular documentary *Grizzly Man* (2005), Herzog managed to receive funding for major Hollywood productions, which began to adhere more closely to the conventions of the American movie industry. At the same time, Herzog's "otherness" also continued to give him a certain edge in Hollywood, and his German accent, which carried the narrative in most of his documentaries, spawned a number of parodies (including his own self-parody in episodes of *Boondocks* and *The Simpsons*).

One of the major differences to mainstream film conventions was Herzog's blurring of "fictional" feature films and "factual" documentary films. In his 1999 Minnesota Declaration, Herzog stated: "There are deeper strata of truth in cinema, and there is such a thing as poetic, ecstatic truth. It is mysterious and elusive, and can be reached only through fabrication and imagination and stylization."[8] Herzog's documentaries used invented quotations and scripted dialogue and connected seemingly disparate elements, while his fictional films involved "real" elements, such as pulling an actual steamboat over a mountain in *Fitzcarraldo* instead of using a scale model, as well as the "authentic" mental health issues presented on screen by actors like Klaus Kinski and Bruno Schleinstein. Herzog's fascination with a dehistoricized ecstasy achieved through conquest and control of nature and people made it difficult to distinguish whether his films were neocolonialist fantasies or critiques of colonialism. It was equally difficult to tell whether he gave a fair representation of people who were physically and mentally challenged and from different national and cultural backgrounds or whether he simply exploited them. In addition, problematic gender politics remained hidden behind the shroud of an elusive male ecstasy. Thus, while Herzog might have abandoned Hollywood conventions, many of his films nonetheless provided narratives firmly rooted in similar Western white male ideologies.

However, the camera work and the soundtracks added other elements to Herzog's films and complicated the problematic politics of his narratives. Breaking with many of Hollywood's conventions, Herzog's soundtracks included silences and nonmusical sound and had unusual musical scores that played a significant role in creating meaning. As Herzog has said: "There is never anything like 'background music' in my films."[9] While the director employed soundtracks ranging from European classical music to different kinds of rock and from world music to selections by German-born Hollywood composer Hans Zimmer, Popol Vuh's music was arguably the most significant sonic contribution to Herzog's highly acclaimed films.

Werner Herzog and Florian Fricke's collaborations dated back to Herzog's first feature film *Signs of Life* (*Lebenszeichen*, 1968), in which Fricke appeared as a pianist playing and discussing Frédéric Chopin. Stavros Xarchakos scored the movie about a German soldier stationed in Greece during World War II who slowly goes insane. Herzog's *Fata Morgana* (1972), for which elderly film critic Lotte Eisner read passages from the *Popol Vuh* to images of desolate North African landscapes, inspired Fricke to name his band after the Mayan book of creation. Spirituality, a key concept in Fricke's music, was also an element in Herzog's films, but it was here that important differences between their visions emerged. Whereas Fricke came to embrace a decidedly religious and particularly Christian musical expression, Herzog's position was more ambivalent. As Brad Prager has observed: "Herzog's beliefs about filmmaking are consistently bound to a quasi-religious language of

revelation, even though he seems neither to go to church nor does he out-
wardly express much belief in God."[10] Religion was the topic of a number
of Herzog's documentaries, but they generally presented spiritual ecstasy
from the perspective of a detached outsider. For Fricke, on the other hand,
musical and spiritual expressions were always connected.

Herzog's second feature film, *Even Dwarfs Started Small* (*Auch Zwerge
haben klein angefangen*, 1970), was about the aftermath of a rebellion in an
unidentified mental institution and featured a cast consisting exclusively of
little people. Unlike Tod Browning in *Freaks* (1932), Herzog did not let them
speak for themselves but devised a world for "dwarfs" that was embedded in
his own privileged position as a normalized spectator. The film primarily
intended to mock the student movement in Germany. As Herzog remarked:
"I was basically accused of ridiculing the world revolution with *Even Dwarfs*
rather than proclaiming it. Actually, that is probably the one thing they might
have been right about."[11] While his skepticism of New Left politics set him
apart from other young German filmmakers during this time, many elements of the film were aimed at making fun of bourgeois culture and the
church and were very much in line with the student movement (these
included scenes of exaggerated table manners, a wedding ceremony, as well
as a procession with a monkey on a crucifix, and a kneeling dromedary def-
ecating). A nihilist spirit mostly absent from Herzog's other works pervaded
the film, and the soundtrack did little to challenge its somewhat limited
vision, although Popol Vuh provided some electronic effects with the Moog
synthesizer. Along with music from the Ivory Coast, these sounds were
meant to further alienate the viewer from the human and animal characters
on the screen.

As Herzog was developing his filmic vision, both as part of and in critical
distance to the New German Cinema, he began to draw increasingly on
Popol Vuh's music as an integral element of this vision. Beginning with
*Aguirre* (1972), Herzog combined Fricke's full-fledged syncretic spirituality
with his own narratives of transnational madness and opened up levels of
meaning not quite present in his earliest films.[12]

## Colonial Fantasies and the Ecstasy of Nature

*Aguirre, the Wrath of God* (*Aguirre, der Zorn Gottes*, 1972) was Herzog's first
film with a musical soundtrack dominated by Popol Vuh and the first of five

films Herzog made with controversial German actor Klaus Kinski (1926–91). Kinski played Lope de Aguirre, a member of a sixteenth-century expedition in the Peruvian highlands led by Gonzalo Pizarro that searches for El Dorado, the mythic city of gold. In the film, Aguirre eventually defies the Spanish crown but ultimately fails in his mission to find El Dorado, as his party is slowly decimated by spears of the native population, by madness, illness, and starvation. The film was very loosely based on historical figures and facts, with the character Aguirre being mostly inspired by Ugandan revolutionary John Okello, who lived four centuries after the real Aguirre. As Brad Prager noted, Herzog's film "both reviles and reveres the main character's unabashed gall, his narcissism, his death drive and his insatiable hunger for power"[13] and was no clear indictment of Aguirre's colonialism, although it presented him as delusional and somewhat ludicrous.

Continuing a theme from *Even Dwarfs Started Small*, *Aguirre* was critical of organized religion, presenting the missionary Gaspar de Carvajal, whose diary narrated the film, as an important member of the greedy party, blindly following the man who declared himself "the wrath of God." Some critics connected the film, which was shot and took place in Peru, to German history and linked Aguirre's character with Adolf Hitler, an interpretation not endorsed by Herzog but plausible. *Aguirre* was clearly an inspiration for Francis Ford Coppola's Vietnam saga *Apocalypse Now* (1979), which had a similar storyline but used sounds and music (by the Doors, Richard Wagner, and others) less subtly—Herzog has described Coppola's movie as a film "where the sledgehammer effects are constantly hitting you over the head."[14]

In *Aguirre*, music, in addition to camera work and dialogue, was integral for the composition of the film, and sound was used sparingly but to great effect. Herzog has noted: "Often I try to introduce into a landscape a certain atmosphere, using sound and vision to give it a definite character."[15] Popol Vuh's main theme appeared in *Aguirre*'s opening shots of a fog-covered mountain with human-like features, slowly cutting to Pizarro's party descending single-file. As Roger Hillman wrote in his essay on Herzog's sonic worlds: "The music descends in register and instrumentation from an ethereal realm until it takes on a fully developed bass line, complementing perfectly the trajectory of the camera (from eye-of-God perspective to eye-level shots of the river at the foot of the opening mountains) and of this ill-fated expedition."[16] In order to produce a hybrid sound between human and artificial that foreshadowed the main character's insanity, Fricke played a so-called choir organ, a Mellotron-like synthesizer that used the sounds of a prerecorded choir (as well as strings, mandolins, and other acoustic sounds). Herzog explained his request for otherworldly voices to Paul Cronin: "For the music, I described to Florian Fricke what I was searching for, something both pathetic and surreal, and what he came up with was not real singing, nor is it completely artificial either. It sits uncomfortably between the two."[17] The result was a sound both cosmic and foreboding, representing the overwhelming nature that would eventually swallow all the members of the expedition except for Aguirre.

*Aguirre*'s soundtrack consisted primarily of two similar eerie themes by Popol Vuh, containing mostly high-pitched and later deep choir organ chords and improvised processed guitar melodies, which appeared multiple times and in key scenes: the coronation of Aguirre's sidekick, Don Fernando de Guzman, by which Aguirre defeats the Spanish crown, the death of his rival Don Pedro de Ursúa, the vision of a ship in a tree as desperation sets in on Aguirre's raft, and the death of Aguirre's daughter with whom he wanted to start a "pure dynasty." The only other musical element in the film was a panpipe melody played on-screen by a mentally impaired Native actor known as *Hombrecito* ("Little Man"). The circularity of the chant-like score denied progress for the main character (which was true for the Kinski features *Fitzcarraldo*, *Nosferatu*, and *Cobra Verde* as well), and the camera indicated a similar move when it circled the raft for the final scene with Aguirre as the only surviving member of the expedition, surrounded by monkeys. Camera work and music reflected the main character's inner landscape, as did other soundscapes. *Aguirre* had many scenes without dialogue or music—featuring instead the sound of rushing or quiet water, of birds, and of complete silence, oftentimes signaling danger. According to Herzog, "we spent weeks recording the birds and the soundtrack was composed from eight different tracks. There is not a single bird that has not been carefully placed as if in a big choir."[18] Along with the unusual camera work, the soundtrack to *Aguirre* aestheticized the fairly generic narrative and added complexity to a deceptively simple story of failed conquest.

*Aguirre*'s complexity became even more apparent in comparison to two other Herzog feature films about colonial fantasies and with Kinski in the leading role, *Fitzcarraldo* (1982) and *Cobra Verde* (1987).[19] *Fitzcarraldo* used the same setting as *Aguirre* and told the story of the ultimately failed attempt of a deranged Irish businessman, Brian Sweeney "Fitzcarraldo" Fitzgerald (played by Kinski), to pull a steamboat over a mountain and build an opera house in the Peruvian jungle. The making of the two-and-a-half-hour movie involved significant technical setbacks and conflicts with the Aguaruna Indians in Peru. Although the public outrage over Herzog was largely based on exaggerated claims about the film's production, the narrative's problematic neocolonial politics remained. Unlike *Aguirre, Fitzcarraldo* ended with a redeeming moment for the main character, who had the Indians assist him in trying to build a temple for European music when an opera troupe performs on the mangled ship. Due to the production scandals, Herzog's depiction of a "conqueror of the useless" (as Fitzgerald is called by another character) is probably his best-known work, but artistically it might not have been one of his most convincing films.

*Fitzcarraldo*'s major flaw was its depiction of the native population, which had merely functioned as an off-screen threat in *Aguirre*. Hundreds of Indians appeared as extras in the slow-moving film but did not get any kind of authentic voice, although Herzog proudly proclaimed the opposite in Les Blank's documentary about the making of *Fitzcarraldo*, the aptly titled *Burden of Dreams*:

> In this case we will probably have one of the last feature films with authentic natives in it. They are fading away very quickly and it's a catastrophe and a tragedy. We are losing [ . . . ] cultures and individualities and languages and mythologies and [ . . . ] we'll end up like all the cities in the world now with skyscrapers and a universal kind of culture like the American culture.[20]

Not only did Herzog invoke the tired disappearing-Indian trope and simultaneously espouse a simplified view of both the Aguaruna Indians and a globalized America, he also completely ignored that his own film was really about an Irish businessman played by a white German actor, not about indigenous populations.

As for *Aguirre*, the camera work and the soundtrack provided more depth to *Fitzcarraldo*'s somewhat narrow neocolonialist narrative. In addition to four tracks from Popol Vuh's 1981 release *Sei still wisse ICH BIN* and jungle soundscapes, as well as silences revived from *Aguirre*, the film contrasted "civilized" European romantic music (including two on-screen opera performances[21]) with the "uncivilized" native drums and chanting. Key scenes showed Fitzgerald exposing indigenous children to the music of Italian tenor Enrico Caruso and later on his ship responding to Indian war drums by blasting Caruso from his gramophone. Seemingly setting up a colonialist discourse, these scenes had ironic elements to them, since Fitzgerald as the harbinger of "civilization" is clearly a madman who is equally attracted by the ecstasy of the jungle as by the ecstasy of Caruso's voice. In addition, Popol Vuh's songs were situated somewhere between European romanticism and the indigenous music of the film. The main theme "Wehe Khorazim" ("Woe to Chorazin") about a cursed city in the New Testament featured a chant by the choir of the Bavarian State Opera, accompanied by a pounding bass drum, and eventually piano, electric guitar, and tambourine. It appeared in the opening shots of another foggy Peruvian landscape with the following epigraph: "Cayahuari Yacu, the jungle Indians call this country, 'the land where God did not finish Creation.' They believe only after man has disappeared will He return to finish His work." In combination with Popol Vuh's "Wehe Khorazim," the epigraph added a syncretic dimension to the film, connecting Christianity and native religion by introducing a place abandoned by God (and later inhabited by a character who unsuccessfully tries to play God). As in *Aguirre*, Popol Vuh's main theme returned in the middle and near the end of the film, reflecting a circular movement and negating any sense of progress. The other three Popol Vuh tracks on *Fitzcarraldo*'s soundtrack were less conspicuous: the single-chord chorus-guitar-driven "Als lebten die Engel auf Erden" ("As If Angels Lived on Earth") accompanied scenes of Fitzcarraldo and his wife (played by Claudia Cardinale), whereas the more ominous oboe melody "Engel der Luft" ("Angels of the Air") was played when Fitzcarraldo was shown by himself. Another guitar-driven theme, "Im Garten der Gemeinschaft" ("In the Garden of Community"), which added minor-mode chants on top of major-mode instrumentation, appeared when the Indians pull the boat up the mountain and returned with choral voices when the boat crashes down the mountain.

    *Cobra Verde* (1987), the final collaboration between Herzog, Kinski, and Popol Vuh, took neocolonialism to yet another level. Loosely based on Bruce Chatwin's 1980 novel *The Viceroy of Ouidah* and set mostly in Dahomey (now Benin), it is the deeply troubling tale of the Brazilian slave trader and bandit Francisco Manoel da Silva, nicknamed "Cobra Verde" ("Green Cobra"), who was played by Kinski. Instead of engaging with European colonial history (and the much-neglected history of German colonialism in particular),

Herzog presented a "sympathetic" slave trader and many "colorful" African extras, including an army of half-naked female warriors led into battle by Silva. After losing his empire, Silva acknowledges that slavery is a "crime" near the end of the film, which visually and aurally celebrated neocolonialist fantasies. Herzog's callous comment that "*Cobra Verde* is about great fantasies and follies of the human spirit, not colonialism"[22] showed his complete ignorance of historical and political implications in making the film.[23]

Popol Vuh's theme for the soundtrack to *Cobra Verde* consisted of another ominous choir, this time accompanied by a synclavier. It most notably orchestrated the opening shots of animal corpses and an arid landscape, Silva's first appearance in a Brazilian village, and the final scene of the film, in which Silva tries in vain to pull a boat to sea. Traditional African drumming and vocal performances dominated much of the soundtrack, as well as soundscapes of birds, insects, rushing water, and silences. Although still mostly avoiding Hollywood clichés, the soundtrack supplemented the *National Geographic*-like aesthetics, the white male gaze of the camera, and the film's neocolonialist narrative. In the case of *Cobra Verde*, the dehistoricized narrative, the stylized acting, and the Orientalist musical and visual spectacle resulted in a film that lacked all the aesthetic complexity of *Aguirre*.

*Aguirre*, *Fitzcarraldo*, and *Cobra Verde* all involved stories of colonialist dreams and failures, featured Kinski in the leading role, and had choir-driven scores by Popol Vuh. Two documentary films Herzog made in 1974 and 1985, *The Great Ecstasy of Woodcarver Steiner* and *The Dark Glow of the Mountains*, presented very similar stories of white men achieving ecstasy through conquering nature and also prominently featured music by Popol Vuh. If one considers the blurring of "fictional" feature films and "factual" documentaries in all of Herzog's work, viewing these two forty-five-minute films in a similar context as the better-known Kinski features makes much sense, even if they substituted the German actor for the Swiss ski jumper Walter Steiner and the Italian mountaineer Reinhold Messner.

Herzog has called *The Great Ecstasy of Woodcarver Steiner* (*Die große Ekstase des Bildschnitzers Steiner*, 1974) "one of my most important films."[24] Superficially an account of the dangers of professional athletics, the documentary about Walter Steiner's "ski flying" heavily aestheticized the ecstatic or religious aspects of the sport through many super-slow-motion jumps and crashes of the Olympic gold medalist. Images of Steiner's open-mouthed in-flight ecstasy were set to simple, tranquil electric guitar, organ, and piano melodies by Popol Vuh and accompanied by some shots of birds in flight. Instead of focusing on the competitive aspect of the sport, the music highlighted its spiritual dimension. As Brad Prager noted: "Drawing an analogy between athletic and religious ecstasies, Herzog employs a synthetic score that recalls cathedral choirs. [ . . . ] The music emphasizes the quasi-religious status of Steiner's accomplishment."[25] In contrast to generic sports documentaries, Herzog's film did little to contextualize Steiner's record-breaking jumps and instead featured interview segments about Steiner's hobby of woodcarving and about a pet bird he had to shoot. A final epigram describing Steiner's fantasy to be alone, naked on a high rock, and without fear was actually written by Swiss writer Robert Walser and reworded by Herzog, who also appeared on-screen as an awestruck spectator, part of the crowd making what he called a "pilgrimage" to see Steiner.

Conquest of nature and ecstasy bordering on a death wish were also major themes in the other Herzog documentary with music by Popol Vuh, *The Dark Glow of the Mountains* (*Gasherbrum, der leuchtende Berg*, 1985). Recalling the German *Bergfilm* ("Mountain Film") genre of the 1920s, *The Dark Glow* chronicled mountaineers Reinhold Messner and Hans Kammerlander's successful attempt to climb Gasherbrum I and II, two 8,000-meter peaks in the Himalayas, in one excursion and without oxygen tanks. As in his documentary about Walter Steiner, Herzog was less interested in factual details than in the inner life and spirituality of his subjects. Herzog also explicitly linked the inner landscapes of the mountaineers with the outer landscapes of the mountains both in his interviews and in the camera work. Popol Vuh's music, consisting of choral chants and electric guitar improvisation, accompanied scenes where the camera slowly panned the majestic, "ecstatic" peaks and others where the mountaineers were shown from a distance, climbing through the snow and representing "the general irrelevance of human life in the face of the overwhelming mountain."[26] Unlike other film scores, no music was played in the most emotionally charged scene of the film, in which Messner talked about his brother's death in an excursion they had undertaken together.

As in Herzog's feature films, ecstasy of nature also involved an element of neocolonialism in *The Dark Glow of the Mountains*. The two white men, Messner and Kammerlander, appeared as the mountain's conquerors, although they relied on the help of indigenous carriers (or Sherpas). While the film featured interviews with the mountaineers, the Sherpas were only shown through an anthropological lens, singing, dancing, and representing part of the nature of the film. Yet like Klaus Kinski's characters, Messner was not necessarily depicted as superior or more civilized, as he openly acknowledged the "insanity" and "degeneration" of his endeavors. Herzog returned to the "man versus nature" theme in the fictional mountain film *Scream of Stone* (1991), based on an idea by Reinhold Messner, and in his hugely popular documentary *Grizzly Man* (2005) about Timothy Treadwell, who lived with and was eventually killed by brown bears.

## The German Heritage

In his three feature films *Aguirre*, *Fitzcarraldo*, and *Cobra Verde*, Werner Herzog presented transnational stories of colonial failure, with Popol Vuh contributing musical soundtracks that both enriched and complicated his narratives. For his documentaries *The Great Ecstasy of Woodcarver Steiner* and *The Dark Glow of the Mountains*, Herzog turned to internationally known German-speaking subjects (the Swiss Walter Steiner and South Tyrolean Reinhold Messner), and Popol Vuh's score complemented scenes depicting the ecstasy of nature. In a number of films he made in the 1970s, Herzog turned more explicitly to his German heritage, with Popol Vuh providing soundtracks for *Heart of Glass* (1976) and *Nosferatu* (1979). Unlike the raging madness of colonialist fantasies, a quieter, more introspective madness characterized these German films, but they also revolved around Western civilization's decline and presented the national as universal.

Herzog's first feature film with explicitly German themes was *The Enigma of Kaspar Hauser* (*Jeder für sich und Gott gegen alle*, 1974), featuring Bruno Schleinstein in the leading role. The film was loosely based on the life of the real Kaspar Hauser, who lived in Nuremberg in the early nineteenth century. Hauser had spent his early life in total isolation and was mysteriously and fatally stabbed five years after appearing in public. In an ironic contrast to its German title, which literally translated to "Every Man for Himself and God against All," Herzog's film had religious undertones and presented Hauser as a Christ-like figure who rejected traditional faith and logic but was deeply spiritual. Florian Fricke appeared in the film as a blind pianist and played his own piece "Agnus Dei" (a similar role as in *Signs of Life*), but the soundtrack was dominated by European classical, baroque, and Renaissance music, in particular works by Wolfgang Amadeus Mozart.

For *Heart of Glass* (*Herz aus Glas*, 1976), Herzog returned to Germany as the setting. With almost the entire cast under hypnosis, the enigmatic and slightly anticapitalist film told the story of futile attempts by the inhabitants of a small town to recover the secret of a deceased ruby glassmaker in eighteenth-century Bavaria. *Heart of Glass* depicted a community unable to face the demands of modernity and which subsequently goes insane. The film contained many dark visions of the seer Hias (Josef Bierbichler), who represented spirituality, even though it was an apparent critique of Catholicism (themes that appeared again three years later in *Nosferatu*). The film ended on a slightly positive note by showing a vision of the last men on Earth rowing out to sea and being followed by high-flying birds, interpreted in an epigram as possibly a "sign of hope." Visually and thematically, *Heart of Glass* was influenced by German romanticism (in particular the paintings of Caspar David Friedrich) and the sentimental German *Heimat* films of the 1950s, but, even more than *The Enigma of Kaspar Hauser*, it presented the national as the universal. This became especially evident in the scenes of "Bavarian" landscapes, which were filmed on the Irish coast and in the United States (Yellowstone National Park, Monument Valley, and Niagara Falls).

Although Popol Vuh's Florian Fricke provided a significant share of the musical soundtrack, *Heart of Glass*, unlike the Herzog movies with Klaus Kinski, was not framed by a theme of the band. The Munich group Studio der frühen Musik ("Studio of Early Music") supplied yodel-like vocals for the opening shots of Hias in contemplation, a haunting lament at the film's end, and other Western art music from the baroque and earlier periods throughout the film. Their instruments, some of which were played onscreen, included lute, vielle, hurdy-gurdy, and harp. While referencing a German heritage, they blended with Fricke's music to create a sense of dreamy timelessness. Popol Vuh's music, dominated by reverbed guitar, Eastern scales, and some electronic sounds, appeared at various points in the film: Hias dreaming, shots of a rushing waterfall and mountains and shots of the furnace where glass is made, a procession of the townspeople, Hias walking through the woods, Hias climbing the mountain to fight an invisible bear. Like the visual images and the soundscapes—the silences, the roar of the furnace, the mad laughter of the factory owner's father, the screams of the maid—the musical score moved the film from a coherent plot into an atmosphere of quiet insanity, which was situated in southern Germany but took on existential or universal qualities.

Not a classic horror film, *Heart of Glass* nonetheless could be viewed as similarly unsettling. Herzog's *Nosferatu the Vampyre* (*Nosferatu, Phantom der Nacht*, 1979), on the other hand, was clearly rooted in the horror film genre, taking its cues from Friedrich Wilhelm Murnau's classic *Nosferatu, eine Symphonie des Grauens* (*Nosferatu, a Symphony of Terror*, 1922). Both Murnau's and Herzog's films were loosely based on Bram Stoker's novel *Dracula* (1897). Herzog's *Nosferatu* told the story of Jonathan Harker (Bruno Ganz), who, on a business visit to Count Dracula (Klaus Kinski) in Romania, is bitten by the vampire. Dracula, smitten with Jonathan's wife Lucy (Isabelle Adjani), travels by ship to Jonathan's hometown Wismar (in northeastern Germany) and brings the plague with him. Lucy sacrifices herself to Dracula, who perishes after staying with her until sunrise. Jonathan survives as the new vampire.

For Herzog, remaking Murnau's silent film as a film with silences and bridging Weimar cinema with the New German Cinema meant writing "the final chapter of the vital process of 're-legitimization' of German culture that had been going on for some years."[27] This "re-legitimization" transcended Germany's borders. The horror genre, and particularly vampire movies, have been an international phenomenon, and *Nosferatu*, while only moderately successful in Germany, eventually became a surprise hit in the United States after it was released on DVD. The transnational aspect of the film was also highlighted by the fact that, like *Heart of Glass*, it was not just shot in Germany (in this case the northern part of the country) but also in the Netherlands, Czechoslovakia, and Mexico. Finally, the universal dimension of *Nosferatu*'s turn to the national was evident in its connection with the colonialist fantasies of Herzog's other movies. Madness was a major theme, again more subtle (like in *Heart of Glass*), and conquest manifested itself in Dracula's attempts to subdue both Jonathan and Lucy.

The music for *Nosferatu* was provided primarily by Popol Vuh but also included pieces by the Georgian Gordela vocal ensemble and composers Richard Wagner and Charles Gounod. The opening scenes of the film set the tone with mummified corpses of various ages and poses, accompanied by Popol Vuh's ominous "Brüder des Schattens" ("Brothers of the Shade") with "medieval chanting based on two notes a tone apart, increasingly supported and overridden by other instruments, most notably oboes and cymbals."[28] This scene was followed by a slow-motion shot of a flying bat that was repeated throughout the film. Popol Vuh's song ended in a scream by Lucy when she awakes from a nightmare. "Brüder des Schattens," the movie's main theme, returned when Jonathan, on his journey to Dracula, approaches the foggy Carpathian Mountains and walks along raging waters, and again when Dracula and Jonathan travel back to Wismar separately. As the complementary theme to "Brüder des Schattens," the lighter, acoustic-guitar- and piano-driven "Söhne des Lichts" ("Sons of the Light") appeared throughout the film—in scenes of marital bliss with Jonathan and Lucy and of Jonathan riding his horse, and in shots of the town of Wismar before the plague. Discordant Moog sounds, taken from 1971's *In den Gärten Pharaos*, created an eerie mood when Jonathan explores the castle and later when Lucy looks for Dracula and awaits him, and the brooding "Höre, der du wagst" ("Hark Thou Who Dares") with its distinctive three-note piano figure was played when Lucy tries to tell others about Dracula's secret and when she sets out to defeat the vampire. Whereas Popol Vuh's music mainly appeared in scenes with Jonathan and Lucy, the drone of Wagner's prelude to *Das Rheingold* accompanied three scenes directly related to Dracula. Charles Gounod's "Sanctus" perversely closed the film when Jonathan, now fully morphed into a vampire, rides into the distance. Like other films by Herzog, *Nosferatu* used silence and nonmusical soundscapes to create atmosphere, encompassing the full range of horror film sounds, like screeching doors, rats, and bats, howling wolves and wind, the echo of footsteps, church bells, screams, insane laughter, and Dracula's breathing and choking.

Popol Vuh's soundtrack for Herzog's *Nosferatu* not only helped to create a frightening atmosphere but, like the aesthetically pleasing images of the film, also challenged the nihilistic tone of the narrative. Unlike Murnau's version, Herzog's *Nosferatu* ended with Lucy senselessly dying, as Jonathan takes Dracula's place. Yet neither the highly stylized cinematography nor Popol Vuh's spiritually driven music fully supported the gloomy turn of events. Although Western civilization's decline and unstoppable madness were major themes in *Nosferatu* (as they were in many other Herzog movies), beauty was at least partly reaffirmed through the aestheticization of sound and visuals.

Immediately after finishing the production of *Nosferatu*, Herzog quickly shot an adaptation of Georg Büchner's 1836 society drama *Woyzeck* (1979) with most of the same cast and crew, including Kinski in the leading role. Concluding Herzog's 1970s run of films engaging with German subjects, *Woyzeck* told the story of a lowly soldier slowly going insane and eventually killing both his mistress and himself. The music for the soundtrack of the film (which was a fairly straightforward adaptation of the play) was taken from works by the Italian composers Benedetto Marcello and Antonio Vivaldi. With *Aguirre*, *Nosferatu*, *Woyzeck*, *Fitzcarraldo*, and *Cobra Verde*, Herzog made a total of five feature films with Klaus Kinski. The stormy relationship between the two was the subject of Herzog's documentary *My Best Fiend* (*Mein liebster Feind*, 1999). Successful both in Germany and abroad, the film presented Kinski's antics in an entertaining, humorous manner and used old Popol Vuh songs, mostly in connection with the films they originally appeared in. The final scene of *My Best Fiend* showed Kinski playing with a butterfly in order to accentuate his tender side (as opposed to the actor's raging fits that dominated the rest of the film) and featured Popol Vuh's "Als lebten die Engel auf Erden," which had previously accompanied upbeat scenes in *Fitzcarraldo*.

Taken together, the films of Herzog that engaged with his German heritage expressed quieter and more introspective forms of madness than his colonialist fantasies. Yet both "German" and "neocolonial" films shared the aestheticization of their subject matter—especially evident in *Heart of Glass* and *Nosferatu* in Popol Vuh's score and the stylized camera work. Their invocation of the national could be seen as taking on transnational or even universal qualities. In addition, these films provided similar narratives of Western civilization's decline as Herzog's more overtly international movies—narratives that were also both challenged and supported by the films' audiovisual aspects.

## America and the World

After *Cobra Verde*, Herzog relied less on Popol Vuh for scoring his films. Coincidentally, Herzog's career suffered a bit between the late 1980s and the mid-1990s, but the success of the documentaries *My Best Fiend* (1999) and *Grizzly Man* (2005) served as a comeback for the director and enabled him to produce Hollywood movies with larger budgets beginning in 2006. Although Popol Vuh's music only played a minor role in the films that best illustrated Herzog's complex relationship with the United States, they are discussed here briefly to show their parallels with discourses of Americanization prevalent in krautrock on a larger scale.

A simultaneous fascination with and rejection of US popular culture, particularly the Hollywood movie industry, characterized the works of many directors of the New German Cinema, with Wim Wenders's *The American Friend* (1977) and *Paris, Texas* (1984) being obvious examples. In Les Blank's documentary *Werner Herzog Eats His Shoe*, the director declared a "holy war against commercials and talk shows and *Bonanza* and *Rawhide*" and instead called for "a new grammar of images." The first feature film in which Herzog explicitly dealt with the United States was *Stroszek* (1977), with Bruno Schleinstein in the leading role. The film told the story of a group of derelicts and loners from Berlin who move to Wisconsin but fail to achieve their dreams in America, with the main protagonist committing suicide at the end. *Stroszek* featured images of German and American landscapes that were equally bleak and used music by Ludwig van Beethoven, Chet Atkins, Tom Paxton, and Sonny Terry and Brownie McGhee. In some of his documentaries, Herzog addressed more spectacular American subjects, like livestock auctioneers and TV preachers. Later, Herzog caused controversies in Europe with two films that could be perceived as unabashedly pro-American: *Ballad of the Little Soldier* (1984), about the Miskito Indians' resistance against the Sandinistas in Nicaragua, and *Lessons of Darkness* (1992), which aestheticized burning oil fields in the wake of the 1991 Gulf War. For Herzog, the United States was just one among many regions of interest, and he increasingly began to make films in remote locations all over the world. *Wheel of Time* (2003), a documentary about the Dalai Lama's Kalachakra initiations, filmed in India and Austria, featured one scene with a Popol Vuh track ("Silence of the Night") set to images of pilgrims. The track was chosen by Herzog after Florian Fricke's untimely death in 2001 but did not have much of an impact on a soundtrack dominated by Buddhist chants. In contrast to Fricke's heart-felt spirituality, *Wheel of Time*, like other Herzog documentaries explicitly dealing with religion, showed a detached view of religious ecstasy's "spectacle."

Although Herzog's films had become increasingly transnational, it came as a bit of a surprise that in later years he was a sought-after Hollywood director for a few productions with fairly big budgets. With this development, he found himself in the company of other German directors that crossed over to American audiences, like Roland Emmerich and Wolfgang Petersen. Herzog maintained some elements of his unique style that defied Hollywood conventions but also compromised some elements of his 1970s films, in particular the unusual camera work and soundtrack choices. An example for this was Herzog's remake of his own documentary *Little Dieter Wants to Fly* (1998) as *Rescue Dawn* (2006). Both films were about German-born Dieter Dengler, who moved to the United States after World War II so he could join the US Air Force. He was shot down on his first mission in Vietnam, captured, and eventually fled his prison camp and survived several days in the jungle before he was picked up by US forces. In another unabashedly pro-American move, Herzog avoided discussing any historical context and instead presented Dengler as a heroic figure who simply "wants to fly." If the documentary's lack of historical context was alarming, *Rescue Dawn* (2006) went even further in its politics of denial. Christian Bale played Dengler as an American devoid of any German accent, and Laotians and North Vietnamese were heavily stereotyped. German-born Klaus Badelt composed the conventional Hollywood soundtrack, and the sole Popol Vuh track orchestrated only one suspenseful scene in which Dieter is captured, a far cry from earlier Popol Vuh soundtracks. Herzog's ambivalent relationship with Hollywood became more apparent in *Bad Lieutenant: Port of Call New Orleans* (2009), starring Nicholas Cage. The film "rethought" a moralistic Hollywood tale (Abel Farrara's *Bad Lieutenant*, 1992) and turned the good cop into a Kinski-esque madman who is not punished but rewarded for his crimes. Mark Isham's soundtrack for the film, however, was another conventional Hollywood score.[29]

Herzog's tales of colonialism and Western civilization's decline were augmented by the aesthetic dimension of his images and of Popol Vuh's music. Similar to the narratives of the films, the music presented German identity as conflicted and unfinished. Like in a Greek or Shakespearean tragedy, Aguirre, Fitzcarraldo, Hias, Jonathan Harker, and Cobra Verde all ultimately failed, and this failure was also present in the deterritorialized unstableness of the musical narrative. With Herzog's significant success as a filmmaker not just within but also outside Germany, Popol Vuh's soundtracks were able to reach an international audience for krautrock only surpassed by Kraftwerk and Giorgio Moroder. Like other transnational movements connected with krautrock, they negated a strict differentiation between internal and external representations of Germanness. It is this complex web of discursive connections that extends to music generally not labeled as "krautrock," such as that of David Bowie and Donna Summer.

# 5 Outside Looking In

## Donna Summer's Sound of Munich and David Bowie's Berlin Trilogy

One of the effects of krautrock's deterritorialization was the transnational reach of artists like Can, Tangerine Dream, and Popol Vuh—artists who themselves had many non-German influences. A rigorous investigation of krautrock should involve a consideration of performers on the fringes of the field, largely due to their perceived national identity as "foreign" from a German perspective. Discussing Donna Summer and David Bowie in the context of krautrock can serve as a further step in disentangling at least part of the complex web of identity formations embedded in musical performances of Germanness.

Working within a similar context as many krautrock artists, African American singer Donna Summer and Italian-German producer Giorgio Moroder challenged the music's fairly narrow confines of "race," gender, and sexuality in their collaborations. As Moroder and Summer showed, the same sounds that represented an abstract straight white Germanness could also suit an African American diva who appealed to gay men. Yet the border-crossing musical productions of Moroder and Summer are generally classified as disco, not as krautrock. Another border-crossing artist, David Bowie engaged with German national identity through both a problematic obsession with fascism and a genuine interest in expressionist film and visual art. Between August 1976 and February 1978, Bowie lived in West Berlin as an expatriate and was confronted with a rather different German reality, fifty years removed from his imagined community. It was this 1970s West Berlin, along with the music of various krautrock groups, that informed the radical sonic experiments Bowie would undertake on the three albums that became known as the "Berlin Trilogy." Whereas Bowie's previous albums had been dominated by folk and rock influences, contained fairly consistent story-based rock songs, and generally could be separated into "hits" and "filler," the Berlin records broke with these conventions in similar ways krautrock had done: by producing a *Gesamtkunstwerk* characterized by fragmentation, minimalism, and the use of synthesizers and vocals as musical instruments.

In the context of German music in the 1970s, blurring the lines between what it meant to be on the inside looking out and to be on the outside looking in reveals how krautrock's processes of reterritorialization and hybridization were taken up by British and American artists. Donna Summer and David Bowie, two of the most successful international pop performers of their time, popularized elements of krautrock while at the same time enriching the music with a stronger emphasis on fluidity, not just of national identity but also of "race," gender, and sexual orientation.

## Donna Summer, Giorgio Moroder, and the History of Disco

There are a number of reasons why the music of Moroder and Summer is rarely thought of as krautrock. The most obvious explanation may be popular appeal: Summer is the only artist who has had three consecutive number-one platinum albums in the United States (the Moroder-produced two-LP-sets *Live and More*, *Bad Girls*, and *On the Radio*). Contrarily, with the exception of surprise hits like Kraftwerk's "Autobahn," krautrock groups drew much of their appeal for later generations from their relative obscurity. Unlike many krautrock artists, whose earliest musical experiences were in conservatories or with rock bands, Moroder began his career by producing schlager hits, and Summer performed in musicals.[1] Summer's and Moroder's "inauthenticity" was affirmed by their embrace of disco music, which openly promoted consumerism and negated rock music's straight white masculinity. In recent years, artists and historians of electronic music have embraced Summer's and Moroder's music and secured its place in popular music history, yet the link to krautrock remains broken.

Situating Moroder and Summer within the context of German 1970s music does not just mean destabilizing krautrock but also disco, generally perceived as quintessentially American. Disco's transnational history began with the French *discothèques* of 1940s Paris and accelerated with the loft parties of gay men in late 1960s New York City. DJs like Francis Grasso introduced the concept of blending songs into each other in clubs like the Sanctuary.[2] Mid- to late 1970s discos—like the Paradise Garage with DJ Larry Levan—and the clubs on Fire Island still featured a predominantly gay crowd. Economic "stagflation" and urban decay set the stage for disco as much as it did for punk, but the post-1960s narcissism of disco catered in particular to gay black and Latino men. In his novel *Dancer from the Dance* (1978), Andrew Holleran described what he viewed as the classless society of New York City's discotheques (in his case the fictitious 10th Floor): "The boy passed out on the sofa from an overdose of Tuinols was a Puerto Rican who washed dishes in the employees' cafeteria at CBS, but the doctor bending over him had treated presidents."[3] Although Holleran downplayed racial segregation, he captured the period after the Stonewall riots and before the spread of AIDS when gay men were seeking spiritual experiences through sex and dancing. Kai Fikentscher has developed similar ideas by showing parallels between African American churches and gay dance clubs.[4] Although commercial exploitation brought the disco era to a close at the end of the 1970s, androgynous performers like Sylvester and Grace Jones were able to offer an alternative to sexist rock culture even during disco's final years.

Musically, disco was clearly influenced by soul and funk musicians like Isaac Hayes and James Brown and by the Philadelphia sound with its lush strings, horns, and Latin percussion, exemplified by artists like the O'Jays and Teddy Pendergrass. Similar strings appeared on an early disco hit by Barry White, "Love's Theme" (1974). Earl Young was credited for inventing the prototypical disco beat by moving Motown's 4/4 from the snare drum and tambourine to the bass drum and by adding hi-hat flourishes. Young's innovative style could be heard on songs like MFSB's "Love Is the Message" (1973) and the Trammps' "Disco Inferno" (1976). With the popularization of the twelve-inch single, extended versions of disco tracks began to appear. European disco artists like Moroder, French producer Cerrone, and German group Silver Connection combined strings with synthesizers in the second half of the 1970s. Hi-NRG, pioneered by Summer's Moroder-produced "I Feel Love" (1977), featured drum machines and faster tempos. The new electronic disco beat did not succeed in New York City's dance clubs but caught on in the rest of the United States and Europe.[5]

Disco's mainstream success was partly brought about by the box-office hit *Saturday Night Fever* (1977), starring John Travolta. In contrast to disco's actual origins, Travolta played a white heterosexual disco dancer, and the music was provided by Australian pop group the Bee Gees. In the same year, the upper-class club Studio 54 opened in New York City. As a dance craze, disco moves (in particular the Hustle) had become as popular as the Charleston had been in the 1920s and the Twist in the 1960s. Different groups criticized the overexposure and commodification of disco. Funk musician George Clinton simply called it "the blahs," and Jesse Jackson's Operation PUSH threatened to boycott what they called "X-rated disco sex-rock."[6] On July 12, 1979, young white male rock and heavy metal fans burned records at an event called Disco Demolition Night, which took place after a baseball game in Comiskey Park, Chicago. The "Disco Sucks" campaign was also fueled by *Rolling Stone* magazine and had anticommercial but also homophobic and racist undertones. Despite the backlash, US acts continued to release some original disco songs like Chic's "Good Times" (1979) and Diana Ross's "Upside Down" (1980). By the mid-1980s, house music, named after The Warehouse nightclub in Chicago and championed by DJs like Frankie Knuckles, had replaced disco as the most popular underground dance music for gay men.

A number of different critiques of disco have been published over the years, starting with Richard Dyer's 1979 article "In Defense of Disco." In the article, Dyer described the music's sensual (rather than phallic) eroticism and what he saw as its subversive capitalism.[7] Responding to scholars like Dyer, Alice Echols has pointed out that "too often disco revisionists, in an effort to debunk the pervasive view of disco as crassly commercial, exclusionary, and politically regressive, have emphasized instead its subcultural purity, democratic beginnings, and transgressive practices."[8] What may be more regrettable than a tendency to overstate disco's liberatory potential is how accounts of the genre tend to downplay its European influences.[9] The transnational aspects of genres spawned by disco are better known, in particular in the case of techno music, which originated in Detroit but quickly moved to Berlin and other German cities. In conjunction with the related genres hip-hop and house, techno truly realized disco's global potential.

Any account of electronic music's transnational history is not complete without Hansjörg "Giorgio" Moroder. He was born in 1940 in a small town in South Tyrol's Dolomites called Urtijëi, a trilingual community with Italian, German, and Ladin heritage. Moroder briefly studied architecture but quickly realized that his passion was music, and he toured across Europe for six years, playing upright bass in a jazz trio. He then moved to West Berlin to work as a sound engineer and composer. In 1966, Moroder began recording bubble-gum pop songs in English, German, Italian, and Spanish as Giorgio. The most successful of these recordings was "Looky Looky" from 1969, a hit in France, Italy, and Spain. As Moroder recalled: "My intention was always to compose with an English or American feeling."[10] This was in opposition to many krautrock musicians of the time, as were his lack of interest in the countercul- ture and his unapologetic embrace of capitalism. According to Moroder, the upheavals of the late 1960s "meant little to me: I guess I have much more of a commercial feeling and so was not greatly affected by them."[11]

Moroder eventually moved to Munich, which was much closer to his childhood home and less isolated than West Berlin, and founded Musicland Studios in 1969. He produced a number of German-language schlager hits, including Ricky Shayne's "Ich sprenge alle Ketten" ("I Break All Chains"), Michael Holm's "Mendocino" (a cover version of a hit by the Sir Douglas Quintet), and Mary Roos's "Arizona Man" (with a very distinctive synthe- sizer part). The German electronic composer Eberhard Schoener had intro- duced Moroder to the Moog, and it prominently appeared on Moroder's own "Son of My Father" (1972), which became a number-one hit in Great Britain in a version by Chicory Tip. The song's success established Moroder as a European producer, and he began assembling a crew at Musicland that reflected his transnational identity. Coproducer Pete Bellotte and drummer and composer Keith Forsey were British; sound engineer Jürgen Koppers and arranger Harold Faltermeyer were German.[12] Session musicians also came from various European countries, including Great Britain, Sweden, West Germany, and Iceland. Musicland Studios later became a household name for major rock productions and brought recording stars like Queen, the Rolling Stones, ELO, Elton John, and Deep Purple to Munich.

Musicland's international success was launched by recordings Moroder made with Donna Summer. Summer was born 1949 as LaDonna Adrian Gaines in Boston. Influenced by Josephine Baker and Janis Joplin, she became the singer in an otherwise all-white and male band called Crow in 1967 ("the crow being me because I was the only black member of the group"[13]). Summer moved to Munich in 1968 to participate in the German production of the musical *Hair* (*Haare* in German). Summer recalled: "Germany repre- sented a movement of personal liberation for me [ . . . ], and I was living in an artistic and cultural bohemia, a creative heaven."[14] Over the next few years, Summer played in *Showboat* and *Porgy and Bess* in Vienna and, back in Germany, in *The Me Nobody Knows* (*Ich bin ich* in German) and *Godspell*. In

1973, Summer, now a single mother living in poverty, responded to an advertisement for a black female singer and signed to Moroder and Pete Bellotte's Oasis label the following year. In her own words, she felt a connection with Moroder because "like me, he was a foreigner."[15] By invoking Moroder's Italian heritage and her own American identity, Summer pointed to the transnational dimension of the music they would produce in Germany. Moroder himself has noted: "Pete [Bellotte] and myself have combined a certain European feeling with Donna's more American experience."[16]

Summer contributed at least as much to the success of her collaborations with Moroder as he did himself. In addition to many songwriting credits, she provided detached vocals of an unembellished and ringing quality, often sung in the head voice, and rarely employed melisma. At times, Summer's approach was almost as far removed from African American soul influences as that of krautrock groups like Kraftwerk and Neu!. Summer was very aware of her own performativity that borrowed from her experiences singing in musicals: "I don't think a lot of people understand where I'm not an artist that's trying to establish a style. I'm an actress who sings, and that is kind of how I view myself. Whoever the character is in the song, that's who I try to become."[17] Album covers of Summer's collaborations with Moroder reflected this attitude: the singer was depicted as a sex kitten, an angel, a fairy, or a princess. Summer's self-awareness did not always prevent her from being sexually exploited, however, as the roles she got to play were traditionally feminine and never allowed her to express the goofy part of her personality.

Both Summer and Moroder can be viewed as transnational artists in the context of krautrock's deterritorialization and reterritorialization, since they both were at the same time German and non-German. Moroder's trans-European identity (Italian/German/Ladin) and his globalized disco sounds were coupled with his penchant for robot voices, synthesizers, and a "German" drug-free work ethic, all of which placed him in close proximity to Kraftwerk. Summer's Afro-German identity, while rarely discussed, was supported by many factors: her father had been stationed in Germany and taught his wife how to speak German; Summer spent six and a half years in Germany between 1968 and 1975 and became fluent in German; Summer was married to Austrian Helmuth Sommer for two years, with whom she had a daughter and from whom she took her stage name (anglicized as Summer); Summer had another long-time German boyfriend, the artist Peter Mühldorfer, who spoke little English. Donna Summer's Afro-German iden-

tity involved a liminal space that was not always comfortable. As Josiah Howard noted:

> In the minds of many, Donna's marriage [to Helmuth Sommer], coupled
> with her seven-year absence from the United States in the late 1960s and
> early 1970s, placed her outside the African American experience. Conse-
> quently, to many African Americans, Donna was only begrudgingly con-
> sidered an "acceptable" black performer. This impression has shadowed
> her entire career.[18]

Possibly related to her racial and national liminality was the perception of
Summer's sexuality. Rumors of Summer's transsexuality, while clearly fabricated, were even picked up by *Ebony*.[19] Inhabiting such liminal spaces,
Moroder and Summer were able to shape German popular music of the
1970s into something that still resembled krautrock's electronic offshoots but
was also significantly different—the European disco that became known as
the "Sound of Munich."

In addition to their liminality, Summer's performances can be historically
linked to what Darlene Clark Hine has called black women's "culture of dissemblance," a direct result of slavery and rape. In this regard, Summer's role-
playing and fluidity of identity worked to reclaim control over her sexuality
as a black woman. As Hine put it:

> Because of the interplay of racial animosity, class tensions, gender role dif-
> ferentiation, and regional economic variations, black women as a rule
> developed a politics of silence, and adhered to a cult of secrecy, a culture
> of dissemblance, to protect the sanctity of the inner aspects of their lives.
> The dynamics of dissemblance involved creating the appearance of dis-
> closure, or openness about themselves and their feelings, while actually
> remaining enigmatic. Only with secrecy, thus achieving a self-imposed
> invisibility, could ordinary black women acquire the psychic space and
> gather the resources needed to hold their own in their often one-sided
> and mismatched struggle to racist oppression.[20]

While it is crucial to discuss the way both Summer and Moroder had similar
transnational leanings as many krautrock artists, it is equally important to
recognize Summer's status as a black woman in the white patriarchal music

industry represented by Moroder. In her performances, Summer's agency indeed often took on some form of dissemblance.

### "Love to Love You Baby" and "I Feel Love"

Moroder first experimented with krautrock-oriented synthesizer sounds on his solo album *Einzelgänger* ("Loner," 1975), an artistic and commercial failure. According to Moroder, "I used beautiful melodies and futuristic sounds, the people called me mad."[21] In his own judgment, the album remained his only connection to krautrock, whereas he described his other music as "the Sound of Munich, synth pop, funk, disco, Italo disco or Eurodisco."[22] Despite Moroder's own assessment, it is remarkable that he not only felt the necessity to experiment with synthesizer sounds reminiscent of Berlin School artists like Tangerine Dream and Klaus Schulze but that these experiments would help him to develop a unique "German" disco sound with Summer's 1978 hit "I Feel Love."

For Summer's first album, *Lady of the Night* (1974), Moroder had provided musical tracks that blended pop with rock, folk, and schlager. On the single "The Hostage" (a minor hit in France and the Netherlands) and on other songs of the album, Summer's mezzo-soprano voice was mostly mid-range and added a soul timbre to the songs. Yet it was very different vocals that brought about Summer's international breakthrough a year later. For the 1975 album *Love to Love You Baby*, Moroder made a distribution deal with Casablanca Records in Los Angeles. Casablanca owner Neil Bogart insisted that the three-minute title track from Summer's *Love to Love You Baby* should be stretched to seventeen minutes.[23] The song consisted of an improvised line sung in breathy, upper-register vocals and orgasmic shrieks inspired by Serge Gainsbourg's "Je t'aime moi non plus." Gainsbourg's version of the song with Jane Birkin from 1969 had been a major European hit.[24] Birkin's lascivious moaning was copied by Summer, whose husband reportedly had to leave the studio. As Summer remembered: "We dimmed the lights, lit a few candles, and I added all those oohs and aahs."[25] In line with her notion of singing as role-playing, Summer, in an act of racial transgression, performed in Marilyn Monroe's "light and fluffy but highly sensitive voice."[26] Moroder then added what he described as "a very catchy bass-line, a very emphatic bass drum part and a funky guitar, sort of Philadelphia feel."[27]

The seventeen-minute "Love to Love You Baby" was clearly the album's standout track and made it to number two on the American Billboard charts (the rather forgettable songs on the album's second side featured hints of country, R&B, rock, and pop balladry). On the album cover, Summer was depicted with eyes closed, mouth open, head thrown back, and a dress that looked like a nightgown. Summer's hands and crotch were not visible, but it was quite clear that the image was meant to be suggestive of masturbation. This was also true of the title song, as "the absence of an instructing male voice gave the record a polyvalent potential."[28] Summer's moaning, banned by the BBC, could indeed be interpreted as both an expression of female sexuality and as sexploitation. Neil Bogart promoted the record as "seventeen minutes of love with Donna Summer" and encouraged people in advertisements to "take Donna home and make love to her—the album, that is."[29] Bogart later admitted: "The sex-image thing didn't concern me as much as it did others—or as much as it did Donna, for that matter."[30] In her autobiography, Summer recalled that "while the overtly sexual content of 'Love to Love You Baby' was a problem for me, the relentless hype by the label to cast me as a real-life sex goddess drove me crazy."[31] In the context of a sexist music industry, Summer chose to actively participate in her sexual objectification by playing a role while trying to keep her inner sanctity intact. As Richard Cromelin reported in *Rolling Stone* about Summer's live performance of "Love to Love You Baby" and other songs: "She sang her numbers with her knees bent and her head thrown back, undulating her crotch in a circular motion at the audience,"[32] while three dancer couples simulated sexual positions in the background.

*Love to Love You Baby* was the first international success of the "Sound of Munich" with its string arrangements, syncopated bass lines, synthesizers, and a four-on-the-floor kick-drum twice as fast as the human heartbeat. In Moroder's own words, he was making "upbeat, real danceable songs" that paved the way for "techno, house and modern dance music."[33] Moroder's disco sound was equally influenced by electronic krautrock groups like Tangerine Dream and by Philadelphia soul artists. Moroder admitted: "There were obvious aspects that we have used from the Philadelphia sound, although this was only successful in the States. We have internationalised it."[34] Moroder's emphasis on internationalization explains why he has downplayed krautrock influences on his sound and even dismissed the sonically similar Kraftwerk: "I don't particularly like their songs. They are sometimes a little too easy in their music."[35] In contrast to Kraftwerk, Moroder felt the need to distance himself from the Germanness of his music so that it could be perceived as European dance music with the potential to permeate the American market. By calling this music "disco," Moroder also challenged krautrock's seriousness. As he put it in an interview: "The disco sound, you must see, is not art or anything so serious. Disco is music for dancing."[36]

Considering his dislike for Kraftwerk, it is quite ironic that Moroder's best-known solo album *From Here to Eternity* (1977) bore strong similarities to *Autobahn* and *Trans Europe Express*. Moroder had made an attempt to sound sultry on his disco album *Knights in White Satin* (1976) but chose a detached man-machine image for his following releases, singing through a vocoder and boasting, on the album cover of *From Here to Eternity*, that "only electronic keyboards were used on this recording." Moroder might have been poking fun at Queen, who routinely stated on their covers that no synthesizers were used on their albums, but he was quite serious about his love for technology. On the cover of $E=MC^2$ (1979), Moroder exposed computer circuitry under his jacket, and the liner notes stated that this was the world's "first electronic live-to-digital album," containing almost fully computerized sounds. Moroder's identification with a man-machine and his interest in musical technology might have brought him in closer proximity to Kraftwerk than he dared to admit.

As a producer, Moroder was able to hide his Germanness behind Summer, who was slowly ascending to become the "Queen of Disco" (Gloria Gaynor, who had a hit with "I Will Survive" in 1978, also claimed this title). After the success of *Love to Love You Baby*, Moroder quickly produced two albums with Summer in 1976. *A Love Trilogy* featured another side-long disco track ("Try Me I Know I Can Make It"), some more moaning, and some liberal borrowing from Bill Withers's "Ain't No Sunshine." The attempt to replicate the success of "Love to Love You Baby" did not fully pay off. The following album *Four Seasons of Love* was more varied in its presentation of a romantic relationship, from "Spring Affair" to "Winter Melody," with Summer's by now obligatory breathy, upper-register vocals. Moroder made no qualms about the strictly commercial nature of these records:

> Our work together was business in the sense that we would go in the studio and get the job done. We wouldn't waste time or fiddle around like

some other groups that take six or seven months to do an album. Most of the time we had the songs ready. We didn't spend too much time composing songs in the studio. We did complete albums in four or five weeks."[37]

Moroder's emphasis on how quickly his records with Summer were made fit with presenting them as toss-off pop products with no traces of (white male) rock music's "seriousness." *I Remember Yesterday* followed in 1977 and included musical styles from the 1930s to the 1970s and beyond. Individual songs incorporated hot jazz, the sound of Phil Spector's girl groups, early Tamla Motown, Philadelphia soul, and various forms of disco. The final song on the album was "I Feel Love." Aimed at representing the future, it turned out to be the most influential collaboration between Summer and Moroder.

For "I Feel Love," Moroder returned to the Moog synthesizer he had not used since the early 1970s. The song was almost entirely electronic and contained only fourteen words and a simple four-chord progression. Apart from Keith Forsey on bass drum, Moroder played all the music, most notably the galloping Moog bass line. Summer provided ethereal vocals, harmonizing with herself throughout the track. "I Feel Love" was a top-ten hit in many countries, number one in Great Britain, number three in West Germany, and number six in the United States. It has been reissued and remixed multiple times. Before its mainstream success, the song had quickly become a hit in gay clubs and heavily influenced the subgenre Hi-NRG. Peter Shapiro called "I Feel Love" a "masterpiece of mechanoeroticism" and compared the song to Donna Haraway's notion of the cyborg: "With songs like this [ . . . ], disco fostered an identification with the machine that can be read as an attempt to free gay men from the tyranny that dismisses homosexuality as an aberration, as a freak of nature."[38] The song's potential of sexual liberation was quite different from the one promoted by heterosexist mainstream rock music at the time and in that sense had many parallels to Kraftwerk's gender politics.

The machine-like quality of "I Feel Love" was augmented by Summer's robotic dance moves when she performed the song live. The song's artificiality made it an international hit but also embodied what some viewed as its German characteristics. Brian Eno said the song had a "mechanical, Teutonic beat," and Peter Shapiro even called Summer a "Teutonic ice queen."[39] Moroder remained ambiguous about his identification with the Kraftwerk-related Germanness: "These ideas the writers are having about us using

machines and becoming like machines—they must be making a joke. I
know for sure that we are [human] and maybe, as I think you say in English,
we are having the last, longest laugh."[40] Yet Moroder had not only made solo
albums that toyed with images of cyborgs, he also recorded three albums
with his studio musicians as Munich Machine (the first of which had dancing robots on the cover) and even wrote a song called "Man Machine"
(which eventually became Blondie's "Call Me"). In interviews, Summer also
used the metaphor of the machine, but in her interpretation it became more
ominous: "Sometimes it gets to the point where you've been pushed for so
long, by this motorous, monstrous force, this whole production of people
and props that you are responsible for, by audiences and everything that rules
you, until you take it upon yourself to be a *machine*."[41] Both Summer and
Moroder saw themselves as machine-like and embraced certain forms of
disidentification, but whereas for Summer as a black woman it was "frightening when you realize you're part of a machine,"[42] Moroder only ostenta-
tiously rejected but generally identified with Kraftwerk's automated and
disembodied high-tech Germanness.[43]

With "I Feel Love," Summer and Moroder had produced a song that
blended krautrock and disco, African American and German aesthetics,
woman and machine. In 1977, they also released the fairy-tale-themed
double album *Once Upon a Time*. It contained both orchestrated and electronic tracks, the nod to gay culture of "If You Got It Flaunt It," as well as
the heterosexual schmaltz of "Sweet Romance." Summer briefly returned
to the formula of "Love to Love You Baby" with similar moaning on the
John Barry-produced theme for *The Deep* (1977), "Down Deep Inside,"
and on a fifteen-minute version of "Je t'aime" for the movie *Thank God It's
Friday* (1978). In the film, Summer also performed "Last Dance," which
became her first hit prominently featuring her chest voice and employing
melisma. As she mentioned in an interview: "It was enough. I couldn't go
on singing those soft songs."[44] Summer also reasserted her black female
identity on her chart-topping 1979 duet with Barbra Streisand, "No More
Tears (Enough is Enough)," and entered her commercially most successful
period with a string of three Moroder-produced number-one double
albums, starting with *Live and More* (1978), which featured number-one
single "MacArthur Park." The song was another example of Summer's turn
toward a more traditional African American style of singing and used
orchestration rather than electronics.

## *Bad Girls* and Beyond

The earlier collaborations of Summer and Moroder, in particular "I Feel Love" with its electronic experimentation and unembellished vocals, had some distinct parallels with krautrock. While Summer described Germany as a refuge, she also maintained a culture of dissemblance as an African American woman in a "foreign" country, working in a sexist music industry. Moroder, while operating in a German context, strove to create music that sold internationally. Interestingly, the liminal space between krautrock and disco and between German and transnational was largely absent in their later and most successful collaborations. *Bad Girls* (1979), a double album that cemented Summer's superstardom with its disco-meets-rock formula, went triple platinum in the United States alone and sold about five million copies worldwide; both the title track and the lead single, "Hot Stuff," reached the top spot in America (the third single, "Dim All the Lights," made it to number two). At this point, Summer had shed her Afro-German persona and, as she claimed in a *New York Times* interview, had finally found her authentic (American) voice: "I really only started saying what I want to say on the *Bad Girls* album."[45]

*Bad Girls'* most striking feature was its ambiguous representation of prostitution on both the title track and the cover art, for which Summer was responsible.[46] Inspired by the story of a Casablanca secretary who had been mistaken for a sex worker, Summer cast herself as a street walker. The back cover invited the male gaze from the perspective of a potential john driving a car with money in hand, watching Summer-as-prostitute through his windshield. In another image, Moroder appeared with an open trench coat, suggestively getting a "hand job" from Summer, and in the liner notes Summer quipped: "Giorgio, you make a great john." Whether Summer meant this image to be a tongue-in-cheek commentary on the slavery-like conditions of the music industry was as unclear as the meaning of the song "Bad Girls," in which Summer claimed sympathy with sex workers on top of funky guitars and horns but also reinforced a patriarchal view of "bad" prostitutes and "innocent" johns. Summer explained the song's "toot toot, beep beep" chants in her autobiography by asking: "How do you get the attention of a hooker?"[47] The accompanying sounds of whistles made light of the police harassment of sex workers and turned prostitution into a party, and, coming right after the come-on of "Hot Stuff" with its disco beat and rock guitar solo, the song did not work as a coherent critique of prostitution.

Yet the unsettling nursery-rhyme melodies in some of the verses and the semiautobiographic quality of the lyrics by an artist who had undoubtedly been sexually and commercially exploited, but who also found agency through her sexuality, told a different story. As Alice Echols has rightfully remarked, Summer, in a gender-specific dilemma, "was attacked for both her [ . . . ] sexual assertiveness and for her sexual submissiveness by male rock critics."[48] Spanning her major hits, from "Love to Love You Baby" to "Bad Girls," Summer invoked a culture of dissemblance by walking a fine line between sexual objectification and sexual agency without ever revealing her "true" self. Unfortunately, some critics have ignored the complexity of this presentation. For instance, Judy Kutulas unfavorably compared Summer to Gloria Gaynor, falsely assuming that Summer had no input in writing her songs and citing the lyrics to "Hot Stuff" as typical of her catering to male fantasies of female promiscuity. For Kutulas, "the looming presence of [Giorgio] Moroder as a kind of producer-pimp consigned her to the category of musical slut. Summer was a commodity, an object."[49] Here Kutulas simply took the lyrics to one song as evidence for judging an artist's life's work, disregarding Summer's agency and even misreading the symbolism of the album cover (Moroder as pimp instead of john).

Summer continued to work within an American context after she switched record companies in 1980 and signed with Geffen. Casablanca quickly rushed out the chart-topping greatest-hits double album *On the Radio* with an airbrushed cover that made Summer appear white. The singer, who had been suffering from depression and drug addiction, had become a born-again Christian in 1979. According to Moroder, "Donna became religious. She wouldn't sing about this, she wouldn't sing about that. Having her biggest hit with a sexy song, she was suddenly saying that she wouldn't sing that type of song anymore, and then she insisted on having a song about Jesus on her album."[50] In fact, "I Believe in Jesus," which closed Summer's new-wave-inspired *The Wanderer* (1980) with melismatic belting, signaled a move away from European disco toward African American gospel, and ultimately a move away from collaborating with Moroder. In 1981, they made one more double album, but *I'm a Rainbow* was rejected by Geffen and not released until 1996. Summer and Moroder remained friends but only produced one more song together, the Grammy-winning Eurodisco hit "Carry On" (1997).

After her departure from Casablanca, Summer continued to release albums and worked with major American producers like Quincy Jones and Michael Omartian. Her most noteworthy hit from this period was her feminist anthem "She Works Hard for the Money" (1983), in which Summer identified with an elderly waitress in a more straightforward way than she had with the sex workers of "Bad Girls." Around the same time, Summer snubbed her gay audiences with remarks about AIDS as God's revenge upon homosexuals and her comment "remember it's Adam and Eve, not Adam and Steve . . . but I love you anyway."[51] Summer later renounced her statements and continued to play benefits for the gay community, but she still occasionally made controversial statements like "I definitely think there ought to be censorship on the radio."[52] Summer's career never returned to the heights of the disco years, and she died in 2012 of lung cancer not related to smoking. Moroder had to cope with the decline of disco in similar ways as Summer but managed more successfully to transition into the 1980s.[53] Ever the acute businessman, Moroder moved on to make movie soundtracks, which earned him three Academy Awards.[54] In a move contrary to his transnational success, Moroder seemingly reconnected to his German heritage with his work on two controversial films—the newly edited and colored version of Fritz Lang's 1924 *Metropolis* (1984) and the last work of former Nazi propagandist Leni Riefenstahl, *Impressionen unter Wasser* ("Underwater Impressions," 2002). Yet the majority of Moroder's later productions were guided by a relatively indistinct internationalism.[55] Consequently, Moroder's legacy has lived on in internationally successful European artists like David Guetta and Daft Punk.[56]

## David Bowie's Berlin

The collaborations between Summer and Moroder hinted at the transnational reach of krautrock, but if there was one international superstar who embodied its deterritorializing potential, it was David Bowie. Bowie's popularity clearly overshadowed that of any of the German groups and musicians of krautrock, even the relatively wide-ranging success of Kraftwerk. Born 1947 in London as David Robert Jones, Bowie launched his career in 1969 with the hit single "Space Oddity" and popularized glam rock with the highly acclaimed *Ziggy Stardust* album in 1972. Bowie's fame continued throughout the 1970s and into the 1980s and only declined somewhat in the decades that followed. In 1976, at one of the most pivotal moments in his career, Bowie decided to move from Los Angeles to Berlin, a move that inspired what many critics and fans now regard as his most important albums, *Low* (1977), *"Heroes"* (1978), and *Lodger* (1979).

Part of Bowie's new approach in Berlin involved continuing a fluidity of gender and national identity that he had begun to express earlier, especially by presenting himself as an alien both on stage and in film. Bowie had come out as bisexual in an interview with *Melody Maker* in January of 1972, performed the role of the gender-ambiguous Ziggy Stardust, and queered heterosexist rock on *Pin Ups* (1973) with cover versions of the Who, the Yardbirds, and Pink Floyd. Bowie had also spent a significant part of his career outside of his home country, particularly in the United States. By turning to Germany and krautrock, Bowie reinforced his stateless identity (which during this time also included an interest in Japanese and Arabic themes) and solidified his rejection of heterosexist "cock rock." While only Rio Reiser had made the queerness of krautrock explicit, the emphasis on keyboards with the simultaneous de-emphasizing of the lead guitar showed a general dissatisfaction with traditional gender roles. Bowie incorporated krautrock's queering of national and gender identity and successfully marketed it for an international pop audience.

Bowie's career had begun in London, but before his move to Berlin he had spent almost a year and a half in the United States, first in New York City and then in Los Angeles. After experimenting with folk rock and heavy metal, Bowie turned to glam rock, which was characterized by a revival of 1950s rock'n'roll structures and an emphasis on androgyny and had been popularized by Marc Bolan.[57] After his breakthrough album *The Rise and Fall of Ziggy Stardust and the Spiders from Mars* (1972), Bowie continued to explore glam rock on two US-influenced albums, *Aladdin Sane* (1973) and *Diamond Dogs* (1974) before switching his attention rather abruptly to soul music for *Young Americans* (1975). Bowie's embrace of a mythic America was apparent in the documentary *Cracked Actor* (1975), in which he was gazing at LA cityscapes from the back of a limousine. Bowie himself called *Young Americans*, somewhat tongue-in-cheek, "the definitive plastic soul record [ . . . ], the squashed remains of ethnic music as it survives in the age of Muzak rock, written and sung by a white limey."[58] Despite their commercial success, Bowie's "American" albums showed that the artist, who was living on a steady diet of milk, cocaine, and French cigarettes, was creatively and mentally exhausted.

Bowie had gone through a number of different stage personas at this point, from "Space Oddity's" Major Tom to Ziggy Stardust and Aladdin Sane (a pun on "a lad insane"). The last of these personas was introduced as "the thin white duke" on the song "Station to Station" and represented, according to Bowie, "a European living in America who wanted to get back to Europe again."[59] Bowie further explored the thin white duke persona in his first major acting role for Nicolas Roeg's *The Man Who Fell to Earth* (1976).[60] Bowie played Thomas Jefferson Newton, an alien who arrives in New Mexico and attempts to find a water source for his home planet but ultimately succumbs to alcoholism and mental distress. Similar to Bowie's public persona, Newton was depicted as alienated and gender-ambiguous. Still images from the film graced the covers of Bowie's next two albums, *Station to Station* (1976) and *Low* (1977).

*Station to Station*, recorded in Los Angeles, was a transitional album. Bowie continued the "plastic soul" of *Young Americans* on "Golden Years" and "Wild Is the Wind," but the ten-minute "Station to Station," with its machine-like beat, electronic effects, and obscure lyrics (drawing on Aleister Crowley, the Stations of the Cross, and the Jewish Kabbalah), was clearly influenced by krautrock. As Bowie remarked: "I think the biggest influence on that album was the work of Kraftwerk and the new German sound. I tried to apply some of the randomness and I utilized a lot of that feeling for especially the title track."[61] For *Station to Station*, Bowie had assembled a versatile rhythm section that remained for all three albums of the Berlin period. Carlos Alomar (rhythm guitar) and Dennis Davis (drums) had already played on *Young Americans*, and George Murray (bass) had just joined Bowie's band. These three African American musicians would often provide a counterpoint to the krautrock explored by keyboards and vocals.

On the song "Station to Station," Bowie proclaimed ambiguously: "The European cannon / canon is here." Incidentally, Bowie's imminent return to Europe would take him to a city that was almost as alien to him as Los Angeles but would help him to create groundbreaking new music: "I'd got tired of writing in the traditional manner that I was writing in while I was in America and coming back to Europe I took a look at what I was writing and the environments I was writing about and decided I had to start writing in terms of trying to find a new musical language for myself to write in."[62] Moving to West Berlin was a return to Europe but also meant entering uncharted territory. In Germany, Bowie would connect past, present, and future, focus on specific locations on Earth as opposed to outer space, and purge his music of the theatrical cabaret elements in favor of a clean, crisp new-wave sound.

Bowie's move to Europe had some practical and personal reasons—being officially registered in Blonay, Switzerland, was useful for tax purposes, and he was slowly separating from his wife, Angela, while trying to curb his drug use. Yet just like Los Angeles, Berlin also represented a mythic landscape that Bowie was drawn to. He had chatted with the British-American writer Christopher Isherwood, who had lived in the city in the late 1920s and early 1930s and had written about his experiences in *Goodbye to Berlin* (1939), which in turn served as the blueprint for the musical and film *Cabaret* (1966 and 1972, respectively). Bowie also admired German expressionist art and the films of Friedrich Wilhelm Murnau, Fritz Lang, and Georg Wilhelm Pabst. Bowie's interest in the Berlin of the past extended to the Weimar Republic but also, in much more unsavory ways, to the Third Reich.

Bowie's interest in fascism already began to appear in his Ziggy Stardust persona, his references to George Orwell's totalitarian dystopia *1984* on the second side of *Diamond Dogs*, and the stage design of his 1974 tour, which was inspired by Robert Wiene's expressionist silent film *The Cabinet of Dr. Caligari* (1920) but also by Albert Speer, Adolf Hitler's chief architect.[63] When Bowie took a trip to Moscow in April of 1976, customs at the Polish-Russian border confiscated Nazi books that, Bowie argued, he had bought for his research on a film project about Joseph Goebbels. On May 2, 1976, Bowie arrived at Victoria Station in London, standing in an open black Mercedes 600 convertible. An image of Bowie in mid-wave was construed by British tabloids as a Hitler salute. Other pictures taken at the event did not confirm these reports. However, Bowie did apparently pose with raised hand in front of Hitler's bunker on his first visit to East Berlin, even if the only pictures published just showed Bowie's emaciated figure in all black with a Gestapo-style trench coat scowling at the camera and trying to irritate a communist guard.[64]

Bowie's comments in interviews further contributed to notions that the pop star had become a Nazi. "I think I might have been a bloody good Hitler," he was quoted. "I'd be an excellent dictator. Very eccentric and quite mad."[65] In another interview he offered the following political analysis: "I believe very strongly in fascism. The only way we can speed up the sort of liberalism that's hanging foul in the air at the moment is to speed up the progress of right-wing totally dictatorial tyranny and get it over as fast as possible. [ . . . ] Rock stars are fascists too. Adolf Hitler was one of the first rock stars."[66] And finally, in yet another 1976 interview, Bowie admitted: "As I see it, I believe Britain could benefit from a fascist leader. After all, fascism is really nationalism."[67] Bowie's controversial, cocaine-fueled political comments (which he later retracted), along with Eric Clapton's public support for British anti-immigration politician Enoch Powell, led to the founding of the Rock Against Racism coalition in the winter of 1976.

When Bowie actually moved to Berlin in August of 1976, he found himself in a place with a much less naïve relationship to the Nazi era than his own. As he recalled: "Suddenly I was in a situation where I was meeting young men of my age whose fathers had actually been SS men."[68] Bowie came to understand that toying with fascism was inappropriate in a country grappling with collective guilt, and he changed his look accordingly, opting for plaid shirts and jeans to blend in. West Berlin in the 1970s was decades removed from both fascism and the German expressionism he had come to look for. As Bowie noticed: "The kind of lush, decadent thing that's thrown around about Berlin [is] entirely wrong."[69] The city was a haven for draft dodgers, left-wing students, artists, and wealthy but inconspicuous citizens, isolated from the rest of West Germany and economically less productive than other major cities. As Bowie described it, rather dramatically, West Berlin turned out to be "a city cut off from its world, art, and culture, dying with no hope of retribution."[70]

After a few weeks at the stately Hotel Gerhus, Bowie took residence in a fairly modest but spacious *Altbau* (period apartment), located above a spare parts store for cars at 155 Hauptstraße in the southwestern district of Schöneberg. The neighborhood was rather nondescript but lively, with the gay bar *Anderes Ufer* ("other shore") right next door. Bowie's roommate was American rock star Iggy Pop, born 1947 as James Osterberg in Muskegon, Michigan. Pop later moved into his own courtyard apartment at the same address but remained Bowie's closest friend during the Berlin years, along with another American, the record producer Tony Visconti. As Bowie stated in 1977, he wanted to "find some people you don't understand and a place you don't want to be and just put yourself into it" and to "force yourself to buy your own groceries," and he had found the right place, since "nobody gives a shit about you in Berlin."[71] As German journalist Tobias Rüther aptly described it, Berlin's residents accepted Bowie "as they had accepted any other freak or interesting weirdo who tried their luck in the city: without questions or concerns, by collectively shrugging their shoulders."[72]

Although Bowie spent a considerable amount of time in West Berlin, he never learned to speak German and did not collaborate with any German musicians. The only Germans he got to know a bit more intimately were Tangerine Dream's Edgar Froese, Froese's wife Monika, transsexual cabaret owner and performer Romy Haag, and Hansa Studios engineer Eduard Meyer.[73] Meyer, who worked on Iggy Pop's *The Idiot* and David Bowie's *Low*, recalled in 2008: "You could sense that [Bowie] was excited to live where Nazi history had taken place."[74] Meyer also stated: "David enjoyed the atmosphere of the 'front-line city' and felt very much at home here. Berlin was very provincial at the time. [ . . . ] With the wall, nobody could get out, and it was like an island, and David loved that very much."[75] Another German acquaintance Bowie made was Antonia Maaß, singer of the Berlin jazz rock group the Messengers, who were recording at Hansa as well. Maaß, who had an affair with Bowie's producer Tony Visconti and provided backing vocals for the album *"Heroes"*, remembered that Bowie only cared about his music and Berlin's museums.[76]

Bowie was particularly interested in the Brücke Museum in Dahlem, where he spent much time studying German expressionist art (*die Brücke*, literally "the bridge," was a movement of Dresden artists from 1905 to 1913). Bowie had taken up painting and used Erich Heckel's *Roquariol* (1917), a portrait of artist Ernst-Ludwig Kirchner, as the inspiration for both the cover of Iggy Pop's *The Idiot* and his own *"Heroes"*. For the album covers, both Pop and Bowie imitated Kirchner's gesture with bended arm; in Bowie's case, his Elvis quiff also expressed the ongoing fascination with American rock'n'roll. Apart from museums, Bowie seemed to have spent most of his time at home or enjoying West Berlin's nightlife, which might explain his rather clumsy statement that Berlin was "a city made up of bars for sad people to get drunk in."[77] Iggy Pop appeared to have had even fewer meaningful interactions with West Berliners than Bowie, and the few comments he made about the city revealed a deeply clichéd gaze: Berlin "hadn't changed since 1910: organ grinders who still had monkeys, quality transvestite shows. A different world."[78]

Bowie only immersed himself in his city of residence in rather selective ways, but the three albums that he later, in keeping with his interest in visual art, referred to as the "Berlin triptych" revealed an astonishing influence of a particularly West German sensibility. Berlin's continually unfinished status meshed with Bowie's artistic self-construction, and he effortlessly incorporated the music of krautrock artists into his own work. Although Bowie did not explicitly reference Berlin in his recordings, the atmosphere and sounds of the city clearly impacted his music. In 1978, Bowie called Berlin "the centre of everything that is happening and will happen in Europe over the next few years."[79] Incidentally, it was West Berlin's gritty minimalism, not its decadent and fascist past, that left traces in Bowie's music. As he stated in an interview with French magazine *Rock et Folk*:

> I've written songs in all the Western capitals, and I've always got to the stage where there isn't friction between a city and me. That became nostalgic, vaguely decadent, and I left for another city. At the moment I'm incapable of composing in Los Angeles, New York or in London or Paris. There's something missing. Berlin has the strange ability to only make you write the important things.[80]

Bowie had come to the city to find the world of *Cabaret*, but instead he discovered an urban wasteland shaped by Cold War geopolitics.

Musically, the minimalism that inspired Bowie was mostly from Düsseldorf, not West Berlin. With the exception of Tangerine Dream, the so-called Berlin School had much less of an impact on Bowie than Neu! and Kraftwerk. Bowie appropriated *Neu! 75*'s concept of one side of ambient and one side of rock for *Low* and *"Heroes"*, and he possibly even took the title of the latter from Neu!'s song "Hero." Like Kraftwerk, Bowie abandoned blues scales and harmonic structures for electronic minimalism and espoused a distinctly European sensibility as well as a conceptualization of a self-referential *Gesamtkunstwerk* that included music, clothes, album covers, concerts, and interviews.[81] In return, Kraftwerk name-checked their famous admirer on "Trans Europe Express" ("from station to station back to Düsseldorf city, meet Iggy Pop and David Bowie"). In addition to Neu! and Kraftwerk, Bowie was clearly influenced by a number of other krautrock bands, such as Can, Faust, and Cluster. Yet instead of collaborating with them while he was in Germany (or with producers like Conny Plank and Dieter

Dierks), Bowie remained secluded on the island of West Berlin, soaking up German influences from afar and choosing musical partners from the United States.[82]

## The Berlin Trilogy

Bowie's initial interest in Berlin had been informed by notions of 1920s expressionism and 1930s fascism, but actually living in the city brought about a shift in his musical expression toward a fragmented personal as well as spatial identity that bore strong resemblances to krautrock's hybridization and deterritorialization. On the "Berlin Trilogy," consisting of *Low*, *"Heroes"*, and *Lodger*, Bowie dramatically broke with conventional rock structures by turning to incomplete songs and instrumental music and by endorsing a synthetic and minimalist sound. Inhabiting a liminal space of national identity as a "Germanized" Brit after World War II, Bowie provided a counter-model to Moroder and Summer's celebratory "Sound of Munich" and emphasized the fragmentation and alienation of transnational identity in his music.

Influenced by krautrock groups and the new environment of West Berlin that he was settling into, *Low* might have been "the most radical departure from charts music ever undertaken by a superstar."[83] As Bowie admitted: "It's influenced by the new wave—not the American new wave bands, the European new wave."[84] For the first time, Bowie did not promote his album and kept, as the cover image suggested, a "low profile" (the cover featured the word "low" above a profile shot of Bowie's head from *The Man Who Fell to Earth* in front of a bright orange sky). Much of *Low*'s new sound was shaped by a new collaborator, Brian Eno (born 1948), who also contributed to Bowie's other two Berlin albums. Eno had begun his career playing keyboards for Roxy Music and had already made four highly acclaimed solo albums of synthetic rock and ambient music. The 1975 releases *Discreet Music* and *Another Green World* served as the blueprint for Eno's parts for *Low*. Like Bowie, Eno was paying attention to the sounds that came out of West Germany, and he would even go on to record a number of albums with Cluster and Harmonia.[85]

Eno's goal was to combine Kraftwerk's rigidity and funk group Parliament's passion (he was also interested in the disco sound of Moroder). Therefore, Eno had already conceptually envisioned *Low*'s combination of a funky African American rhythm section (Carlos Alomar, George Murray, and Dennis Davis) and "Germanic" keyboards and vocals (provided by the Englishmen Bowie and Eno).[86] Another element that Eno brought to Bowie's music was chance. With his artist friend Peter Schmidt, he had invented the *Oblique Strategies*, a set of about one hundred cards that gave individual musicians seemingly random advice like "work at a different speed" or "use an old idea." The cards inspired many tracks on Bowie's Berlin albums and complemented William S. Burroughs's cut-up technique that Bowie was now using to write most of his lyrics (by cutting words out of a book or newspaper and reassembling them). On *Low*, Eno played many instruments that also dominated the sound on krautrock albums, such as ARP and EMS synthesizers, the Minimoog, and the Chamberlin.

In addition to singing, Bowie played an array of instruments on *Low*. These included saxophone, guitar, various keyboards and synthesizers, xylophone, and harmonica. Most of the album was instrumental, which showed a focus on sound instead of lyrical content. In addition, the album included what *Rolling Stone* called "one of rock's all-time most imitated drum sounds."[87] Producer Tony Visconti used an Eventide harmonizer, a proto-sampler that, like Auto-Tune decades later, could change the pitch without altering the tempo. Visconti applied the Eventide to the sound of Dennis Davis's drums, which were also foregrounded in the mix. As Visconti put it, the harmonizer "fucks with the fabric of time," a description that could also be applied to the music of Neu! or Faust.[88] For better or worse, the resulting crashing snare drum sound became a staple of 1980s pop music. Along with Eno's swirling synthesizers, disjointed and cacophonous guitar solos by Alomar and Ricky Gardiner, and Bowie's withdrawn vocals and paranoid lyrics, Visconti's production added to "that amalgam of the darkest and most enticing elements of American and German musical cultures: the robotic, the escapist, the ethereal, the direct, all conveying a state of emotional dissonance, in which depression could be uplifting and boredom became transparent."[89]

*Low* was divided into one side of song fragments with sparse lyrics and one side of ambient instrumentals.[90] Side one was bookended by "Speed of Life" and "A New Career in a New Town," two wordless songs heavy on electronics but with traditional verse-chorus structures, the latter's title commenting on Bowie's move to Berlin. Both tracks contained quieter passages clearly influenced by Kraftwerk's synthetic sound. Sandwiched between the two instrumentals were five relatively short songs with vocals by Bowie. "Breaking Glass" referenced the Tree of Life from the Kabbalah, had more melody in the bass line than the vocals, and ended abruptly after one verse and what might have been the chorus. "What in the World" featured angular rhythms, atonal lead guitar, and Iggy Pop's slightly off-key backup vocals. The more melodic "Always Crashing in the Same Car" rephrased the paranoia of the other pieces as a dreamscape. "Sound and Vision" had the elements of a more pop-oriented song but deconstructed them: its first half was purely instrumental, it foregrounded the background vocals by Mary Hopkin, and it contained only one verse. Finally, "Be My Wife," the second single after "Sound and Vision," had Bowie singing about deterritorialization: "I've lived all over the world, I've left every place." It may have been the most conventional song on the album, but its vocal melody seemed deliberately unambitious, and consequently it was the first Bowie single in five years that failed to enter the UK charts.

If side one of *Low* was already confusing for many of his fans, side two with its four electronic instrumental pieces was where Bowie truly defied expectations and showed his appreciation of krautrock and his newfound European sensibility. "Warszawa," which Bowie wrote after gazing at bleak Polish landscapes and cities on his trip to Moscow (he hardly left the train), was comprised of synthesizers that blended Eastern European music with Kraftwerk and featured phonetic singing with pitch manipulations that made Bowie's voice sound like a Bulgarian boys choir. "Art Decade" (a pun on "art decayed" and "art deco") was a somber ambient piece with layers of synthesizer about the Berlin Bowie had discovered. "Weeping Wall" contained more wordless vocals by Bowie, synthesizers, as well as percussive xylophone and vibraphone and was written about what he perceived as the "misery" of the Berlin Wall. Finally, "Subterraneans," yet another ambient piece with phonetic singing, featured reversed recordings of instruments over synthesizer tracks reminiscent of Tangerine Dream. According to Bowie, the song dealt with the people caught in East Berlin after the Wall was built. The faint jazz saxophone solo was a nod to the East Berlin jazz scene.

However cursory Bowie's engagement with Berlin and Eastern Europe was when he recorded *Low*, his compositions still managed to capture a sensibility that was both locally grounded and transcendental. Initially, the critical response to the album was mixed, with the *New Musical Express* printing both a positive review by krautrock advocate Ian MacDonald and a negative review by Jimi Hendrix biographer Charles Shaar Murray side-by-side. Yet over time the album has been regarded as one of the most, if not the most important album of Bowie's career.[91] Bowie popularized the sounds of krautrock (and, to some extent, of electronic composers of minimalism) by connecting them with an African American rhythm section. As Phil Doggett put it: "For those who had taken little notice of the computerized rhythms of Kraftwerk, the apparently seamless patterns of Philip Glass and Steve Reich, the sparse landscape of NEU! and the deconstructive impulses of Faust, *Low* sounded completely revolutionary."[92]

The second album of the Berlin triptych, *"Heroes"*, was the first to be entirely conceived and recorded in Berlin, this time at the Hansa Studio right by the inner-German border, which Bowie had dubbed "the Hall by the Wall" (*Low* had been partly recorded in France). It repeated the concept of Bowie's previous album with one side of fragmented rock songs and one side of (mostly) ambient instrumentals. Musically, *"Heroes"* was as uncompromising as *Low* but also contained a major pop hit with the title track, which became one of Bowie's signature songs. In addition to Eno and *Low*'s rhythm section, consisting of Alomar, Murray, and Davis, *"Heroes"* featured Robert Fripp of British art rock group King Crimson on lead guitar. The album was released in 1978. *"Heroes"* was musically not the same watershed moment as *Low*, but it represented the full realization of Bowie's engagement with krautrock and German identity.

"Beauty and the Beast" and "Joe the Lion" opened the album with motorik beats, discordant guitars, and lyrics that made no sense, a combination somewhat akin to some of Faust's recordings. Transnational German/American themes surfaced when Antonia Maaß could be heard singing the word *Liebling* ("darling") on "Beauty and the Beast" and when "Joe the Lion" referenced American performance artist Chris Burden, who had nailed himself to the top of a Volkswagen Beetle in 1974. Bowie was inspired by Iggy Pop to make up the lyrics as he recorded them. With the exception of "'Heroes,'" which he wrote down on paper first, Bowie would sing a line, stop the tape, record the next line, and repeat this process. The album's fourth song, "Sons of the Silent Age," was an overall more conventional composition that could have fit on older Bowie albums but also possibly referenced German silent movies like Fritz Lang's *Metropolis* (1927). The last song on side one, "Blackout," contained distorted vocals and more disjointed guitars and synthesizers. The song had autobiographical allusions to Bowie's disintegrating marriage and his binge-drinking and described the narrator as being "under Japanese influence," possibly a reference to hara-kiri by an artist who musically was more under German influence at the time.

The title track "'Heroes,'" which appeared right in the middle of the album's first side, deserves further attention. A retro-romantic story of love and loss, its earnestness was somewhat diminished by the quotation marks in the title. The six-minute track contained layers of guitar feedback and synthesizers and was recorded with three microphones placed at varying distances from Bowie. They were gradually opened one after the other, resulting in his vocals moving from quiet lament to melodramatic scream. The relatively coherent lyrics depicted a passionate but hopeless love affair "by the wall" amidst gun shots, where "shame was on the other side." The song clearly referenced the Berlin Wall (Bowie has repeatedly mentioned armed border guards visible from the studio where the song was written and recorded) but was also inspired by Otto Mueller's painting *Lovers Between Garden Walls* (1916) and the short story "A Grave for a Dolphin" (1956) by Alberto Denti di Pirajno.

The single version of "'Heroes,'" edited from six to three minutes, was initially not a hit, but the song quickly became a live favorite and one of Bowie's best-known recordings (it has even appeared in TV commercials). Bowie also recorded versions of the song in German and French. Although "'Heroes'" was a universal tale of love, its connection to Berlin was evoked again when it was featured in the film *Christiane F.* (1981), and when Bowie performed the song at the Concert for Berlin for seventy thousand fans in front of the Reichstag in 1987. Before playing the song, he read a message in German, dedicating it to his "friends on the other side of the wall," and a few hundred young people listening on the East side rioted that same night and during the next few days.[93] By immersing himself as an outsider in German culture, Bowie had become versed in the fragmented identity of a divided nation, and his music was resonating among members of the culture he was representing.

Side two of Bowie's *"Heroes"* contained four synthesizer-driven instrumentals and ended with one more conventional song. "V-2 Schneider" began with the sound of an airplane landing and morphed into an upbeat saxophone-synthesizer theme with a lively bassline and Bowie singing the title repeatedly through what sounded like a vocoder. The title referenced Kraftwerk's Florian Schneider and German V-2 missiles from World War II.

As Tobias Rüther observed: "The song reduces the world that surrounded Bowie, the Federal Republic of Germany, to the Fleet Street code, the stereotype which British tabloid reporters use to play off their home country against the Germans, then and now."[94] One could argue, however, that "V-2 Schneider" was not merely reaffirming Bowie's British national identity but could also have been his reaction to British critics who feared by moving to Berlin he had turned into a "Hun" himself.[95]

In "Sense of Doubt," Bowie and Eno employed call-and-response patterns with eerie-sounding synthesizers over a descending four-note piano motif after *Oblique Strategies* cards had given each of them contradictory instructions, explaining the tension of the song. It morphed into the more serene "Moss Garden," on which Bowie played *koto*, a Japanese zither-like instrument, on top of synthesizer washes reminiscent of Klaus Schulze. Bowie unintentionally misspelled "Neuköln," a district of West Berlin with a large Turkish immigrant population, for the song of the same name (it should have been *Neukölln*). On the song, Bowie played saxophone using a Middle Eastern modal scale amid ambient synthesizer sounds. Explaining the motivations behind the track, Bowie stated: "The Turks are shackled in bad conditions. They're very much an isolated community. It's very sad."[96] As with his impressions of Poland and the Berlin Wall, all that Bowie could see was sadness, a sadness that might have been more his own than that of others. After all, while staying in Berlin, Bowie was mostly isolated from both German and Turkish communities. For the last song of *"Heroes"*, Bowie returned to Middle Eastern themes. "The Secret Life of Arabia" was a rather conventional rock composition with a disco beat and lyrics that seemed a bit misplaced but already signaled the travel focus of the more song-oriented follow-up album, *Lodger*.

Overall, *"Heroes"* explored similar musical themes as *Low* but also developed them further. Bowie's transnational identity was expressed through both closeness to and distance from Germany. His music was rooted in African American sensibilities while still embracing the synthetic sounds of krautrock in a city that was both at the heart and on the border of Germany. Bowie, who had not promoted *Low*, toured *"Heroes"* extensively. After taking his son on a six-week safari to Kenya, Bowie played in the United States, Europe, Australia, and Japan. Later in 1978, he released the double live album *Stage*. It was recorded in Philadelphia, Boston, and Providence and consisted of one album of older material and one album with songs from the first two parts of the Berlin Trilogy. After the isolation of the divided city, Bowie was in the process of exposing a global audience to his version of krautrock.

*Lodger* (1979), the third part of the Berlin Trilogy, reflected Bowie's transient identity and, although conceptually linked to *Low* and *"Heroes"*, was not recorded in Germany but in New York City and Montreux, Switzerland. The album title was a bit misleading—while Bowie had been a lodger and a traveler during his Berlin years, he appeared more like a tourist on his latest record, which featured many of the same musicians he had been working with (Eno, Alomar, Murray, Davis) as well as some new additions, like Frank Zappa's guitarist Adrian Belew. *Lodger* did not contain any ambient instrumentals and developed some of the sonic experimentation of *Low* and *"Heroes"* into more conventional but still daring pop songs.

The cover of *Lodger* was, fittingly, in the form of a postcard, with Bowie made up as an accident victim. On "Move On," Bowie described himself as a "traveling man" and name-checked Africa, Russia, Kyoto, and Cyprus. Musically, the biggest influence was still krautrock, but two songs brought in other elements. "Yassassin (Turkish for Long Live)" was an odd mix of Middle Eastern melodies, funk bass, and a Caribbean reggae rhythm (the correct spelling would have been *yaşasın*), and "African Night Flight" incorporated tribal chants, percussion, and the synthetic chirping of crickets. Phil Doggett compared the song's appropriation of African sounds unfavorably to Can's E.F.S. series, but Bowie's angular rhythms and detached vocals displayed a similar tongue-in-cheek approach to world music to that of the German group.[97] It seemed that, after having engaged with the culture of West Berlin more in depth, Bowie was aware that he was only scratching the surface in his new cultural explorations.

Interestingly, Bowie referenced Neu! even more explicitly on *Lodger* after having left Germany. The most obvious example was "Red Sails," which copied Michael Rother's echo-filled rhythm guitar and Klaus Dinger's precise drumming and off-key singing and featured a narrator sailing to the "hinterland" and caught in a "struggle with a foreign tongue." On other songs, Bowie seemed to have incorporated the idea of recycling from *Neu! 2*. "Move On" was created from an older Bowie composition, "All the Young Dudes," played backwards. "Red Money" used the backing track from Iggy Pop's "Sister Midnight," slowed down slightly. Finally, two songs, "Fantastic Voyage" and "Boys Keep Swinging," were almost identical, except that the latter had a more ragged sound because the musicians had switched instruments after some advice from the *Oblique Strategies*. The self-referential, ironic approach that Bowie shared with Neu! was also apparent in many of the lyrics, which were somewhat more straightforward but detached: "Repetition" and "Fantastic Voyage" tackled domestic violence and nuclear war from utterly impassionate-sounding narrators, and the singles "D.J." and "Boys Keep Swinging" were merely parodies of disc jockeys and masculine identity, respectively.

Bowie's *Lodger* might not have had quite the same impact as the first two parts of the Berlin Trilogy and was not received very well by critics at the time, but the album has recently been rediscovered as an underappreciated continuation of radical ideas. Bowie's next album, *Scary Monsters* (1980), was the last one to use the well-tried rhythm section of the Berlin years, but Eno's absence led to a more polished sound and well-crafted pop songs, including one with overlaid Japanese vocals ("It's No Game Part 1"). It represented the transition from krautrock-inspired music to the mainstream pop of multimillion-selling *Let's Dance* (1983), recorded with a brand new band that included aspiring blues guitarist Stevie Ray Vaughan.

Bowie's representation of a restless, unstable identity on the Berlin Trilogy drew heavily on krautrock's deterritorialization, hybridity, and fragmentation. This becomes even more apparent when one compares the trilogy to Bowie's collaborations with Iggy Pop on two albums that were both released in 1977, *The Idiot* and *Lust for Life*. Pop's engagement with German music and transnational themes was negligible, and it therefore serves as a counterexample to the significant impact krautrock had on Bowie's work. On Pop's two "German" albums, it was only through Bowie's participation that the country they were both living in left any noticeable traces in the musical production, and Bowie's ambition in his own work to create new music through an act of border-crossing became even more apparent.

Iggy Pop had recorded three proto-punk albums with the Stooges beginning in 1969, and Bowie, who had coproduced the group's *Raw Power* (1973), sought to revive Pop's career by working on *The Idiot*.[98] Bowie cowrote and produced all the songs for the album, provided backing vocals, and played guitar, electric piano, synthesizer, saxophone, and drum machine. He also tried out new sounds that he would further develop on *Low*, which explains Pop's description of the music as "a cross between James Brown and Kraftwerk."[99] Compared to Pop's Stooges albums, *The Idiot* had a more refined sound, which provided a contrast to his deep *sprechgesang*. The music on *The Idiot* was quite eclectic. It ranged from the funk bass and syncopated riffs of "Sister Midnight" to the cabaret singing of "Baby" and the doo-wop elements of "Tiny Girls" (saxophone and 6/8 time), from the motorik drum machine beat and wailing electric guitar of "Nightclubbing" to the distorted garage rock of "Funtime." On "China Girl," which prominently featured toy piano and synthesizers and which Bowie rerecorded and turned into a worldwide hit in 1983, the line "visions of swastikas in my head and plans for everyone" recalled his toying with fascism. On "Dum Dum Boys," Pop recounted the story of the Stooges over a simple arpeggio riff. The album ended with the eight-minute, mostly one-chord "Mass Production," which prefigured the sound of 1990s alternative rock with a tape loop of industrial noise on top of a relentless beat. Some of the music's minimalism could be seen as krautrock-influenced, but overall there was no clear indication that Pop felt any connection to German musicians.

Less than a year after *The Idiot*, Pop released *Lust for Life*, another Bowie production. Bowie played keyboards and cowrote seven of the nine songs. The album's sound was much more straightforward, tighter, and suited Pop's limited vocal range well. It also contained two of his most recognizable songs, the title track and "The Passenger." The powerful, driving "Lust for Life" used the rhythm from the Supremes' "You Can't Hurry Love" to support Pop's monotone vocal and was part of the singer's 1990s comeback when it appeared in the film *Trainspotting* (1996). "The Passenger" had an infectious four-chord guitar riff by Ricky Gardiner and lyrics that were inspired by the experience of riding the subway in West Berlin. It was the only song on Pop's two albums with Bowie that had any meaningful connection to Germany. Unlike Bowie, Pop seemed unable to infuse his Detroit rock'n'roll with much local color.[100] In comparison to Pop's Berlin albums, Bowie's development of his previous glam rock queerness into a deterritorialized, krautrock-infused art form on *Low*, *"Heroes"*, and *Lodger* is even more striking.

## German Afterthoughts

In his final months in Berlin in early 1978, Bowie returned to his earlier fascination with the 1920s when he played a German soldier and dandy in his second movie production, David Hemmings's *Schöner Gigolo, armer Gigolo* (the English title was *Just a Gigolo*). The film featured famous German actors

such as Marlene Dietrich, Maria Schell, and Curd Jürgens, as well as Hollywood veteran Kim Novak. *Just a Gigolo* was unanimously panned as a hope-
lessly stereotypical portrayal of 1920s Berlin with clumsy acting. Bowie, who
had successfully played an alien in *The Man Who Fell to Earth*, later referred
to the film as "all my thirty-two Elvis movies rolled into one."[101] Considering how well Bowie had connected to the time and place he had entered by
making music that was both forward-looking and rooted in West German
realities, *Just a Gigolo* represented an uncritical return to his pre-Berlin fascination with the Weimar Republic and Nazi Germany.

After leaving Germany, Bowie occasionally revisited his time in Berlin in
various songs. His 1978 single "Alabama Song," written by Bertolt Brecht
and Kurt Weill, had previously been recorded by the Doors but was also a
staple of Romy Haag's cabaret show, and Bowie sang it more like Haag than
like Jim Morrison. Haag also influenced Bowie's performance in the music
video for "Boys Keep Swinging," where he embodied 1950s rock'n'roll masculinity but also appeared in three different drag costumes as his own
"female" backup singers.[102] For his 1979 guest spot on *Saturday Night Live*,
Bowie hired another gender-ambiguous performer, German-American
Klaus Nomi, along with New York City drag artist Joey Arias. For Bowie's
memorable renditions of "The Man Who Sold the World," "TVC15," and
"Boys Keep Swinging," Nomi and Arias provided operatic background
vocals and robotic movements.[103] Bowie returned to German themes again
in 1981 with a BBC production of Bertolt Brecht's *Baal*, in which the singer
played the leading role, and for which he recorded an EP at Hansa Studios
in Berlin. Finally, after a ten-year recording hiatus and three years before his
untimely death, Bowie released the song "Where Are We Now?" in 2013, on
which he name-checked several places in Berlin and looked back on his
time in the city with nostalgia.

Bowie's German afterthoughts were not as relevant and cutting-edge as
the "krautfunk" of his Berlin triptych but showed his ongoing fascination
with themes related to his extended stay in the country. Ultimately, the most
meaningful connection between Bowie's music and West Berlin was not
made by the singer himself but by German director Uli Edel in his 1981 film
*Wir Kinder vom Bahnhof Zoo* (*We Children from Bahnhof Zoo*). Christiane F.'s
first-person account of one of the young teenage drug addicts and prostitutes who gathered at West Berlin's subway station Zoologischer Garten had
shocked audiences in 1979. In the book, Christiane F. declared herself a

Bowie fan: "David Bowie was our only hero, the coolest of them all. His music was the best. All the guys wanted to look like David Bowie."[104] Two years after the book, the film utilized this connection by using Bowie's music for the atmospheric soundtrack. The singer also had a guest appearance in the film.

The *Christiane F.* soundtrack included two tracks from *Lodger* ("Boys Keep Swinging" and "Look Back in Anger"), three tracks from *"Heroes"* (the title track, "V-2 Schneider," and "Sense of Doubt"), one track from *Low* ("Warszawa"), two tracks from *Station to Station* ("TVC15" and "Stay"), and a live version of "Station to Station" from *Stage* that was used for the concert scene of the film. The restaging of Bowie's show at the Deutschlandhalle on April 10, 1976, corresponded with a scene in the book where the singer's rendition of the cocaine-fueled song directly spoke to the underage heroin addict: "When David Bowie began, it was almost as cool as I had expected it to be. It was insane. But when he started singing 'it's too late,' it brought me right down. Suddenly I felt like crap. [ . . . ] I thought the song accurately described my situation. [ . . . ] I could have used some valium."[105] The distance between the performer and the fan, despite their shared addictive personality, became even more apparent in the filming where Bowie did not directly interact with Natja Brunckhorst, who played Christiane F. The part in the film where Bowie performed the song "Station to Station" was actually shot in a New York club and then intercut with audience footage from an AC/DC concert in Berlin. Bowie was spatially removed from the narrative of the film, but conceptually his music made perfect sense.

In addition to the concert scene, Bowie's music from his Berlin Trilogy was used throughout the film to underscore both Christiane's fascination with drugs and the desperation of her addiction. "Sense of Doubt," in particular, worked exceptionally well to orchestrate the film's underworld of subway tunnels, public restrooms, empty downtown streets lined with underage prostitutes, and the desolate high-rise buildings of the Gropiusstadt where Christiane grew up. The despair of "'Heroes'" also took on a different meaning in the context of the many teenage drug addicts overdosing in the film who dream about being "heroes just for one day." With his recordings at Hansa Studios, Bowie had unintentionally provided the ideal soundtrack for Uli Edel's gritty tale of 1970s West Berlin.

Bowie's *Christiane F.* soundtrack recast his music in a local context, but the greatest achievement of his Berlin years was his popularization of krautrock and his successful integration of synthesized sounds into Anglo-American rock. In a 1997 interview with *Mojo*, Bowie discussed how his interest in krautrock inspired him to bypass punk rock, a move that in turn made him an influence for post-punk: "I was a big fan of Kraftwerk, Cluster and Harmonia, and I thought the first Neu! album, in particular, was just gigantically wonderful. Looking at that against punk, I had no doubts where the future of music was going, and for me it was coming out of Germany at the time."[106] Bowie's influence was most apparent in British pop groups from the 1980s like Ultravox, ABC, and the Human League, but it also extended to the Talking Heads and Joy Division, who were originally called Warsaw in reference to Bowie's "Warszawa," and even to 1990s groups like Blur, Radiohead, and Nine Inch Nails. U2 recorded *Achtung Baby* (1991) in collaboration with Brian Eno at Hansa Studios, and Nick Cave, Depeche Mode, and R.E.M. also went to Berlin to record in the "Hall by the Wall." Along with Kraftwerk's and Giorgio Moroder's international successes, Bowie's Berlin years were the closest that krautrock ever got to mainstream popularity.

While Bowie's preconceived notions of 1920s and 1930s Germany gradually made way for the reality of 1970s West Berlin and resulted in a fragmented identity that found its expression in the Berlin Trilogy, the "Sound of Munich" created in the collaborations between Donna Summer and Giorgio Moroder inhabited a liminal space between krautrock and disco, between German and transnational. To some extent, Bowie's and Summer's role-playing represented two different versions of a conflicted and unstable identity, alienation, and celebration of difference. The collaborations between Moroder and Summer and the music Bowie made in connection with Berlin have generally not been considered in the context of krautrock, largely because transnational, female, gay, and black identities have been systematically excluded from notions of German identity. Yet many of their productions show striking parallels to various forms of krautrock, particularly in their deterritorialization and reterritorialization of German identity after World War II. Therefore, including artists like Summer and Bowie in an analysis of krautrock can serve to show that its complex web of discursive identity formations clearly extended beyond the borders of Germany itself. For a discursive formation like krautrock, there were no sharp distinctions between being inside looking out and being outside looking in.

# 6 After Krautrock

## The Neue Deutsche Welle and Beyond

Krautrock affected music both inside and outside Germany. In the wake of the British and American punk revolutions of the late 1970s, the *Neue Deutsche Welle* ("German New Wave") emerged across various local scenes in West Germany. Spanning roughly from 1979 to 1983, the Neue Deutsche Welle (NDW) picked up some of krautrock's ideas and developed them further, but it also applied reterritorialization more narrowly by focusing on German themes and lyrics. Along with its quick appropriation by the music industry, this led to NDW's fairly short lifespan and its relatively minor impact outside Germany.[1] Nonetheless, the Neue Deutsche Welle marked the moment in the history of West German popular music that reformulated krautrock for the post-punk generation.[2]

Internationally, krautrock's abandonment of Anglo- and African American structures created a fertile ground for groups both spatially and temporally removed from the music's origins. The renewed interest in German music from the 1970s has had an impact on many contemporary fields of production. Perhaps most strikingly, krautrock's shadow looms large in the imagination of current American indie rock writers, musicians, and audiences. The popular webzine *Pitchfork Media* exemplifies how deterritorialized sounds that disavowed American influences attained subcultural capital in the United States. While some meanings might have gotten lost over time and in translation, both rearticulations of some of krautrock's fragmented identity formations—nationally and transnationally—show the continued relevance of the music's politics.

## The Neue Deutsche Welle

The term *Neue Deutsche Welle* was popularized by music journalist Alfred Hilsberg in two articles for the German edition of *Sounds* in 1979.[3] Hilsberg had also used the word *krautpunk* in the same magazine a year earlier to describe the early stirrings of German punk rock.[4] Neue Deutsche Welle simply added "German" to the term for American (and British) new wave music (which itself was derived from the *Nouvelle Vague* of 1950s and 1960s French filmmakers[5]). Early German punk and NDW scenes developed in Düsseldorf, Berlin, Hamburg, and Hanover (the first two being important for krautrock as well, the other two less so). NDW typically featured shorter pop songs with synthetic sounds and German lyrics, but the diverse genre encompassed the industrial noise of Einstürzende Neubauten as well as the puerile schlager of Andreas Dorau, the hypermasculinity of DAF, and the feminism of Östro 430. As the music evolved from regional scenes and small independent labels to major record companies, many of the original NDW bands began to reject the NDW label. Simultaneously, record companies rebranded older, existing bands as NDW. Thus, some of the genre's biggest commercial successes had only German-language lyrics in common and differed in almost every other way—such as the glib synthetic pop of studio musicians Spliff, the Bavarian rockabilly of the Spider Murphy Gang, and the apocalyptic hard rock of Extrabreit.

With the possible exception of the Nina Hagen Band, German groups were relatively late to adopt punk rock but quick to adopt British new wave. German punk swiftly shifted to NDW, which retained punk's humor and do-it-yourself ethics, especially in the cassette-tape scene.[6] Yet NDW was overall more positive and more heavily middle-class than punk, which had at least some ties to the working class.[7] One could also claim that NDW moved from punk's collectivism to a focus on individualism and hedonism, which found its most popular expression in Markus's 1982 song "Ich will Spaß" ("I Want to Have Fun"), lyrically the German equivalent to Sammy Hagar's ode to speeding on the interstate, "I Can't Drive 55."

The Neue Deutsche Welle was different from krautrock but not a radical departure, and there were many connections between the two formations. The Ratinger Hof in Düsseldorf, the most important early NDW venue (besides other clubs like the SO36 in Berlin and the Markthalle in Hamburg) was frequented by members of early NDW bands like S.Y.P.H., KFC,

ZK, and Male but also catered to members of Neu!, La Düsseldorf, and Kraftwerk.[8] In fact, the three Düsseldorf groups had anticipated NDW's emphasis on sleek visuals and German lyrics. In addition, independent NDW labels like Ata Tak, No Fun, and ZickZack were clearly modeled after Ton Steine Scherben's David Volksmund Produktion. Finally, musicians occasionally overlapped: Can's Jaki Liebezeit played drums on Joachim Witt's NDW hit from 1981, "Goldener Reiter" ("Golden Rider"); Conny Plank produced major NDW acts DAF and Ideal, the latter of which had released their first LP on Klaus Schulze's IC label; Can's Holger Czukay produced S.Y.P.H.; both Plank and Czukay were involved with NDW group Die Krupps; Helmut Hatler, the guitarist of Fehlfarben, had played with krautrock group Kraan; and Bodo Staiger of NDW group Rheingold had played with Klaus Dinger protégés Lilac Angels and successfully plagiarized Kraftwerk on the 1981 hit "Dreiklangsdimensionen" ("Triad Dimensions"). In turn, Kraftwerk rereleased their 1978 song "Das Model," which became an NDW hit in 1982. This was not surprising, since at that point countless NDW bands had already imitated Kraftwerk's synthesizer sound and their monotonous vocal delivery.[9]

Despite these connections between krautrock and the Neue Deutsche Welle, the two formations were separated historically and politically by NDW's articulation of apocalyptic notions common in the 1980s and by its more decisive break with the hippie counterculture.[10] NDW audiences also tended to be much younger (between ten and sixteen years old), and the genre allowed for much more female participation than krautrock had. Finally, unlike many krautrock musicians, most NDW artists had no formal musical education. As Margita Haberland, singer and violinist for Hamburg post-punk group Abwärts noted: "We no longer felt the need to deal with the junk of history, conservatories and such."[11] NDW's break with the past was evident in a special edition of German music monthly *Musikexpress* from 1982 in which "krautrock" was used repeatedly to describe sounds that were considered passé. Historically, NDW looked more to the 1950s than the 1960s and 1970s. Unlike krautrock's dramatic break with postwar popular culture, NDW referenced the 1950s in both fashion and music, and its affinity to schlager eventually made it so commercially viable that it temporarily entered West Germany's pop mainstream.[12]

Musically, NDW artists continued to explore synthesizers, which in the 1980s had become much more affordable and therefore more accessible to amateur musicians. Whereas krautrock musicians like Florian Fricke, Klaus Schulze, and even Giorgio Moroder had experimented with big Moog synthesizers, NDW groups like DAF or Der Plan favored the smaller and cheaper Korg MS-20. NDW novelty act Trio even popularized a children's toy, the Casio VL-1, on their 1982 hit "Da Da Da."[13] The further development of krautrock's synthetic sounds by DAF, Einstürzende Neubauten, Der Plan, Die Krupps, and Pyrolator were probably NDW's most important contribution to popular music. Unlike krautrock, which often consciously broke with African American and Anglo-American musical traditions, NDW's musical influences included ska (Fehlfarben), British punk (Mittagspause, Male), rap (Falco), and new wave groups like Wire and Gang of Four. NDW artists like Andreas Dorau also looked for inspiration in German musical traditions, primarily schlager but also the *Kinderlied*, nineteenth-century children's songs. Moritz R® of Der Plan talked about his disappointment when he found out that most schlager were only cover versions of American songs, which led him to explore *Kinderlieder* as the only accessible indigenous form of music.[14]

NDW's reterritorialized inward look was most clearly expressed by the previously unheard-of prevalence of German-language lyrics. Krautrock groups like Ton Steine Scherben, Kraftwerk, and La Düsseldorf had prominently featured German lyrics, as had some other German rock musicians like Udo Lindenberg and Nina Hagen. Yet much of German rock history had been "the history of escaping its own language."[15] To some extent, the newfound interest in the German language was inspired by punk's embrace of British accents.[16] As Alfred Hilsberg noted in a 1981 interview: "The German groups now sing in German, and why should Germans sing in English? German speech rhythm does not adapt well to standard rock music. Therefore, German groups now often choose a more appropriate musical accompaniment and rhythm."[17] Hilsberg traced the machine-like quality of the newer German groups back to Can and Kraftwerk. Singing in German involved a complicated process, as NDW scholar Frank Apunkt Schneider has pointed out: "In some cases—the best cases—NDW's reappropriation of German language doubled the alienation of pop music being inherently 'un-German.'"[18] Drawing on Gilles Deleuze and Félix Guattari, Schneider went on to say that this "alienation within one's own language" was comparable to Czech writer Franz Kafka's *Pragerdeutsch* ("Prague German").[19]

Some of NDW's song lyrics specifically addressed a reterritorialized

German national identity, often in the context of alienation. Mittagspause's "Herrenreiter" (1979) was an early example in which the colors of the German flag were dissected so that black represented "the sky of our future," red "the soil of our past," and gold "the teeth of our fathers." The references here were to Germany's bleak future (black) due to its violent and bloody past (red), in particular Germans profiting from exploiting Jews during the Nazi era (gold).[20] Another NDW song, Nichts' "Ein deutsches Lied" ("A German Song," 1982), put the national identity crisis more bluntly and equated being German with "not telling anybody," being "afraid of questions," and feeling "ashamed of my country." In some NDW songs, reterritorialized national consciousness was expressed through anti-American sentiments. The most famous examples were Ideal's "Keine Heimat" ("No Home")—in which the Berlin-based band asked "Who saves us from America?"—and Fee's "Amerika." In Fee's song the United States consisted of "bubble gum and Coke," "Mickey Mouse and Marilyn," and a "western hero as president" who was "so good for business but too slow for Afghanistan." Fehlfarben also referenced US president Ronald Reagan in "Ein Jahr (Es geht voran)" ("One Year [Moving Forward]") with lines like "mountains explode, the president's to blame" and "pale B movie stars will soon rule the entire world."[21]

Whereas some NDW songs explicitly discussed national identity, others simply described West Germany in a deterritorialized state of paranoia and doom. For instance, Abwärts created dystopian, synthesizer- and violin-infused soundscapes about a German "Computerstaat" ("Computer State") and "Maschinenland" ("Machine Land"); the angular post-punk of Fehlfarben discussed personal alienation; punk group S.Y.P.H. celebrated industrial wastelands in "Zurück zum Beton" ("Back to Concrete"); finally, Einstürzende Neubauten (appropriately translated as "Collapsing New Buildings") had similar connections to the squatter movement as Ton Steine Scherben and blended the vocal delivery of Blixa Bargeld, which was almost identical to that of Rio Reiser, with Faust's industrial sounds. Recording their first album under a freeway bridge, the Neubauten celebrated destructive energy as an end in itself. This meant breaking with Ton Steine Scherben's notion of "destroying what destroys you" (and thereby potentially changing the social situation).[22] Similar to the Neubauten, Die Krupps from Düsseldorf featured apocalyptic industrial sounds on their *Stahlwerksinfonie* ("Steel Works Symphony"). Einstürzende Neubauten and Die Krupps were internationally successful and influenced electronic body music (EBM); the more humorous and less stereotypically German sounds of other experimental groups like Der Plan, Palais Schaumburg, and The Wirtschaftswunder hardly transcended Germany's borders.

In krautrock, international participation had largely been limited to Can's lead singers, but a few bands of the Neue Deutsche Welle began to extend notions of deterritorialized identity by explicitly engaging with migration. In the 1960s and 1970s, millions of workers from countries like Turkey, Italy, and Greece immigrated to West Germany, many of whom eventually brought their families, settled permanently, and challenged what it meant to be German. NDW band The Wirtschaftswunder (named after the "Economic Miracle" of the 1950s), with members from Italy, Czechoslovakia, Canada, and Germany, expressed language confusion in broken German on their jittery song "Analphabet" ("Illiterate"). The new waves of immigration that had begun with the *Gastarbeiter* ("guest workers") later became an integral part of German hip-hop with its high involvement of Turkish Germans and Afro-Germans.

The NDW group that represented renewed struggles over migration and national identity most poignantly and also achieved significant popularity outside of Germany was Deutsch-Amerikanische Freundschaft ("German-American Friendship"), or DAF. Between 1979 and 1982, the Düsseldorf group released five albums. They started as a full band with five members but gradually became an all-electronic duo consisting only of Gabriel "Gabi" Delgado-López (vocals) and Robert Görl (drums, sequencers, and synthesizers). Delgado-López self-identified as a *Gastarbeiterkind*, a child of Spanish guest workers. He grew up in the Düsseldorf housing projects after his anti-fascist parents had been forced to leave Spain under Franco's dictatorship.[23] DAF's name mocked anti-American sentiments with the Cold War alliance or "friendship" between Germany and the United States, but lyrically they rejected any "foreign" influences. As Gabi Delgado-López pointed out in a 1979 interview with the German *Sounds*: "We are consciously opposing the rules dictated by English pop imperialism that say that pop groups are required to speak and sing in English and are reduced to imitating English bands."[24] In another interview, Delgado-López described how his perspective as a *Gastarbeiterkind* shaped his particular approach to German-language lyrics: "I arrived in Germany when I was eight years old and therefore saw things differently. That's why I really wanted to make aggressive music with German lyrics. I thought: 'This works so well with the language. Why isn't anybody doing it?'"[25]

DAF's music was characterized by Delgado-López's machine-like *sprech-gesang* and the sequenced drum sounds of classically trained Robert Görl. Largely abandoning verse–chorus structures and rock harmonies, the duo set the stage for 1990s techno music. Delgado-López mentioned that they shared an interest in machines and technology with Kraftwerk but dismissed the krautrock group as "boring old farts."[26] DAF wanted to replace the dis-embodied quality of Florian Schneider and Ralf Hütter's music with physi-cality: "The machines were always close to breaking down. Unlike Kraft-werk, our machines had to sweat."[27] DAF's deterritorialized and hybridized man-machine sound was augmented by the visuals of the group—their shaved heads, half-naked, sweaty bodies, Doc Marten's boots, and shiny black leather, which mirrored skinhead culture with all its political ambiguities.[28] Delgado-López, who was openly bisexual, aptly described DAF's aesthetics as "fist-fuck-like."[29]

DAF started on the small independent label Ata Tak and subsequently went to Great Britain to record their second album for Mute. The group was then signed by major label Virgin, where they released their next three albums. On their early hit "Kebab-Träume" ("Kebab Dreams"), which was also recorded as "Militürk" by Mittagspause and Fehlfarben, Delgado-López connected Cold War paranoia and anti-Russian sentiments with Turkish immigration, obscuring any clear political message and hybridizing national identities with ambiguous lines like "Germany, Germany, it's all over" and "we are the Turks of tomorrow." DAF had already toyed with Nazi imagery in a song that referenced Germany's 1939 invasion of Poland, "Die lustigen Stiefel marschieren über Polen" ("The Funny Boots March over Poland"), but their 1981 hit "Der Mussolini" created even more controversy and was banned on German radio stations. Over a monotonous sequenced beat, Delgado-López encouraged listeners to dance the "Mussolini," the "Jesus Christ," the "Adolf Hitler," and the "Communism." In Delgado-López's own words, DAF wanted to show "the interchangeability of ideologies,"[30] but as with their skinhead posturing, some people saw fascist and blasphemous tendencies in the song.[31] DAF's ambiguous transcultural politics, which also involved a blurring of sexual identities in the allusions to gay S&M in their song "Der Räuber und der Prinz" ("The Robber and the Prince"), were successfully revived by East German group Rammstein in the mid-1990s, who also blended pseudo-fascism with homoeroticism and became one of the most successful German bands of all time.

DAF proved to be very influential in particular for the British post-punk scene. Other groups like Einstürzende Neubauten and the all-female Mania D developed a cult following in the United States. Only a few NDW groups achieved mainstream success but were often perceived as one hit wonders or novelty acts outside of Germany. Most noteworthy was Nena's "99 Luftballons" (also recorded in English as "99 Red Balloons"). Perceived in the United States as "new wave," the mainstream NDW song reached number two on the Billboard charts in 1984 and was the first German-language hit in the United States since Kraftwerk's "Autobahn" ten years earlier. Other international NDW hits included three songs by Austrian rapper Falco ("Der Kommissar," "Rock Me Amadeus," and "Vienna Calling"), Trio's minimalist "Da Da Da" (which made it to number one in ten European countries), United Balls' "Pogo in Togo" (which reached number one in Australia and New Zealand), and Peter Schilling's "Major Tom," lyrically a remake of David Bowie's "Space Oddity" (which went to number one in Canada). These songs were surprise hits that failed to leave much of a musical legacy outside Germany. On the other hand, the radical sound experiments of DAF, Einstürzende Neubauten, and Die Krupps, which did not dominate the charts, have been cited as influences by British and American artists, along with many krautrock groups.

In its home country, NDW's reappropriation of German lyrics was its most important legacy. An album like Fehlfarben's *Monarchie und Alltag* ("Monarchy and Daily Routine," 1980), regularly listed as one of the most important German-language recordings in rock history, was difficult to appreciate outside its country of origin, as the lyrics were its most original contribution. NDW albums like *Monarchie und Alltag* inspired later artists of the guitar-heavy *Hamburger Schule* ("Hamburg School"), like Blumfeld and Tocotronic, German hip-hop artists, and female-fronted pop acts like Juli and Silbermond. NDW's rediscovery of schlager also led to a major revival of the genre in the 1990s among younger audiences. It is quite remarkable how much of an impact the Neue Deutsche Welle had on German music and how little krautrock is remembered, whereas the opposite is true outside Germany.

## Krautrock's Return

Initially, krautrock did not leave much of a legacy in its country of origin. Artists who had been commercially successful—like Kraftwerk, La Düsseldorf, and Michael Rother—gradually retreated from the scene, while other artists like Faust are still virtually unknown in their home country. Some groups—like Tangerine Dream—remained successful throughout the 1980s but were rarely associated with their 1970s output or any concept of "krautrock." The term itself, which had never been accepted by most of the musicians associated with it, was increasingly used by publications like the German *Sounds* in the 1980s to classify music that was overblown and deemed passé—the bloated progressive rock of bands like Eloy, Grobschnitt, and Triumvirat. German punk and NDW, in contrast, briefly appeared as a fresh alternative that responded to the trends coming from the UK and even to Germany's schlager legacy.

The significant political changes in Europe that ultimately led to Germany's reunification in 1990 called for new kinds of music to emerge that expressed national identity in somewhat different ways than krautrock and NDW had done. Reunification emphasized national (instead of binational or postnational) thinking, yet the German nation-state as a whole continued to be devoted to European integration and remained decentered from above and below.[32] Consequently, in popular music from the 1990s German national identity was aggressively celebrated but also ironically inverted and questioned, for instance by immigrant voices heard in hip-hop or by East German heavy metal band Rammstein.[33] These coping strategies did not radically diverge from those of krautrock but were generally not perceived in the same context. Krautrock as a musical formation has only recently been remembered in Germany. Examples are the first book-length account of the music in German, Henning Dedekind's *Krautrock* (2008), Kraftwerk's performance of eight albums for their "Retrospective 1 2 3 4 5 6 7 8" in Düsseldorf in January 2013 (nine months *after* the same performance at the Museum of Modern Art in New York City), and the emergence of younger German bands like Von Spar, Stabil Elite, and Space Debris that clearly reference older groups like Can, Faust, and Neu!.[34]

In some ways, the rediscovery of krautrock in Germany in recent years is only a response to the massive influence that the music has had internationally. Bands like Faust, Tangerine Dream, and Can were successful in Great

Britain before Germans took notice, and their influence on British punk and post-punk was significant. In the 1990s, krautrock's influence shifted toward the United States, partly due to British musician Julian Cope's *Krautrocksampler* (1996), which was popular among American music insiders and indie bands. As Cope pointed out, his main reason for writing the book was "to introduce the word 'Krautrock' in a more positive, pouting glamrock way."[35] Entire genres of British and American popular music openly borrowed from krautrock groups like Can, Kraftwerk, Neu!, and Tangerine Dream, including, but not limited to, punk, post-punk, post-rock, industrial, disco, various forms of electronica like techno, ambient, and house, hip-hop, and indie rock. Even bestselling groups like Radiohead and Wilco clearly indicated that they were indebted to West German music from the 1970s.

While krautrock's influence on British and American music was more pronounced, the music has had other international followers, including groups like Föllakzoid from Chile, Marbeya Sound from Mexico, and Air Structures from Russia. The most overtly krautrock-inspired band may be Japan's Yellow Magic Orchestra, which formed in 1977 and has blended Kraftwerk's electronics with Eastern scales on songs like "Firecracker," "Computer Games," and "Tong Poo." Lead singer Ryuichi Sakamoto cited similar reasons for abandoning Anglo-American song structures as many krautrock artists: "We were tired of being told the Japanese were copying everything—the cars and TVs—at that time. So we thought it was time to make something very original from Japan."[36] Like Kraftwerk, Yellow Magic Orchestra was a surprise hit among African American audiences and even appeared on the legendary *Soul Train* TV show in 1980. Geopolitical affinities between Germany and Japan after World War II serve to explain the musical links between the two countries, which were also expressed by the Japanese groups Acid Mothers Temple and Boredoms that recycled Amon Düül I, Popol Vuh, Can, and Tangerine Dream. Both Can and Klaus Schulze collaborated with Japanese musicians, and, until recently, Tokyo Tower's wax museum boasted life-size models of Schulze, Manuel Göttsching, and members of Faust.

## Pitchfork Media

Krautrock's popularity in Japan notwithstanding, its continued appeal for American indie rock musicians, writers, and fans has probably been the music's most striking transnational impact in recent years. The popular webzine *Pitchfork Media* exemplifies how music that arrived at a specific moment in West German history and disavowed American influences attained subcultural capital among later generations in the United States. *Pitchfork* was founded in 1995 by Ryan Schreiber and gradually developed into "a fully fledged indie institution, with its own dedicated following, house-style and lucrative spin-off music festivals."[37] Written for a predominantly young, white, and male audience, *Pitchfork* was and is "both beloved and loathed for its long, complex reviews and unfailingly elitist stance as a tastemaker in the fickle community it serves, where bands of varying visibility rapidly go in and out of style."[38] Over the years, *Pitchfork* has featured many reviews of krautrock reissues and newer releases by musicians associated with the music. In 2004, *Pitchfork* published their "Top 100 Albums of the 1970s." With a disproportionate amount of German music, the list included three LPs by Can (*Ege Bamyasi, Tago Mago,* and *Future Days*), two by Kraftwerk (*Trans Europe Express* and *The Man Machine*), one each by Cluster (*Zuckerzeit*), Neu! (*Neu!*), Faust (*Faust IV*), and Giorgio Moroder (*From Here to Eternity*). Also included were the two krautrock-inspired LPs by Iggy Pop (*The Idiot* and *Lust for Life*), as well as David Bowie's *Low,* which topped the list. Krautrock clearly played an important role in staking out a musical past for writers of one of indie rock's premier publications.

Most of the early *Pitchfork* reviews of krautrock albums were written by Dominique Leone, now a professional musician. For Leone, the appeal of krautrock was what he perceived as its affinity to minimalist music and Miles Davis's jazz fusion on *In a Silent Way.* For Leone, "it 'made sense' in a cool way, a way that I hadn't heard a lot of other music make sense before. It *sounded* interesting, cool production, a lot of repetition and synthesized atmosphere, but with unabashedly beautiful parts, and just as bizarre cut-and-paste ADD sections."[39] Krautrock offered nontraditional song structures and an emphasis on ambient sound that young *Pitchfork* writers could connect with newer strands of indie rock and electronica. Although he wrote most of the early reviews on krautrock, Leone was not alone in his love for the music. According to Brent Sirota, another former contributor and now a history professor at North Carolina State University, "when I moved to Chicago in summer 1999 for grad school and became friends with *Pitchfork* founder Ryan Schreiber, one of the first things he burned for me was a copy of Manuel Göttsching/Ash Ra Tempel's *Best of the Private Tapes*. We both loved this collection."

Some *Pitchfork* writers became interested in krautrock by way of its connection with British post-punk and, later, American post-rock; for others, it was a fascination with psychedelic rock, jazz, and music from outside of the Anglo-American spectrum. In listing their favorite krautrock albums, *Pitchfork* writers chose relatively well-known groups like Can, Faust, Tangerine Dream, and Amon Düül II but also very obscure artists like German Oak, Kalacakra, Pell Mell, Rufus Zuphall, and Bokaj Retsiem.[40] The obscurity and assumed Otherness of krautrock added to its subcultural cachet. In describing the music, many *Pitchfork* writers used the term "weird" with positive connotations: krautrock was "the wiggy, weird stuff that only Germany in the early 70s could have produced in any quantity" (Joe Tangari); krautrock "tends to be expansive, repetitive, spacey in that weird early synthesizer kind of way, or just plain weird" (Nick Sylvester); or krautrock was simply "weird bands from Germany" (Dominique Leone). Generally very knowledgeable about the history, sound, and cultural context of krautrock, *Pitchfork* writers still described the music from a US-specific context as inherently "other." Nick Neyland reminisced about the "pre-Internet days," when "even the names Dieter Moebius and Hans-Joachim Roedelius had a certain exotic appeal. They almost seemed like characters in a sci-fi film."

Even if krautrock's "weirdness" and subcultural cachet were entry points for many *Pitchfork* writers, they often developed a deeper understanding of the sonic and conceptual qualities of the music. As Joe Tangari, an early reviewer who still contributes to the webzine, stated:

> Krautrock has its Germanness in its favor, but I think it stands the test of time because of its willful oddness and inventive spirit. You put on Kraftwerk and maybe you can tell when it was made, but it doesn't sound dated. An Amon Düül II album will never sound like a relic of its era because it never worried about achieving any kind of wide acceptance in its era. It was music designed not to fit in, and that ironically means it fits fine in any era.

While Tangari understood the specific national and cultural context in which krautrock had evolved, he also pointed to its transcendence of both time and space: "To me, krautrock is more of an attitude or an approach to music than a particular sound. Krautrock is about experimenting, dismantling boundaries, and reconsidering what pop music can be and do." Nick Neyland, a younger *Pitchfork* writer, specified that sonically, krautrock oftentimes was "driving, repetitive music," spinning "a kind of intense, hypnotic spell over an audience." Neyland used Klaus Dinger of Neu! and Jaki Liebezeit of Can as examples, "two entirely different drummers, one straight-down-the-line, the other wildly improvisational. That contrast is a useful indication of how broad krautrock could be."

Whereas an earlier generation of *Pitchfork* contributors had connected with a music that was largely forgotten even in its country of origin, a younger generation of writers still cared about krautrock, but not always as passionately. As Tangari speculated, "krautrock lingers in the backs of younger reviewers' minds, but their familiarity might be second-hand, or limited to major releases." As a somewhat younger writer on *Pitchfork*'s staff list, Brian Howe described krautrock with a critical distance, very well-informed about the particulars of the music but also less personally involved: "It seems like more of a marketing construct than a coherent genre—a catch-all term for German experimental music with a certain emphasis on analog electronic technology and mechanized repetition, particularly in the form of a drum machine pounding in 4/4 time." Kosmische Musik, on the other hand, was "more heavily associated with the New Age electronic-ambient side of German experimental music than [its] psychedelic rock side." The repetitive structure of some krautrock, particularly in terms of the motorik beat, appeared to be the major identifier for the music and its influence. Howe pointed out that "'krautrock' is frequently used in the North American press as a shorthand for anything with a motorik pulse. It probably took me quite a while to realize there was more to it than that."

As tastemakers and gatekeepers, *Pitchfork* contributors have helped to popularize krautrock among indie rock audiences in the United States, but they have also responded to and reflected the interest of British and American indie and electronica artists in the music. Never shy about dropping names, *Pitchfork* writers cited many influential artists who drew on krautrock in the 1990s. These included in particular post-rock groups Tortoise and Gastr del Sol and indie bands Stereolab and Sonic Youth, all of whom made their indebtedness to krautrock explicit.[41] Many *Pitchfork* writers also agreed that late 1970s and early 1980s British post-punk was deeply influenced by German bands, and they referenced Public Image Limited, Gang of Four, and Wire as examples. Finally, various forms of electronic music bore some resemblance to krautrock's experimentation with synthesizers and repetitive structure. As Nick Neyland put it: "It's hard to tell if the heavy reliance on repetition in club culture is a direct descendent of krautrock, but I think the influence is in there somewhere."

Individual *Pitchfork* writers listed a myriad of other krautrock-influenced groups related to indie rock in addition to post-rock, post-punk, and electronica. Incidentally, these groups did not include well-known indie band Radiohead but artists as far apart musically as Mogwai, Pavement, Boards of Canada, Nurse with Wound, Wooden Shjips, and Primal Scream. According to Tangari, krautrock's influence extended to rap and synth pop. Brent Sirota heard traces of the German groups in "drone and the New Age revival and all that retro analogue synth stuff that is being produced these days." For Nick Sylvester, "krautrock is baked into the DNA of pretty much all experimental synthesizer-based and underground noise music." Sirota also pointed out that sometimes it was not clear whether British and American musicians were actually influenced by krautrock or whether this reference was "cited largely after the fact, like discovering you have a famous ancestor." Sirota's example was Wilco's 2004 release *A Ghost Is Born*, "an album crammed with facile Neu! references."

Genuine influence or not, what was clear from the plethora of indie and electronica artists mentioned by the contributors to *Pitchfork* was how much subcultural cachet krautrock acquired in the United States throughout the 1990s and early 2000s. For music that decidedly broke with Anglo- and African American traditions and left relatively few traces in the country in which it originated, this was quite an achievement. It appears that despite some missing subtleties that got lost in translation, krautrock has finally received the recognition it deserves through the appreciation of British and American musicians, cultural brokers, and audiences.

# Appendix: The 50 Most Important Krautrock Albums

This admittedly highly subjective list, while far from exhaustive, gives an overview of the broader spectrum of krautrock. It serves as an audio companion to the book and includes the major releases discussed throughout the chapters but also some noteworthy minor contributors like Agitation Free, Jürgen Müller, and Wolfgang Riechmann. Most of these albums have been rereleased and are readily available. I have listed the most recent vinyl and CD versions for each entry.

### Agitation Free: *Malesch* (Vertigo, 1972)
LP: Made in Germany, 2012
CD: Revisited, 2008

Agitation Free, a psychedelic rock band from West Berlin, was one of the earliest krautrock groups. However, they did not release their first album until 1972. *Malesch* (Arabic for "it doesn't matter" or "take it easy") was heavily influenced by the band's Goethe Institute-sponsored trip to Egypt, Lebanon, Cyprus, and Greece. Similar to Can, Agitation Free forewent a colonial gaze and organically blended field recordings with their instrumental pieces, which ranged from Grateful Dead-like guitar solos to pulsating synthesizer drones. Agitation Free recorded two more albums before disbanding, but *Malesch* was their most varied effort.

### Amon Düül II: *Phallus Dei* (Liberty, 1969)
LP: Revisited, 2009
CD: Revisited, 2006

Amon Düül I were historically important, but the music they left behind was poorly executed and barely listenable. The more professional approach of Amon Düül II, on the other hand, allowed for some music that remains relevant. Their first album, *Phallus Dei* (Latin for "God's penis"), was a taste of what was to come. It contained one side of shorter songs and the title track on side two, a suite that easily moved from free jazz to psychedelic rock and from heavily percussive passages to violin-tinged progressive rock. Rhythmic complexity, guitar solos, and over-the-top vocals dominated the album.

## Amon Düül II: *Yeti* (Liberty, 1970)
LP: Revisited, 2009
CD: Revisited, 2006

Generally regarded as the high point of Amon Düül II's career, *Yeti* took *Phallus Dei*'s ideas and expanded on them. The latter had been recorded over two days and on two tracks; *Yeti* was recorded over two weeks and on sixteen tracks. The double album consisted of one record of compositions and one of improvisations, somewhat similar to Can's *Tago Mago*. Complex song suites with off-kilter vocals abounded, and Renate Knaup finally sang lead on the manic "Archangel's Thunderbird." Blending psychedelic folk with hard-hitting progressive rock and noisy drones with acoustic bliss, Amon Düül II made many references to recreational drugs, particularly LSD.

## Amon Düül II: *Tanz der Lemminge* (United Artists, 1971)
LP: Purple Pyramid, 2014
CD: Revisited, 2006

Amon Düül II followed their magnum opus *Yeti* a year later with another double album, *Tanz der Lemminge* (also known as *Dance of the Lemmings*). Each of the first three side-long tracks showcased a different musician. The album contained two complex suites with an eclectic mix of acoustic and electric rock, followed by Falk Rogner's synthesizer washes on "The Marilyn Monroe Memorial Church," which was reminiscent of Klaus Schulze's works. Three shorter improvised pieces completed the two-LP set, the last experimental release of the band. On their subsequent albums, Amon Düül II moved more toward mainstream rock structures.

## Ash Ra Tempel: *Ash Ra Tempel* (Ohr, 1971)

LP: Spalax, 2004

CD: Made in Germany, 2012

Ash Ra Tempel's original lineup (Manuel Göttsching, Klaus Schulze, and Hartmut Enke) only recorded one album together. The self-titled debut showcased the band's versatility on its two side-long instrumentals, the Jimi Hendrix-inspired heavy rock of "Amboss" and the meditative drones of "Traummaschine." Notoriously hard to find (especially with its original fold-out cover), Ash Ra Tempel's first album was a major statement for the band, which after Schulze's departure continued in a similar vein on albums like *Schwingungen* and *Join Inn*.

## Ashra: *New Age of Earth* (Isadora, 1976)

LP: Spalax, 1997

CD: Virgin, 1990

By the time *New Age of Earth* was released, Manuel Göttsching had essentially become a solo artist and had developed a dramatically different sound than on the records released with Ash Ra Tempel. *Inventions for Electric Guitar* and the soundtrack for *Le Berceau de Cristal* had already featured heavily processed, serene guitars and synthesizers. Göttsching perfected the New Age sound for his 1976 Ashra album, an early ambient prototype. It stands with some of Tangerine Dream's and Klaus Schulze's works as the fullest realization of kosmische Musik. Göttsching would turn heads again in 1984 with his proto-techno album *E2-E4*.

## David Bowie: *Low* (RCA, 1977)

LP: —

CD: Parlophone, 1999

David Bowie began to move toward krautrock with the title track from 1977's *Station to Station*. With support from a crew that included Tony Visconti, Brian Eno, and Carlos Alomar, Bowie undertook what may have been his most radical sonic reinvention on *Low*. The album, heavily influenced by Neu! and Kraftwerk, was split into one side of frantic art rock fragments and one side of synthesizer-heavy, mostly instrumental pieces. As the first and most consistent part of Bowie's Berlin Trilogy, *Low* brought Krautrock sounds into the rock mainstream and probably directly influenced more British and American artists than any of the German groups.

### David Bowie: *"Heroes"* (RCA, 1977)

LP: —
CD: Parlophone, 1999

The only part of David Bowie's Berlin triptych entirely envisioned and recorded in the divided city, *"Heroes"* might not be as consistent as *Low*, but with the title track it contained one of the British pop star's best-known songs. The angular rock on side one, with the added guitar of Robert Fripp, was again contrasted with a mostly tranquil and occasionally brooding side two. Bowie's references here were Cluster and Tangerine Dream. By the time Bowie recorded the last part of the Berlin triptych, *Lodger*, he had already checked out of the city by the wall.

### Can: *Soundtracks* (Liberty, 1970)

LP: Mute, 2014
CD: Mute, 2009

Can's debut album *Monster Movie* with vocalist Malcolm Mooney had been the first taste of the group's unique sound. For the transitional *Soundtracks*, a compilation of the band's work for TV and film, they recruited their new singer, Damo Suzuki. Two tracks with Mooney were still included (one of them was the unusually melodic "She Brings the Rain"), the rest featured Suzuki whispering and screaming. *Soundtracks* contained one of Can's best-known songs with the largely improvised fourteen-minute "Mother Sky" from the movie *Deep End*.

### Can: *Tago Mago* (United Artists, 1971)

LP: Mute, 2014
CD: Mute, 2008

Can demonstrated the full scope of their sonic repertoire on the double album *Tago Mago*. Holger Czukay edited the sprawling sessions into two LPs, one that was somewhat more conventional and one that was experimental avant-garde. "Halleluwah" chugged on for more than eighteen minutes, and "Aumgn" was of similar length but took the idea of post-rock even further by dispensing with any conventional song structure. *Tago Mago* included music ranging from tight jazz grooves to overtone singing and from jittery drum machine loops to mellow keyboard washes. Often cited as one of the most important krautrock releases, *Tago Mago* still sounds current.

### Can: *Ege Bamyasi* (United Artists, 1972)
LP: Mute, 2014
CD: Mute, 2008

Can followed *Tago Mago* with the more compact *Ege Bamyasi*. The group showed their versatility on both funky rock songs like "Vitamin C" and "I'm So Green" and on the *musique concrète* of "Soup." Since the album with its iconic cover of a can of okra was not long enough, the hit single "Spoon" was tacked on to the end. *Ege Bamyasi* may have been hastily assembled, but its influence was long lasting. Stephen Malkmus of Pavement even went so far as to re-record the album in its entirety with the German band Von Spar in 2012.

### Can: *Future Days* (United Artists, 1973)
LP: Mute, 2014
CD: Mute, 2008

Can's sound changed significantly for 1973's *Future Days*, the last album with Damo Suzuki on vocals. Gone were the hectic *musique concrète* passages. Instead, slower grooves dominated all songs with the exception of funky single "Moonshake." Prior to recording, the band members had been on vacation in southern Europe, and the result was a more laid-back, ambient sound. Without Damo Suzuki and with Holger Czukay gradually retreating, Can's sound became a bit more conventional on their following albums.

### Cluster: *Zuckerzeit* (Brain, 1974)
LP: Lilith, 2012
CD: Lilith, 2007

Hans-Joachim Roedelius and Dieter Moebius had been recording experimental synthesizer music as Cluster (and Kluster) for a few years when

*Zuckerzeit* was released in 1974. Produced by Michael Rother, the album marked a shift toward short, rhythmic, and more pop-oriented instrumentals. It was packaged like candy and laden with cheap drum machines, sugary synthesizers, and Moebius's oddball sound effects. Its impact on electronic music was significant, and many more contemporary groups have copied *Zuckerzeit*'s low-fi sound.

## Cluster: *Sowiesoso* (Sky, 1976)
LP: Bureau B, 2016
CD: Bureau B, 2016

After the pop references on *Zuckerzeit*, Cluster returned to somewhat more experimental and meditative sounds for the follow-up *Sowiesoso*. Ambient textures dominated the album's electronic aural landscape, but it also featured many bizarre sound effects. Whenever the music threatened to fade into the background, some bubbling or gurgling synthesizer appeared in the mix. Hans-Joachim Roedelius, Dieter Moebius, and producer Conny Plank's seven instrumental pieces would not seem out of place among the more ambient side of contemporary electronica.

## Cluster & Eno: *After the Heat* (Sky, 1978)
LP: Bureau B, 2009
CD: Bureau, 2009

Released as "Eno Moebius Roedelius," Cluster's second collaboration with Brian Eno was more varied and textured than 1977's *Cluster & Eno* and the 1976 Harmonia-Eno session, which came out in 2009 as *Tracks and Traces*. Blending the gentle sounds of *Sowiesoso* with Eno's ambient style was a logical step for the electronic musicians of Cluster. None of the three players—Eno, Moebius, or Roedelius—dominated the sound, which combined synthesizers with piano and processed guitar. Can's Holger Czukay made a guest appearance on "Tzima N'arki."

## Cosmic Jokers: *Galactic Supermarket* (Kosmische Musik, 1974)

LP: Spalax, 1997
CD: Spalax, 1994

Rolf-Ulrich Kaiser released four unauthorized LPs with recordings from the krautrock "supergroup" that featured Klaus Schulze, Manuel Göttsching, Dieter Dierks, Harald Großkopf, and others. The same sessions produced official albums by Ash Ra Tempel, Walter Wegmüller, and Sergius Golowin. All four Cosmic Jokers LPs are notoriously hard to find, but *Galactic Supermarket* was the most varied. Vocals by Gille Lettmann and Rosi Müller were used sparingly and effectively, and the jam session of the assembled musicians alternated psychedelic rock with atmospheric synthesizer drones.

## DAF: *Alles ist gut* (Virgin, 1981)

LP: —
CD: Mute, 1998

DAF took krautrock's synthesizer sound in a new direction on the Neue Deutsche Welle hit album *Alles ist gut* ("Everything's Fine"). Reduced to a duo consisting of Gabi Delgado-López on grunt-like vocals and Robert Görl on drums and synthesizers, the Düsseldorf group continued toying with fascist and gay images on songs ranging from the relentless beat of "Der Mussolini" to the mellow fairy tale "Der Räuber und der Prinz." Produced by Conny Plank, *Alles ist gut* influenced various electronic genres like EBM and techno. The provocative play with German national identity was later successfully revived by heavy metal group Rammstein.

## Deuter: *Aum* (Kuckuck, 1972)

LP: Cherry Red, 2011
CD: Kuckuck, 1998

Multi-instrumentalist Georg Deuter might not have been one of the key players in krautrock's history, but his New Age forays into Indian classical music and free improvisation helped him gain a substantial following. Nature sounds and an array of instruments (sitar, drums, flute, guitar), all played by Deuter himself, created a spiritually driven musical experience reminiscent of some of Popol Vuh's works. Deuter's later albums turned to more generic

New Age, but *Aum* in particular highlighted the important connection between krautrock and world music.

## Einstürzende Neubauten: *½ Mensch* (Some Bizarre, 1985)
LP: —
CD: Potomac, 2009

Einstürzende Neubauten's industrial post-punk was the logical consequence of ideas started by Faust. Musically, *½ Mensch*, the group's third LP, was more diverse than its predecessors and included not just noise but also haunting quiet passages and a cappella singing. "Seele brennt" ("Soul Is Burning") showed the newfound wide sonic spectrum. Neubauten's radical avant-garde approach, Blixa Bargeld's tortured vocals, and the group's martial, synthetic beats won the band many admirers in the United States and Great Britain and influenced countless groups that included Depeche Mode and Nine Inch Nails.

## Faust: *Faust* (Polydor, 1971)
LP: Lilith, 2007
CD: Recommended, 2015

Faust's debut album was likely the most dramatic departure from conventional rock structures in the history of krautrock. This departure began with the cover art, an x-rayed fist on a transparent cover with a transparent lyric sheet and a transparent and unmarked vinyl record inside, and extended to the music. With their deconstructive collage of odd sounds, song fragments, Dada lyrics, and noise, Faust made clear that they were not simply the German Beatles (as their record company Polydor had hoped). The group's avant-garde music would influence numerous indie, post-rock, and industrial bands in the years to come.

## Faust: *So Far* (Polydor, 1972)
LP: 4 Men with Beards, 2009
CD: Polydor, 2010

Faust's second album had a black cover containing art prints for each song. Pressured by Polydor, the band strove for a slightly more commercial sound than on their debut release, resulting in nine pieces of music with distinctive styles and recurring melodies. While *So Far* was more accessible, it was still sonically radical, from the monotonous drone of "It's a Rainy Day Sunshine Girl" and the abrasive synthesizers of "Mamie Is Blue" to the Frank Zappa homage "I've Got My Car and My TV." This album offered an easier entry point to explore Faust's unique soundscapes than the debut.

## Faust: *The Faust Tapes* (Virgin, 1973)
LP: Recommended, 2010
CD: Recommended, 2001

After their first two albums, Faust changed labels. Their first release on Virgin was a collage of mostly short pieces of highly experimental sounds and music. A few distinctive folk and art rock songs were hidden within the two tracks, which each took up an entire side. Sold for only forty-nine pence in the United Kingdom, *The Faust Tapes* was the first "hit" for the group, reportedly selling fifty thousand copies. This success helped to popularize the band among aficionados of unusual sounds, but in their home country Faust remained largely unknown until they reformed in the 1990s.

## Faust: *Faust IV* (Virgin, 1974)
LP: Virgin, 2009
CD: Caroline, 2007

All four releases of the original Faust contributed to their mystique. *Faust IV* was another turn to song-like structures after a thoroughly experimental album (just like *So Far* had been after their debut). Opener "Krautrock" negated any overly commercial direction with nearly twelve minutes of instrumental drones, but some of the following seven tracks were as close to pop music as Faust would ever get, adding reggae, jazz rock, and acoustic folk akin to the Canterbury scene to the mix. After *IV*, Faust did not release another album for twenty years.

## Fehlfarben: *Monarchie und Alltag* (EMI, 1980)
LP: —
CD: EMI, 2000

Highly regarded by German critics but little known outside of the country, Fehlfarben's *Monarchie und Alltag* ("Monarchy and Daily Routine") proved that the Neue Deutsche Welle had depth and focus. The group combined angular post-punk guitars and ska rhythms with Peter Hein's staccato vocals and his lyrics about suburban boredom and Cold War angst. Hein quit the band after the album and gave up a successful pop career to keep his low-paying office job. He resurfaced decades later to reunite with Fehlfarben after having deeply influenced German rock bands throughout the 1980s and 1990s.

## Guru Guru: *UFO* (Ohr, 1970)
LP: ZYX, 2008
CD: ZYX, 2008

Guru Guru were one of the earliest krautrock groups. The southern German band's original lineup consisted of Mani Neumeier on drums, Ax Genrich on electric guitar, and Uli Trepte on bass. Musically, their psychedelic rock instrumentals were fairly close to the music of Anglo-American artists, in particular the guitar solos of Jimi Hendrix—only much looser and leaning more toward free improvisation. On their first album *UFO*, Guru Guru plowed through five tracks of heavily distorted guitar and bass, feedback noise, and expansive drumming. The group went on to record more than ten other albums in the 1970s alone.

## Harmonia: *Musik von Harmonia* (Brain, 1974)
LP: Grönland, 2016
CD: Grönland, 2016

Harmonia was a krautrock "supergroup" that added Michael Rother of Neu! to Cluster's lineup of Hans-Joachim Roedelius and Dieter Moebius. Simply titled "Music by Harmonia," their first album had an iconic cover with a blue detergent bottle and sounded much like a continuation of the three musicians' collaboration on Cluster's *Zuckerzeit*. It featured Rother's processed guitar on top of electronic percussion and synthesizers and also included one longer, meditative piece, the tongue-in-cheek "Sehr kosmisch" ("Very Cosmic"). Entirely instrumental, *Musik von Harmonia* effortlessly blended pop and avant-garde.

## Harmonia: *Deluxe* (Brain, 1975)

LP: Grönland, 2016
CD: Grönland, 2016

Intentionally more commercial than their first album, Harmonia's *Deluxe* featured vocals and live drums played by Guru Guru's Mani Neumeier. The production was also much slicker than on the debut, giving the group a more professional air. Although widespread success did not ensue for the band, the more rock-oriented format of songs like "Monza" showcased Harmonia's broad musical spectrum. Cluster and Michael Rother parted ways after one more collaboration, which was not released until 1996 (*Tracks and Traces* with Brian Eno).

## Michael Hoenig: *Departure from the Northern Wasteland* (Warner Brothers, 1978)

LP: —
CD: Kuckuck, 2001

Michael Hoenig was a former member of Agitation Free and Tangerine Dream, but on *Departure from the Northern Wasteland* he developed his own realization of the Berlin School sound. Driven by sequencers and synthesizers, the music on the album evoked the northern German landscape that Hoenig knew from his childhood. The keyboarder had worked on his solo effort for two years, and the resulting four tracks bore many similarities to Klaus Schulze's and Edgar Froese's 1970s albums. Hoenig did not release another solo album for ten years, making *Departure* a rare glimpse into the work of a lesser known krautrock musician.

## Kraftwerk: *Autobahn* (Philips, 1974)

LP: EMI, 2009
CD: EMI, 2009

It took Kraftwerk three albums to develop the distinctive sound of *Autobahn* (four if one counted their debut as Organisation). The album was divided into two very different sides: an A-side with the twenty-two minute title track (which in edited form became a surprise hit in the United States) and a B-side with instrumental sketches that combined the ominous with the sentimental. The A-side's monotonous vocals, electronic percussion, and detached synthesizer melodies were the model for Kraftwerk's later works. *Autobahn* was a pop record but also still had Florian Schneider and Ralf Hütter dabbling in avant-garde music.

## Kraftwerk: *Trans Europe Express* (Kling Klang, 1977)
LP: EMI, 2009
CD: EMI, 2009

Kraftwerk failed to produce a commercially viable successor to *Autobahn* with the quirky and experimental *Radio Activity*. Yet with *Trans Europe Express* they established themselves as cutting-edge electronic pop stars. The title track featured their catchiest melody yet, and other songs like "Europe Endless" and "Showroom Dummies" reflected the group's maturity and diversity. It was this album that caught the attention of early techno and hip-hop artists, making Kraftwerk an unlikely sensation in Detroit and the South Bronx.

## Kraftwerk: *The Man Machine* (Kling Klang, 1978)
LP: EMI, 2009
CD: EMI, 2009

For *The Man Machine*, Kraftwerk incorporated some of the African American music that they themselves had influenced. Their sound in turn became more immediate, danceable, and futuristic. On "The Robots" and "The Model," Kraftwerk crafted their music into single-length pop hits, and the ethereal "Neon Lights" was the blueprint for the British New Romantic groups of the 1980s. *The Man Machine* was a mere thirty-six minutes long, but the album was an important moment in Kraftwerk's long career both conceptually and aesthetically.

## Kraftwerk: *Computer World* (Kling Klang, 1981)
LP: EMI, 2009
CD: EMI, 2009

It took Kraftwerk three years to produce a follow-up to *The Man Machine*. Florian Schneider and Ralf Hütter updated their sound for their first digital-age album. *Computer World* featured both tongue-in-cheek humor ("Pocket Calculator") and sentimental longing ("Computer Love"). Kraftwerk generally tried to make concept albums, and *Computer World*, with its focus on various aspects of a highly technological society, might have been the most consistent one. In the following decades, Kraftwerk continued to release albums, but their impact on popular music was less dramatic.

## La Düsseldorf: *La Düsseldorf* (Nova, 1976)
LP: 4 Men with Beards, 2008
CD: Eastwest, 2005

On his first LP with La Düsseldorf after the demise of Neu!, Klaus Dinger still embraced some of his former group's aesthetics (motorik rhythms, few harmonic changes), but a stronger focus on electronics and German-language lyrics foreshadowed the Neue Deutsche Welle. Dinger and his bandmates celebrated the city of Düsseldorf and reflected on the passage of time on the album's four songs. 1978's *Viva* was commercially more successful than *La Düsseldorf*, but Dinger had arguably realized the band's concept most fully on their debut album.

## Moebius & Plank: *Rastakraut Pasta* (Sky, 1980)
LP: Bureau B, 2012
CD: Bureau B, 2010

Krautrock producer Conny Plank and Cluster member Dieter Moebius released the collaboration *Rastakraut Pasta* at the tail end of the movement. At a time when the Neue Deutsche Welle was in full swing, Moebius & Plank showed that krautrock still had sonic worlds to explore. As the title suggested, the instrumental pieces on the album blended off-kilter electronica with reggae. Holger Czukay of Can played bass on four of the seven tracks. Moebius & Plank recorded another collaborative album, *Material*, which was released a year later.

## Giorgio Moroder: *From Here to Eternity* (Casablanca, 1977)
LP: —
CD: Repertoire, 1999

Giorgio Moroder may be most famous for his work as a producer, but he also made a number of solo albums. These included the disco funk of *Knights in White Satin*, $E=MC^2$, and the two Munich Machine releases, as well as the synthesizer experiments of *Einzelgänger*. 1977's *From Here to Eternity* was arguably Moroder's most fully developed solo work, sonically akin to Kraftwerk's *Trans Europe Express* from the same year but with an incessant disco beat and livelier vocals. Generally not regarded as krautrock, this album nonetheless featured a similarly bold exploration of electronic sounds.

## Jürgen Müller: *Science of the Sea* (self-released, 1982)
LP: Digitalis, 2011
CD: Digitalis, 2012

According to a press release, Jürgen Müller, a student of oceanic science at the University of Kiel who taught himself how to play synthesizers, recorded *Science of the Sea* as the soundtrack for a deep sea documentary that was never made. Allegedly only one hundred copies were produced in 1982, but the album was rereleased to critical acclaim in 2011. The twelve tracks of "underwater music" had similarities with the *kosmische* sounds of the Berlin School. Some blogs have questioned the authenticity of the story and have suspected that *Science of the Sea* might be a more recent recording.

## Neu!: *Neu!* (Brain, 1972)
LP: Grönland, 2012
CD: Grönland, 2012

The first LP Klaus Dinger and Michael Rother released as Neu! in 1972 deliberately moved away from rock music's appropriation of blues scales. Deceptively simple, Neu!'s self-titled debut opened with the hypnotic one-chord groove of "Hallogallo." The experimental "Sonderangebot" and the serene "Weissensee" followed. The album's second side featured three abstract songs about a failed relationship, from a blissful beginning to rejection to yearning desire. *Neu!* was not the most accessible record, but patient listeners were rewarded with the realization that this was one of the most radical and innovative albums in the history of popular music.

## Neu!: *Neu! 2* (Brain, 1973)

LP: Grönland, 2012
CD: Grönland, 2012

Neu!'s second album conceptually advanced what their debut had started. It contained more one-chord jam sessions with guitar and drums and other, quieter pieces. *Neu! 2*'s newness was in the tape-splicing, playback speed variations, and the remixing of the second side. It might have been more interesting in theory than in practice, but it showcased Neu! as radical sound innovators. For Klaus Dinger and Michael Rother, necessity had become the mother of invention when they decided to recycle their own music after the record company had pulled their funding.

## Neu!: *Neu! 75* (Brain, 1975)

LP: Grönland, 2012
CD: Grönland, 2012

Consistent with their conceptual framework, Neu!'s third offering was more of the same—guitar-driven rock songs and moody, reverbed soundscapes. On most tracks, Klaus Dinger and Michael Rother refined and streamlined their sound and refrained from overtly experimental pieces, but *Neu! 75* also included two proto-punk songs by Dinger with unintelligible vocals, "Hero" and "After Eight." It was Neu!'s last album for many years. Dinger and Rother continued to make music separately, but the chemistry of their first three albums remained their greatest legacy.

## Popol Vuh: *Einsjäger und Siebenjäger* (Kosmische Musik, 1974)

LP: Wah Wah, 2013
CD: SPV, 2004

Popol Vuh began their career with two seminal Moog albums, *Affenstunde* and *In den Gärten Pharaos*, which were highly experimental and relatively inaccessible for casual listeners. In turning to acoustic instruments and Christian messages, they found a musically more balanced sound, and 1974's *Einsjäger und Siebenjäger* was its most fully developed expression. A number of short pieces and the twenty-minute title track combined meditative guitar runs by Daniel Fichelscher with Florian Fricke's piano and Djong Yun's angelic soprano. Popol Vuh also made a number of similar instrumental albums in the 1970s.

## Popol Vuh: *The Best Soundtracks from Werner Herzog Films* (ZYX, 1982)
LP: —
CD: —

Popol Vuh's soundtracks for Werner Herzog's films have only been partly issued on vinyl and CD, and some, like the well-received *Great Ecstasy of Woodcarver Steiner*, have never been officially released. The most diverse compilation remains a German LP from 1982 that included many tracks from *Fitzcarraldo*, the long "Brüder des Schattens, Söhne des Lichts" from *Nosferatu*, the main theme from *Aguirre*, and a very short piece from *Heart of Glass*. These songs offered a glimpse into the vast repertoire of acoustic and electronic sounds Popol Vuh employed to accompany Herzog's images.

## Wolfgang Riechmann: *Wunderbar* (Sky, 1978)
LP: Bureau B, 2009
CD: Bureau B, 2009

As one of the members of the Düsseldorf scene, Wolfgang Riechmann had played with Michael Rother (of Neu!) and Wolfgang Flür (of Kraftwerk) and had recorded an album with the group Streetmark. He was employed as a social worker when he was senselessly stabbed and killed in 1978. His posthumously released solo album *Wunderbar* was comprised of synthesizer-dominated instrumentals that bridged the sounds of Kraftwerk and Klaus Schulze. Meditative yet rhythmically driven, the six tracks were an important addition to the krautrock catalog and showed much promise for a career that ended prematurely.

## Klaus Schulze: *Timewind* (Brain, 1975)
LP: —
CD: Revisited, 2007

Determining which Klaus Schulze album was his most important is an impossible task, given the keyboard player's prolific career. After his early recordings as a drummer for Tangerine Dream and Ash Ra Tempel, Schulze found his calling when he discovered synthesizers. 1975's *Timewind* was already his fifth solo album. It contained two long electronic tracks that made use of the full arsenal of electronic sound. With its vague references to Richard Wagner and the surrealist cover, this was cosmic music disguised as high art. Other Schulze releases from the mid-1970s—*Picture Music*, *Moondawn*, and *Mirage*—had a very similar concept and sound.

## Klaus Schulze: *X* (Brain, 1978)

LP: Made in Germany, 2009
CD: Revisited, 2005

Klaus Schulze's most ambitious project was the double album *X* from 1978. The connections between the tracks and the predominantly German artists they were named for were not always apparent, but musically *X* incorporated a vast array of both electronic and acoustic instruments. Schulze blended synthesizers, strings, and drums into massive soundscapes. In many ways, *X* was the culmination of Schulze's 1970s work. He continued to release albums throughout the decades that followed, but they did not always live up to the epic proportions of his earlier work.

## Donna Summer: *Once Upon a Time* (Casablanca, 1977)

LP: —
CD: Mercury, 2008

Generally not considered krautrock, Donna Summer's work with Giorgio Moroder was more pop-oriented but had many similarities with electronic artists like Kraftwerk. Both Summer and Moroder spent a considerable amount of time in Germany. The double album *Once Upon a Time* might not have included Summer's greatest hits like "I Feel Love" or "Bad Girls," but artistically it was one of Moroder's most mature productions. The disco sounds contained on the four sides were quite diverse and included both orchestral and synthesizer-dominated tracks. On songs like "Working the Midnight Shift" and "I Love You," Summer and Moroder had perfected their collaborative craft.

## Tangerine Dream: *Zeit* (Ohr, 1972)

LP: Esoteric, 2011
CD: Esoteric, 2011

On their third album *Zeit*, Tangerine Dream moved from avant-garde art rock to fully realized kosmische Musik. The double album had only four tracks, which stretched synthesizer drones and atmospheric bleeps to seemingly infinite dimensions. Tangerine Dream's uncompromising cosmic sound was all the more surprising because they had just released the hard-rocking single "Ultima Thule." *Zeit* was Tangerine Dream's first album as a trio comprised of Edgar Froese, Peter Baumann, and Christopher Franke. Florian Fricke of Popol Vuh played Moog on "Birth of Liquid Plejades."

## Tangerine Dream: *Phaedra* (Virgin, 1974)

LP: Virgin, 2014
CD: Virgin, 2012

With *Phaedra*, Tangerine Dream had a surprise hit in Great Britain. They had updated their sound with sequencers, but the result was still an experimental instrumental synthesizer album. In contrast to albums like *Zeit*, the side-long title track epitomized the group's new rhythmically driven approach. Tangerine Dream would produce a number of other electronic ambient releases and develop much more commercial music for their 1980s soundtrack work, but *Phaedra* was arguably their most refined exploration of the Berlin School sound.

## Ton Steine Scherben: *Keine Macht für Niemand* (David Volksmund, 1972)

LP: David Volksmund, 2015
CD: David Volksmund, 2015

Ton Steine Scherben, generally considered one of the most important rock bands in Germany, are virtually unknown elsewhere. This is partly due to their politically charged German lyrics, which were an essential component of their music. Their double album *Keine Macht für Niemand* ("No Power for Nobody") established their proto-punk sound. Shorter songs with chanted vocals alternated with longer, musically expansive pieces, which ventured more into krautrock territory. *Keine Macht für Niemand* was a landmark album because it was proof that German lyrics and rock music could mesh, and that songs with strong political messages could find a sizeable audience.

### Ton Steine Scherben: *Wenn die Nacht am tiefsten* (David Volksmund, 1975)

LP: David Volksmund, 2015
CD: David Volksmund, 2015

After *Keine Macht für Niemand*, Ton Steine Scherben took three years to record another album. Moving from West Berlin to the northern German countryside went hand in hand with a less dogmatic approach to political lyrics. The double album *Wenn die Nacht am tiefsten* ("When It's Darkest Night") was also more diverse musically than its predecessor, featuring the driving rhythm of "Heut' nacht" ("Tonight") as well as the tender "Halt dich an deiner Liebe fest" ("Hold On to Your Love"). Reminiscent of some of the Rolling Stones' 1970s work, *Wenn die Nacht* added more musical depth to the band's exploration of German lyrics.

### Xhol Caravan: *Electrip* (Hansa, 1969)

LP: Tripkick, 1997
CD: Garden of Delights, 2003

With *Electrip*, Xhol Caravan (formerly known as Soul Caravan) from Wiesbaden recorded one of the earliest albums generally identified as krautrock. This might be a bit of a misnomer since the group, which included African American drummer and occasional singer Skip van Wyck, was not really moving away from American song structures but embracing psychedelic rock and jazz. Xhol Caravan's music had layers of organ, flute, and saxophone on top of funky rhythm tracks. Resembling some of the German jazz rock bands that followed, they also managed to infuse their music with some krautrock elements.

# Notes

## Introduction

1. David Stubbs, *Future Days: Krautrock and the Building of Modern Germany* (London: Faber & Faber, 2014); Nikos Kotsopoulos, *Krautrock: Cosmic Rock and its Legacy* (London: Black Dog, 2010).

2. Julian Cope, *Krautrocksampler* (London: Head Heritage, 1996).

3. Cope, *Krautrocksampler*; Lester Bangs, "Kraftwerkfeature," in *Psychotic Reactions and Carburetor Dung*, ed. Greil Marcus (New York: Vintage, 1988), 154–60; Jim DeRogatis, *Turn On Your Mind: Four Decades of Great Psychedelic Rock* (Milwaukee, WI: Hal Leonard, 2003).

4. Henning Dedekind, *Krautrock: Underground, LSD und kosmische Kuriere* (Höfen: Hannibal, 2008); Alexander Simmeth, *Krautrock Transnational: Die Neuerfindung der Popmusik in der BRD, 1968–1978* (Bielefeld: Transcript, 2016).

5. Michel Foucault, *The Archaeology of Knowledge* (New York: Pantheon, 1972), 32.

6. Ibid., 37.

7. See Pierre Bourdieu, *The Field of Cultural Production: Essays on Art and Literature* (New York: Columbia University Press), 33–34.

8. Barry Shank, *The Political Force of Musical Beauty* (Durham, NC: Duke University Press, 2014), 1.

9. Ibid.

10. See Ian Biddle and Vanessa Knights, "National Popular Musics: Betwixt and Beyond the Local and the Global," in *Music, National Identity and the Politics of Location: Between the Global and the Local*, ed. Ian Biddle and Vanessa Knights (Burlington, VT: Ashgate, 2007), 1–15.

11. See Arjun Appadurai, *Modernity at Large: Cultural Dimensions of Globalization* (Minneapolis: University of Minnesota Press, 1996); Fredric Jameson, "Notes on Globalization as a Philosophical Issue," in *The Cultures of Globalization*, ed. Fredric Jameson and Masao Myoshi (Durham, NC: Duke University Press, 1998), 54–77; John Tomlinson, *Globalization and Culture* (Chicago: University of Chicago Press, 1999); Anthony Giddens, *Runaway World: How Globalization Is Reshaping Our Lives* (New York: Routledge, 2000).

12. See Ulf Hannerz, "The World in Creolization," *Africa* 57 (1987): 546–59; Roland Robertson, *Globalization: Social Theory and Global Culture* (London: Sage, 1992); Néstor García Canclini, *Hybrid Cultures: Strategies for Entering and Leaving Modernity* (Minneapolis: University of Minnesota Press, 1995).

13. See Jonathan Xavier Inda and Renato Rosaldo, "A World in Motion," in *The Anthropology of Globalization*, ed. Jonathan Xavier Inda and Renato Rosaldo (Malden, MA: Blackwell, 2002), 1–34.

14. Canclini, *Hybrid Cultures*, 229.

15. Ibid., 243.

16. See Nikos Papastergiadis, "Tracing Hybridity in Theory," in *Debating Cultural Hybridity: Multi-Cultural Identities and the Politics of Anti-Racism*, ed. Pnina Werbner and Tariq Modood (London: Zed Books, 1997), 257–81.

17. George Lipsitz, *Dangerous Crossroads: Popular Music, Postmodernism and the Poetics of Place* (New York: Verso, 1994), 3–4.

18. Josh Kun, *Audiotopia: Music, Race, and America* (Berkeley: University of California Press, 2005), 2.

19. Ibid., 20.

20. See John O'Flynn, "National Identity and Music in Transition: Issues of Authenticity in a Global Setting," in *Music, National Identity*, 26.

21. John Connell and Chris Gibson, *Sound Tracks: Popular Music, Identity and Place* (New York: Routledge, 2003), 143. The concept of "imagined communities" was developed by Benedict Anderson. See Benedict Anderson, *Imagined Communities: Reflections on the Origin and Spread of Nationalism* (London: Verso, 1983).

22. Connell and Gibson, *Sound Tracks*, 143.

23. It is beyond the scope of this book to look at the way the Nazi past was handled in East Germany. In a somewhat simplistic analysis, Siobhan Kattago has discussed strategies of the East German government to universalize the past in its Marxist critique of capitalism, unlike West Germany's internalization of the past. See Siobhan Kattago, *Ambiguous Memory: The Nazi Past and German National Identity* (Westport, CT: Praeger, 2001).

24. See *America and the Shaping of German Society, 1945–1955*, ed. Michael Ermath (Oxford: Berg, 1993), 2.

25. Nick Thomas, *Protest Movements in 1960s West Germany: A Social History of Dissent and Democracy* (Oxford: Berg, 2003), 13.

26. See Dörte von Westernhagen, *Die Kinder der Täter: Das Dritte Reich und die Generation danach* (Munich: Kösel, 1987).

27. More recently, a number of controversial books and movies have dealt with complex issues of responsibility, guilt, and punishment. Among these are Bernhard Schlink's novel *Der Vorleser* (*The Reader*, 1995) about the love affair between a young German boy and a former concentration camp guard, the Oscar-winning film *Der Untergang* (*The Downfall*, 2004), humanizing Adolf Hitler in a depiction of his final days, and the bestseller *Die vergessene Generation* (*The Forgotten Generation*, 2005), an attempt to recount the trauma of Germans who were children during World War II.

28. See Thomas, *Protest Movements*.

29. Some APO members would later become well-known politicians, a prime example being Green Party member and former foreign minister Joseph "Joschka" Fischer.

30. See Dieter Rucht, "Protestbewegungen," in *Die Geschichte der Bundesrepublik Deutschland, Bd. 3: Gesellschaft*, ed. Wolfgang Benz (Frankfurt: Fischer, 1989), 311–44.

31. Jakob Tanner, "'The Times They Are A-Changin'": Zur subkulturellen Dynamik der 68er Bewegungen," in *1968: Vom Ereignis zum Mythos*, ed. Ingrid Gilcher-Hotley (Frankfurt: Suhrkamp, 2008), 276–77. All translations from German to English in this book are my own.

32. See Dedekind, *Krautrock*, 59.

33. See Detlev Mahnert and Harry Stürmer, *Zappa, Zoff und Zwischentöne: Die internationalen Essener Songtage 1968* (Essen: Klartext, 2008), 58.

34. Quoted in Jugendamt der Stadt Essen, ed., *Song Magazin 1968 für IEST 68* (Essen, 1968), 12.

35. Ibid., 103–4.

36. See Detlef Siegfried, *Time Is on My Side: Konsum und Politik der westdeutschen Jugendkultur der 6oer Jahre* (Göttingen: Wallstein, 2006), 607.

37. Timothy S. Brown, "'The Germans Meet the Underground': The Politics of Pop in the Essener Songtage of 1968," in *Musikkulturen in der Revolte: Studien zu Rock, Avant-garde und Klassik im Umfeld von '1968'*, ed. Beate Kutschke (Stuttgart: Steiner, 2008), 163.

38. See Mahnert and Stürmer, *Zappa, Zoff*, 145.

39. See Christoph Wagner, *Der Klang der Revolte: Die magischen Jahre des westdeutschen Musik-Underground* (Mainz: Schott, 2013), 198.

40. Brown, "The Germans," 169.

41. Mahnert and Stürmer, *Zappa, Zoff*, 230.

42. In this context, I want to take up Kevin Fellezs's discussion of fusion jazz and expand his ideas about an "in-between" genre to the realm of spatiality. See Kevin Fellezs, *Birds of Fire: Jazz, Rock, Funk and the Creation of Fusion* (Durham, NC: Duke University Press, 2011).

43. Winfried Trenkler, liner notes for *Kraut-Rock: German Rock Scene* (Brain, 1974).

44. See *Music and German National Identity*, ed. Celia Applegate and Pamela Potter (Chicago: University of Chicago Press, 2002), 2–3.

45. Schlager, perceived by the 1960s counterculture as reactionary, but really a hybrid of many different influences and styles, remained hugely popular in West Germany throughout the 1970s and 1980s and were revived by a younger generation in the decades that followed.

46. Paul Griffiths, *Modern Music and After* (New York: Oxford University Press, 2010), 35.

47. In departing from a blues-based approach, krautrock bands and fans differed significantly from the rock music scene in Germany at large. For instance, the American Folk Blues Festival brought many African American blues performers to both West and East Germany in the 1960s and was hugely successful. See Ulrich Adelt, *Blues Music in the Sixties: A Story in Black and White* (New Brunswick, NJ: Rutgers University Press, 2010).

48. See Michael Rauhut, *Rock in der DDR: 1964–1989* (Bonn: Bundeszentrale für politische Bildung, 2002).

49. See Rüdiger Ritter, "'1968' und der Wandel der Protestkultur in der Musik im Ostblock: Ausgewählte Beispiele (CSSR, DDR, Polen, Ungarn)," in *Musikkulturen*, 209.

50. Ibid., 212.

## Chapter One

1. In light of the lengthy process in which Germans had to and in many ways still have to grapple with the Nazi past, *Stunde Null* is a somewhat misleading term for the end of World War II or should at least be applied more flexibly. Christa Hoffmann has also

noted the parallels to another *Stunde Null* in German history, the fall of the Berlin Wall in 1989, which posed comparable challenges of dealing with the past. See Christa Hoffmann, *Stunden Null?: Vergangenheitsbewältigung in Deutschland 1945 und 1989* (Bonn: Bouvier, 1992).

2. Quoted in Nikos Kotsopoulos, *Krautrock: Cosmic Rock and its Legacy* (London: Black Dog, 2010), 22.

3. Quoted in Pascal Bussy and Andy Hall, *Das Can Buch* (Augsburg: Sonnentanz, 1992), 67.

4. Quoted in Frank Sawatzki, "Die Seele der Mathematik oder wie die Rockmusik zu Can kam," in *Pop am Rhein*, ed. Uwe Husslein (Cologne: König, 2007), 94.

5. Quoted in *Kraut und Rüben*, directed by Stefan Morawietz (WDR, 2006).

6. Quoted in Karlheinz Borchert, "Can mit neuer Platte: Zukunftstage haben begonnen," *Musikexpress* 216 (December 1973), 61.

7. Quoted in *Kraut und Rüben*.

8. See David Stubbs, *Future Days: Krautrock and the Building of Modern Germany* (London: Faber & Faber, 2014).

9. Holger Czukay, "Holger Czukay über das Can-Studio," *Riebe's Fachblatt* 2 (1973), 12.

10. Quoted in *Can Box Book*, ed. Hildegard Schmidt and Wolf Kampmann (Münster: Medium Music Books, 1998), 70.

11. Ibid., 217.

12. As Jaki Liebezeit noted: "Malcolm was very American. That's why the first album was still fairly American. Later that disappeared." Ibid., 306.

13. Ibid., 132.

14. Quoted in Henning Dedekind, *Krautrock: Underground, LSD und kosmische Kuriere* (Höfen: Hannibal, 2008), 69.

15. Quoted in Bussy and Hall, *Das Can Buch*, 134.

16. Quoted in Schmidt and Kampmann, *Can Box Book*, 55.

17. Quoted in Bussy and Hall, *Das Can Buch*, 28.

18. Quoted in Tim Barr, *Kraftwerk: From Düsseldorf to the Future (with Love)* (London: Ebury Press, 1998), 64.

19. On "Vom Himmel hoch" ("From Heaven Above") from the first Kraftwerk album, the group used sounds reminiscent of falling bombs, explosions, and air raid signals. These references to World War II were unusual for explicitly invoking and critically engaging with the Nazi past.

20. Quoted in Pascal Bussy, *Kraftwerk: Man, Machine and Music* (London: SAF, 1993), 100.

21. In a slight departure from my analysis, Melanie Schiller views Kraftwerk's "Autobahn" as "a simultaneous (re)construction and dissemination/disjunction of national identity" through spatiality, temporality, and subjectivity. See Melanie Schiller, "'Fun Fun Fun on the Autobahn': Kraftwerk Challenging Germanness," *Popular Music and Society* 37, no. 5 (December 2014): 618–37.

22. Bussy, *Kraftwerk*, 59.

23. John T. Littlejohn, "Kraftwerk: Language, Lucre, and Loss of Identity," *Popular Music and Society* 32, no. 5 (December 2009), 643.

24. Wolfgang Flür, *Kraftwerk: I Am a Robot* (Bodmin: MPG Books, 2000), 52.

25. Quoted in Bangs, "Kraftwerkfeature."

26. Quoted in Barr, *Kraftwerk*, 74.

27. In their analysis of Kraftwerk's music, Sean Albietz and Kyrre Tromm Lindvig have commented on the group's "self-aware, satirical and ironic critiques of socially constructed markers of Germanness." Ralf Hütter emphasized the humorous side of Kraftwerk in an interview with the *Hot Press* in 1981: "We have a special type of black humour. We always wear black. It has to do with truth and certain aspects of the truth. Funny and serious at the same time. Revolutionary and funny." Sean Albietz and Kyrre Tromm Lindvig, "*Autobahn* und Heimatklänge: Soundtracking the FRG," in *Kraftwerk: Music Non-Stop*, ed. Sean Albietz and David Pattie (New York: Continuum, 2011), 15. Hütter quoted in Barr, *Kraftwerk*, 137.

28. Littlejohn, "Kraftwerk," 647.

29. Bussy, *Kraftwerk*, 82.

30. Quoted in Barr, *Kraftwerk*, 130.

31. Quoted in David Buckley with Nigel Forrest, *Kraftwerk: Publikation* (London: Omnibus, 2012), 95.

32. Ralf Hütter quoted in Bussy, *Kraftwerk*, 164.

33. Quoted in Barr, *Kraftwerk*, 156.

34. Ibid., 142.

35. Ibid., 137.

36. Quoted in "Computer-Welt," EMI press release (1981), Günther Ehnert collection, Klaus Kuhnke Archive, Bremen.

37. Quoted in Dankmar Isleib, "Kraftwerk," *Musikexpress* 5 (1981), 13 and 14.

38. Quoted in Buckley, *Kraftwerk*, 126. In a similar move, Mark Duffett has claimed that Kraftwerk's white masculinity helped to de-essentialize black masculinity. While he completely ignores national identity (Kraftwerk's white Germanness), Duffett helps to understand the group's gender politics when arguing that "Kraftwerk lived out a conception of masculinity that was cerebral, collective, strategic and peppered with ironic, self-deprecating humour." Mark Duffett, "Average White Band: Kraftwerk and the Politics of Race," in *Kraftwerk: Music Non-Stop*, 202.

39. Barr, *Kraftwerk*, 3.

40. Derrick May famously described techno as "George Clinton and Kraftwerk stuck in an elevator with only a sequencer to keep them company." Quoted in Barr, *Kraftwerk*, 183–84.

41. Ibid., 172.

42. Although the significance of Neu! has become much clearer over the years and music publications like *Pitchfork Media* regularly name-check the group in reverent tones, academic scholarship is largely nonexistent. The only scholarly essay on Neu! is Lloyd Isaac Vayo's piece in a special krautrock issue of *Popular Music and Society*. Vayo invokes Walter Benjamin's famous essay "The Work of Art in the Age of Mechanical Reproduction" and convincingly argues that Neu! can be seen as "rubble music that takes the best from the German past and reassembles it into a road map for a new way forward." Vayo's essay is strong on theory and weak on historical context and specific musical analysis. Given Neu!'s continued popularity, more scholarship on the group is likely to appear in

the near future. Lloyd Isaac Vayo, "What's Old is NEU!: Benjamin Meets Rother and Dinger," *Popular Music and Society* 32, no. 5 (December 2009), 617.

43. Quoted in Ax Genrich, "Interview mit Conny Plank," *Riebe's Fachblatt* 11 (November 1974), 17.

44. Ibid.

45. Quoted in Stefan Morawietz, "Klaus Dinger Interview 2005," http://www.you tube.com/watch?v=r32KZhgIAC0.

46. Ibid.

47. Quoted in Dr. Rock, "Kosmische Polymath Michael Rother: Eno, Bowie & Making Peace with Dinger," *The Quietus* (3 November 2009), http://thequietus.com/ articles/03128-michael-rother-of-neu-and-kraftwerk-interv.

48. Quoted in Kotsopoulos, *Krautrock*, 120.

49. *Krautrock: The Rebirth of Germany*, directed by Benjamin Whalley (BBC, 2009).

50. Quoted in Vayo, "What's Old," 621.

51. Quoted in Edgar Smith, "Neu!," *Loud and Quiet* 3, no. 17 (May 2010), http:// www.loudandquiet.com/2010/07/neu-michael-rother-interview/.

52. Quoted in Wilson Neate, "Krautrock Deluxe: Michael Rother," *Blurt*, http:// blurtonline.com/feature/krautrock-deluxe-michael-rother-part-1-2/.

53. Ibid.

54. Quoted in Biba Kopf, "Klaus Dinger Interview Transcript," *The Wire* 208 (June 2001), http://thewire.co.uk/articles/1042/.

55. Ibid.

56. Ibid.

57. Julian Cope, *Krautrocksampler* (London: Head Heritage, 1996), 42.

58. Ibid., 125.

59. *Kraut und Rüben*.

60. For a good overview of this scene, see Marc Masters, *No Wave* (London: Black Dog, 2007).

61. The album was finally released in 1997 and again in an extended edition in 2009.

62. Ingeborg Schober, "La Düsseldorfs neu-es Kraftwerk," *Sounds* 4 (April 1979), 40.

63. Ibid.

64. For a more thorough investigation of Düsseldorf's role in musical history, see Rüdiger Esch, *Electri_City: Elektronische Musik aus Düsseldorf* (Frankfurt: Suhrkamp, 2014).

65. Asked about their contemporaries, Michael Karoli stated: "Kraftwerk were very German. I think that we were more open." Similarly, Irmin Schmidt noted: "Kraftwerk were the perfect antithesis of Can. I find their music as impersonal as it is original, but it is saved by its humorous side." Quoted in Bussy, *Kraftwerk*, 22.

## Chapter Two

1. Despite their importance, scholarship on these groups is scarce. See Timothy Brown, "Music as a Weapon?: *Ton Steine Scherben* and the Politics of Rock in Cold War Berlin," *German Studies Review* 32, no. 1 (February 2009), 1–22; Michael T. Putnam, "Music as a Weapon: Reactions and Responses to RAF Terrorism in the Music of Ton Steine Scherben and their Successors in Post-9/11 Music," *Popular Music and Society* 32,

no. 5 (December 2009), 595–608; Arne Koch and Sei Harris, "The Sound of Yourself Listening: Faust and the Politics of the Unpolitical," *Popular Music and Society* 32, no. 5 (December 2005), 579–94.

2. Karl-Ludwig Schibel, "Kommunebewegung," in *Die sozialen Bewegungen in Deutschland seit 1945: Ein Handbuch*, ed. Roland Roth and Dieter Rucht (Frankfurt: Campus, 2008), 528.

3. Timothy Miller, *The 60s Communes: Hippies and Beyond* (Syracuse, NY: Syracuse University Press, 1999), xxi.

4. See Ron E. Roberts, *The New Communes: Coming Together in America* (Englewood Cliffs, NJ: Prentice-Hall, 1971), 12–13.

5. See *Creating and Managing the Collective Life*, ed. Rosabeth Moss Kantner (New York: Harper, 1973), 2; *Communes: Historical and Contemporary*, ed. Ruth Shonk Cavan and Man Singh Das (New Delhi: Vikas, 1979).

6. Robert P. Sutton, *Communal Utopias and the American Experience: Secular Communities, 1824–2000* (Westport, CT: Praeger, 2004), x.

7. Miller, *The 60s Communes*, xiii.

8. Ibid., xxiv.

9. See Dennis McNally, *A Long Strange Trip: The Inside History of the Grateful Dead* (New York: Broadway, 2002).

10. Miller, *The 60s Communes*, 142.

11. See Schibel, "Kommunebewegung," 534; Martin Klimke, *The Other Alliance: Student Protest in West Germany and the United States in the Global Sixties* (Princeton: Princeton University Press, 2010).

12. Quoted in Ulrich Enzensberger, *Die Jahre der Kommune I: Berlin 1967–1969* (Cologne: Kiepenheuer & Witsch, 2004), 181.

13. Ibid., 98.

14. See Detlef Siegfried, *Time Is on My Side: Konsum und Politik der westdeutschen Jugendkultur der 60er Jahre* (Göttingen: Wallstein, 2006), 647.

15. See Gerhard Augustin, *Der Pate des Krautrock* (Berlin: Bonsworth, 2005), 100.

16. Quoted in Edwin Pouncy, "Amon Düül II: Communing with Chaos," *The Wire* 144 (February 1996), http://www.thewire.co.uk/articles/60.

17. See Ingrid Schober, *Tanz der Lemminge: Amon Düül, eine Musikkommune in der Protestbewegung der 60er Jahre* (Reinbek: Rowohlt, 1979), 44.

18. Quoted in Henning Dedekind, *Krautrock: Underground, LSD und kosmische Kuriere* (Höfen: Hannibal, 2008), 123.

19. Quoted in Schober, *Tanz*, 40.

20. Ibid., 39–40.

21. Quoted in Dedekind, *Krautrock*, 55.

22. David Stubbs, "Amon Düül," in *Krautrock: Cosmic Rock*, 54.

23. Quoted in Pouncy, "Amon Düül II."

24. Quoted in Augustin, *Der Pate*, 134–35.

25. See Schober, *Tanz*, 135.

26. Quoted in Raoul Hoffmann, *Zwischen Galaxis & Underground: Die neue Popmusik* (Munich: dtv, 1971), 199.

27. Quoted in Pouncy, "Amon Düül II."

28. Quoted in Raoul Hoffmann, *Rock Story: Drei Jahrzehnte Rock & Pop Music von Presley bis Punk* (Frankfurt: Ullstein, 1980), 255.

29. Quoted in Schober, *Tanz*, 69.

30. Quoted in Stefan Gnad, "Bloß kein Krautrock: Amon Düül II im Interview," *Zine with no Name* (April 2009), http://www.zine-with-no-name.de/musikm/amon_%20 duul_%20II_interview_john_weinzierl_april_2009.htm.

31. Quoted in Schober, *Tanz*, 31.

32. Ibid., 69.

33. Julian Cope, *Krautrocksampler* (London: Head Heritage, 1996), 61.

34. Quoted in Schober, *Tanz*, 106.

35. Ibid.

36. Lester Bangs, "Amon Düül: A Science Fiction Rock Spectacle," in *Eurock: European Rock and the Second Culture*, ed. Archie Patterson (Portland, OR: Eurock Publications, 2002), 4.

37. Ibid., 5.

38. Quoted in Michael Fuchs-Gamböck, "Eternal Underground," Amon Düül II, *Yeti* (SPV, 2009).

39. Quoted in Schober, *Tanz*, 70.

40. "Neues auf dem Plattenteller," *Sounds* 17 (April 1970), 20.

41. Quoted in Pouncy, "Amon Düül II."

42. Quoted in Dedekind, *Krautrock*, 132.

43. Amon Düül II, "Was wir waren, was wir wollen," *Sounds* 30 (June 1971), 22.

44. Ibid.

45. In addition to *Chamsin*, Amon Düül II also participated in other films of the New German Cinema. In 1970, they appeared in Rainer Werner Fassbinder's *Niklashausen Journey* (1970) and in Wim Wenders's filming of their song "Phallus Dei," and they received the German Film Prize for their soundtrack to Hans-Jürgen Syberberg's *San Domingo*.

46. Bangs, "Amon Düül," 7. Only Julian Cope, otherwise devoted to Amon Düül, panned the album and inexplicably called it "a pile of pedestrian shit." Cope, *Krautrocksampler*, 64.

47. See Schober, *Tanz*, 288.

48. See Christoph Wagner, *Der Klang der Revolte: Die magischen Jahre des westdeutschen Musik-Underground* (Mainz: Schott, 2013), 374–75.

49. Cope, *Krautrocksampler*, 67.

50. Manfred Gillig, "Amon Düül II: Made in Germany," *Sounds* 10 (1975), 66.

51. Quoted in Andy Wilson, *Faust: Stretch Out Time, 1970–1975* (London: The Faust Pages, 2006), 1.

52. Ibid.

53. Quoted in Blow Upffertig, "Jürgen Irmler Interview" (2004), http://faust-pages. com/publications/jochen.blowupffertig.html.

54. Quoted in Wilson, *Faust*, 14–15.

55. Quoted in Jim DeRogatis, *Turn On Your Mind: Four Decades of Great Psychedelic Rock* (Milwaukee, WI: Hal Leonard, 2003), 268.

56. See Wilson, *Faust*, 155.

57. Quoted in Wilson, *Faust*, 156.

58. Quoted in Ian MacDonald, "The Sound of the Eighties," *New Musical Express* (3 March 1973), http://faust-pages.com/publications/macdonald.soundeighties.html.

59. Quoted in Dedekind, *Krautrock*, 110.

60. Quoted in Wilson, *Faust*, 15.

61. Ibid., 129.

62. Wilson, *Faust*, 25–26.

63. Quoted in Wilson, *Faust*, 27.

64. Wilson, *Faust*, 25.

65. Quoted in Wilson, *Faust*, 24.

66. See Chris Cutler, *Faust: The Wümme Years, 1970–73* (Recommended Records, 2003).

67. Wilson, *Faust*, 31.

68. See Wilson, *Faust*, 33.

69. "Faust Press Release," Polydor, March 1971, http://faust-pages.com/publications/polydor.pressrelease.html.

70. "Faust (1971, Rare Footage Documentary)," http://www.youtube.com/watch?v=C6huQHDcjWY.

71. Quoted in Wilson, *Faust*, 47.

72. MacDonald, "The Sound."

73. Quoted in Dedekind, *Krautrock*, 202.

74. Wilson, *Faust*, 56.

75. Quoted in Wilson, *Faust*, 57.

76. UL, "Faust: So Far," *Sounds* 1 (January 1973), 34.

77. Quoted in Wilson, *Faust*, 72.

78. Quoted in MacDonald, "The Sound."

79. See Wilson, *Faust*, 160. Faust also sampled the German radio time signal service on the album.

80. Quoted in MacDonald, "The Sound," 56.

81. Ibid.

82. MacDonald, "The Sound," 56.

83. Quoted in Dedekind, *Krautrock*, 17.

84. Hermann Haring, *Rock aus Deutschland West* (Reinbek: Rowohlt, 1984), 102–3.

85. Cope, *Krautrocksampler*, 21.

86. Olaf Reuther, "Polit-Rock in Deutschland," *Sounds* 2 (February 1974), 23.

87. Wolfgang Seidel, "Scherben . . . ," in *Scherben: Musik, Politik und Wirkung der Ton Steine Scherben*, ed. Wolfgang Seidel (Mainz: Ventil, 2005), 102.

88. See Kai Sichtermann, Jens Johler, and Christian Stahl, *Keine Macht für Niemand: Die Geschichte der Ton Steine Scherben* (Berlin: Schwarzkopf & Schwarzkopf, 2008), 14.

89. Rio Reiser took his name from the nineteenth-century novel *Anton Reiser* by Karl Phillipp Moritz.

90. Rio Reiser and Hannes Eyber, *König von Deutschland: Erinnerungen an Ton Steine Scherben und mehr* (Berlin: Möbius Rekords, 2001), 242.

91. Ibid., 256.

92. Quoted in Sichtermann, *Keine Macht*, 160.

93. Sichtermann, *Keine Macht*, 161.

94. In an interesting move across communes, Kommune 1 helped to realize the single by providing their printing press. See Albrecht Koch, *Angriff auf's Schlaraffenland: 20 Jahre deutschsprachige Popmusik* (Frankfurt: Ullstein, 1987), 53.

95. Seidel, "Scherben . . . ," 92.

96. See Seidel, "Scherben . . . ," 92.

97. Hartmut El Kurdi, *Schwarzrote Pop-Perlen: Ton Steine Scherben, Keine Macht für Niemand* (Hannover: Wehrhahn, 2001), 45.

98. Reiser, *König*, 212–13.

99. See Sichtermann, *Keine Macht*, 162 and 223.

100. Seidel, "Scherben . . . ," 102. In German, the term *anderes Ufer* ("other shore") is commonly used to connote gay identity.

101. Reiser, *König*, 294.

102. Quoted in Sichtermann, *Keine Macht*, 185.

103. Ibid., 196.

104. Ibid., 252.

105. See Ralf Fischer, "Lechts und Rinks sind nicht zu verwechseln: Aufklärung über einen weitverbreiteten Irrtum," in *Scherben: Musik*, 215–27.

## Chapter Three

1. See Paul Heelas, *The New Age Movement: The Celebration of Self and the Sacralization of Modernity* (Cambridge, MA: Blackwell, 1996), 17; Wouter J. Hanegraaff, *New Age Religion and Western Culture: Esotericism in the Mirror of Secular Thought* (Albany: State University of New York Press, 1998), 1.

2. See Sarah M. Pike, *New Age and Neopagan Religions in America* (New York: Columbia University Press, 2004).

3. Heelas, *New Age*, 3.

4. See Heelas, *New Age*, 2.

5. See Suzanne Owen, *The Appropriation of Native American Spirituality* (London: Continuum, 2008), 89.

6. Stuart Rose, *Transforming the World: Bringing the New Age into Focus* (Bern: Peter Lang, 2005), 37.

7. Paul Théberge, *Any Sound You Can Imagine: Making Music/Consuming Technology* (Hanover, NH: Wesleyan University Press, 1997), 4.

8. Quoted in Heelas, *New Age*, 18.

9. Gilles Deleuze and Félix Guattari, *Anti-Oedipus: Capitalism and Schizophrenia* (Minneapolis: University of Minnesota Press, 1983), 2.

10. Donna Haraway, *Simians, Cyborgs and Women: The Reinvention of Nature* (New York: Routledge, 1991), 150.

11. Trevor Pinch and Frank Trocco, *Analog Days: The Invention and Impact of the Moog Synthesizer* (Cambridge, MA: Harvard University Press, 2002), 7.

12. Théberge, *Any Sound*, 54.

13. Ken McLeod, "Space Oddities: Aliens, Futurism and Meaning in Popular Music," *Popular Music* 22 (2003), 340.

14. See Steve Waksman, *Instruments of Desire: The Electric Guitar and the Shaping of Musical Experience* (Cambridge, MA: Harvard University Press, 2001), 244.

15. Pinch and Trocco, *Analog Days*, 138.

16. Quoted in Werner Pieper, "Kaiser Schmarrn süß/sauer," in *Alles schien möglich . . . 60 Sechziger über die 6oer Jahre und was aus ihnen wurde*, ed. Werner Pieper (Heidelberg: The Grüne Kraft, 2007), 51.

17. Rolf-Ulrich Kaiser, *Das Buch der neuen Pop-Musik* (Düsseldorf: Econ, 1969), 172.

18. Ibid., 103.

19. Rolf-Ulrich Kaiser, *Rock-Zeit: Stars, Geschäft und Geschichte der neuen Pop-Musik* (Düsseldorf: Econ, 1972), 58.

20. Ibid., 68.

21. Ibid., 270.

22. Ibid., 263.

23. Ibid., 124.

24. In his later years, Leary became actively involved in neopaganism. See Robert Greenfield, *Timothy Leary: A Biography* (Orlando, FL: Harcourt, 2006).

25. Rolf-Ulrich Kaiser, "Kosmische Musik: Die Reise durch die Zeit," *Kosmische Musik* (Ohr, 1972).

26. Quoted in "Rolf-Ulrich Kaiser: Ohrenschmerzen & Pilzvergiftung," *Sounds* 9 (September 1973), 39.

27. Quoted in "Tangerine Dream: In Münchens Benno-Kirche wurden Träume realisiert," *Musikexpress* 235 (July 1975), 39. The backlash against kosmische Musik did not only come from the musicians on Rolf-Ulrich Kaiser's label. Udo Lindenberg, the best-known German-language rock singer of the time, recorded the song "Gerhard Gösebrecht" in 1974 as a rockist statement against "space music."

28. Julian Cope, *Krautrocksampler* (London: Head Heritage, 1996), 86.

29. Quoted in Jan Eric Reetze, "Rolf-Ulrich Kaiser and Gille Lettmann," *Music, Media & More* (23 May 2011), http://janreetze.blogspot.com/2011/05/rolf-ulrich-kaiser-gille-lettmann_1460.html.

30. Gille Lettmann and Rolf-Ulrich Kaiser, "Star Sounds: Discover the Galaxy Sound of Cosmic Music," in *Eurock: European Rock and the Second Culture*, ed. Archie Patterson (Portland, OR: Eurock Publications, 2002), 61.

31. Ibid., 62.

32. Ibid., 61.

33. See Pieper, "Kaiserschmarrn."

34. Cope, *Krautrocksampler*, 88.

35. Paul Stump, *Digital Gothic: A Critical Discography of Tangerine Dream* (Wembley: SAF, 1997), 13.

36. Quoted in Cope, *Krautrocksampler*, 30. Emphasis in the original.

37. See Rainer Blome, "Tangerine Dream," *Sounds* 29 (May 1971), 16; Michael Schwinn, *Klaus Schulze: . . . eine musikalische Gratwanderung* (Neustadt: Michael Schwinn, 1986), 29.

38. Albrecht Piltz, "Klaus Schulze, 1947–2250," Klaus Schulze, *Blackdance* (SPV, 2007). The same could be said about the other clearly defined regional scene in krautrock, the Düsseldorf sound of Kraftwerk and Neu!. While these groups emphasized a robotic 4/4

beat, the Berlin School artists generally abandoned rigid rhythms in favor of "dark, sequentially-based sound and dramatic melody lines." The limitations of categorizing krautrock groups by region are evident when one looks at Ton Steine Scherben, who, while from Berlin, had politically motivated lyrics but musically were strongly indebted to Anglo-American traditions and therefore are not considered part of the Berlin School. See Patterson, *Eurock*, 497.

39. Quoted in Hoffmann, *Rock Story*, 248.

40. Quoted in Patterson, *Eurock*, 373.

41. *Kraut und Rüben*, directed by Stefan Morawietz (WDR, 2006).

42. Ibid.

43. Quoted in Schwinn, *Klaus Schulze*, 24.

44. Quoted in Blome, "Tangerine Dream," 16.

45. Ibid.

46. In addition, Florian Fricke contributed Moog sounds on "Birth of Liquid Plejades."

47. Cope, *Krautrocksampler*, 133.

48. In 1973, Tangerine Dream recorded another album, *Green Desert*, but it was only released with overdubs in 1986, and it is impossible to tell what the album would have sounded like had it actually been released right after *Atem*.

49. Quoted in Manfred Gillig, "Tangerine Dream: Träume von synthetischen Mandarinen?," *Sounds* 7 (1975), 37.

50. Jim DeRogatis, *Turn On Your Mind: Four Decades of Great Psychedelic Rock* (Milwaukee, WI: Hal Leonard, 2003), 264. As another noteworthy release, one of Tangerine Dream's former musicians, Michael Hoenig, produced a seminal Berlin School recording with *Departure from the Northern Wasteland* in 1976. Edgar Froese died in 2015.

51. See Winfried Trenkler, "Die kosmische Reise," *Sounds* 12 (December 1972), 24. "Ashra" could also be a reference to the ancient Goddess Asherah or to Indian ashrams.

52. Quoted in Patterson, *Eurock*, 555.

53. Ibid., 558.

54. See Jason Gross, "Klaus Schulze," *Perfect Sound Forever* (1997), http://www.furious.com/perfect/kschulze.html.

55. Quoted in Trenkler, "Die kosmische Reise," 23.

56. Quoted in Patterson, *Eurock*, 343.

57. This is true even for Pink Floyd at their most "krautrock" on *Ummagumma* (1968). The double album contained experimental studio recordings, but two of them still had vocals, and the live recordings on the second record were more traditional rock pieces.

58. Edgar Froese of Tangerine Dream, for one, did not like Schulze's invocation of German classical music, calling it "bullshit." Quoted in Patterson, *Eurock*, 374.

59. The most important example is the debut album of Neue Deutsche Welle band Ideal, which sold seven hundred thousand copies.

60. "I never played a concert in the U.S.A. And I don't think there's a chance that I will ever play there. Just listen to my albums and imagine the 'typical' American taste. The two just don't match. I don't want to change, and I suppose the Americans won't change either. Their view of art is not mine. Not to mention the business side." Klaus Schulze ended this diatribe by noting that neither Beethoven nor Bach nor Mozart had ever

performed in the United States, connecting his invocation of European classical music with his rejection of Americanization. Schulze quoted in Patterson, *Eurock.*, 574.

61. Quoted in Greg Allen, *Klaus Schulze: Electronic Music Legend* (Victoria, BC: Trafford, 2008), 292.

62. In their soundtracks for Werner Herzog, Popol Vuh incorporated organ and, in 1987, Fricke also reintroduced synthesizers. See the following chapter.

63. The other owner of a Moog was Eberhard Schoener, a composer with an interest in popular music who later worked with rock groups like Deep Purple and the Police.

64. Popol Vuh, "Selbstbildnis einer deutschen Gruppe," *Sounds* 25 (January 1971), 16.

65. Ibid.

66. See Christoph Wagner, *Der Klang der Revolte: Die magischen Jahre des westdeutschen Musik-Underground* (Mainz: Schott, 2013), 93–94.

67. See Trenkler, "Die kosmische Reise," 25.

68. Quoted in Patterson, *Eurock*, 62.

69. See Gerhard Augustin, *Der Pate des Krautrock* (Berlin: Bonsworth, 2005), 243.

70. *Kraut und Rüben.*

71. Quoted in Rainer Langhans, "Musik ist für mich eine Form des Gebets," *Sounds* 3 (March 1973), 36.

72. In addition to these musically and spiritually eclectic albums, Popol Vuh contributed a number of soundtracks for the films of Werner Herzog (see the following chapter). In the 1990s, Florian Fricke turned to slicker New Age music, dabbled in electronica, and recorded a CD with straightforward piano interpretations of Wolfgang Amadeus Mozart. Fricke passed away in 2001.

## Chapter Four

1. As an oftentimes instrumental and atmospheric music, krautrock has been employed as soundtrack music for many films. As mentioned in other chapters, Can, Klaus Schulze, Tangerine Dream, and Amon Düül II have all done soundtrack work.

2. Soundtrack albums by Popol Vuh have been released for *Aguirre, Heart of Glass, Nosferatu, Fitzcarraldo,* and *Cobra Verde.* They do not contain all of Popol Vuh music from the films and include many tracks that are not in the films. Some vital soundtrack music, like that of *The Great Ecstasy of Woodcarver Steiner,* has never been officially released. In my discussion, I focus on the actual music heard in Werner Herzog's films, not the soundtrack albums.

3. Kara Keeling and Josh Kun, "Listening to American Studies," *American Quarterly* 63, no. 3 (September 2011), 451.

4. For a history on the New German Cinema, see for example: Julia Knight, *New German Cinema: Images of a Generation* (London: Wallflower Press, 2004); Hans Günther Pflaum and Hans Helmut Prinzler, *Film in der Bundesrepublik Deutschland: Der neue deutsche Film von den Anfängen bis zur Gegenwart* (Bonn: Inter Nationes, 1985).

5. Quoted in Paul Cronin, *Herzog on Herzog* (London: Faber and Faber, 2002), 33.

6. Ibid., 25. See also Chris Wahl, ed., *Lektionen in Herzog: Neues über Deutschlands verlorenen Filmautor Werner Herzog und sein Werk* (Munich: Richard Boorberg, 2011).

7. Wahl, *Lektionen.* The hyperbolic self-presentation in some of Herzog's films can

also be interpreted as a "parody of an auteur." See Timothy Corrigan, "Producing Herzog: From a Body of Images," in *The Films of Werner Herzog: Between Mirage and History*, ed. Timothy Corrigan, (New York: Methuen, 1986), 6.

8. Quoted in Cronin, *Herzog on Herzog*, 301.

9. Quoted in Brad Prager, *The Cinema of Werner Herzog: Aesthetic Ecstasy and Truth* (New York: Wallflower Press, 2007), 92.

10. Prager, *Cinema*, 121.

11. Quoted in Cronin, *Herzog on Herzog*, 55.

12. According to K. J. Donnelly, Werner Herzog used Popol Vuh's songs in his movies "not to heighten tension in the mainstream sense of film music, but essentially to cut across the image and add a sense of emotional and spiritual death." K. J. Donnelly, "Angel of the Air: Popol Vuh's Music and Werner Herzog's Films," in *European Film Music*, ed. Miguel Mera and David Burnand (Burlington, VT: Ashgate, 2006), 123.

13. Prager, *Cinema*, 26.

14. Quoted in Cronin, *Herzog on Herzog*, 257.

15. Ibid, 81.

16. Roger Hillman, "Coming to Our Senses: The Viewer and Herzog's Sonic Worlds," in *A Companion to Werner Herzog*, ed. Brad Prager (Malden, MA: Blackwell, 2012), 170.

17. Quoted in Cronin, *Herzog on Herzog*, 80.

18. Ibid.

19. *Aguirre*'s complexity also stood in marked contrast to the collaboration of Popol Vuh's Florian Fricke and Daniel Fichelscher with Conny Veit of krautrock group Gila on the album *Bury My Heart at Wounded Knee*, which was released in 1973, only one year after *Aguirre*. Based on white historian Dee Brown's 1970 bestseller about Native American struggles, the album by the former psychedelic rock group Gila, joined by Sabine Merbach on vocals and the two main members of Popol Vuh on guitar and keyboards, invoked notions of noble savages, contained *faux* Indian drums, flute, and chanting, and featured sentimental lyrics about romanticized Native Americans reminiscent of German author Karl May's nineteenth-century hero Winnetou and sung with a German accent: "In a sacred manner I live, to the heavens I gaze, in a sacred manner I live, my horses are many." The second side of the concept album contained "Black Kettle's Ballad" about the Sand Creek Massacre in 1864, sung from the perspective of the pacifist Cheyenne chief who was killed four years after the massacre by George Custer's troops: "Here I stand on my land, dying people all around me, here I stand, my bloody hand holding an arm of an Indian squaw, her body ripped by a white man's sword and her unborn child is lying beside her in the sand."

20. *Burden of Dreams*.

21. Incidentally, Werner Herzog would choreograph operas by Richard Wagner and other composers later in his career.

22. Quoted in Cronin, *Herzog on Herzog*, 212.

23. Werner Herzog's dehistoricization of "Africa" occurred in his documentaries, too, examples being in particular *Wodaabe, Herdsmen of the Sun* (1989) and *Echoes from a Somber Empire* (1990).

24. Quoted in Cronin, *Herzog on Herzog*, 95.

25. Prager, *Cinema*, 24.

26. Ibid., 110.

27. Werner Herzog quoted in Cronin, *Herzog on Herzog*, 151.

28. Donnelly, "Angel," 124.

29. Werner Herzog's uneven Hollywood career has continued with the two films *My Son, My Son, What Have Ye Done?* (2009) and *Queen of the Desert* (2015).

### Chapter Five

1. Tellingly, Giorgio Moroder's early recordings have been rereleased under the title *Schlagermoroder* (Repertoire Records, 2013).

2. For the disco history that follows, I draw on the following: Alice Echols, *Hot Stuff: Disco and the Remaking of American Culture* (New York: Norton, 2010); Kai Fikentscher, *"You Better Work!": Underground Dance Music in New York City* (Hanover, NH: Wesleyan University Press, 2000); Tim Lawrence, *Love Saves the Day: A History of American Dance Music Culture, 1970–1979* (Durham, NC: Duke University Press, 2003); Johnny Morgan, *Disco* (New York: Sterling, 2011); Peter Shapiro, *Turn the Beat Around: The Secret History of Disco* (New York: Faber and Faber, 2005).

3. Andrew Holleran, *Dancer from the Dance* (New York: Perennial, 2001), 40.

4. See Fikentscher, *"You Better Work!"*

5. Morgan, *Disco*, 98.

6. Echols, *Hot Stuff*, xxv.

7. See Richard Dyer, "In Defense of Disco," in *On Record: Rock, Pop, and the Written Word*, ed. Simon Frith and Andrew Goodwin (New York: Pantheon, 1990), 410–18.

8. Echols, *Hot Stuff*, xxvi.

9. For instance, Alice Echols has claimed that "disco did not arrive on American shores courtesy of Giorgio Moroder, the Bee Gees, and Abba" (Echols, *Hot Stuff*, 11). As I argue in this chapter, Moroder in particular did contribute to a transnational development of disco early on.

10. Quoted in Angus Mackinnon, "Der Munich Mensch Machine," *New Musical Express* (9 December 1978), http://homepage.ntlworld.com/clive.hocker/moroder/mor_1978/part01.htm.

11. Ibid.

12. Harold Faltermeyer scored an international hit in 1985 with the theme song for the movie *Beverly Hills Cop*, "Axel F."

13. Donna Summer quoted in Mikal Gilmore, "Donna Summer: Is There Life After Disco?," *Rolling Stone* (23 May 1978), http://www.rollingstone.com/music/news/donna-summer-is-there-life-after-disco-20120517.

14. Donna Summer with Marc Eliot, *Ordinary Girl: The Journey* (New York: Villard, 2003), 65.

15. Ibid., 101.

16. Quoted in Mackinnon, "Der Munich Mensch."

17. Quoted in Josiah Howard, *Donna Summer: Her Life and Music* (Cranberry Township, PA: Tiny Ripple Books, 2003), 26.

18. Howard, *Donna Summer*, 20. For instance, Donna Summer was interrogated about her blackness by *Jet* magazine in 1976.

19. See James Haskins and J. M. Stifle, *Donna Summer: An Unauthorized Biography* (Boston: Little, Brown and Company, 1983), 74.

20. Darlene Clark Hine, *Hine Sight: Black Women and the Re-Construction of American History* (Brooklyn, NY: Carlson, 1994), 41.

21. Giorgio Moroder, e-mail conversation with author, 28 April 2013.

22. Ibid.

23. Neil Bogart named both his company and himself after the 1942 Hollywood movie (his real name was Bogatz). Apart from Donna Summer, Bogart counted George Clinton's Parliament, Kiss, and the Village People among his artists. For a more detailed view of Casablanca, see Larry Harris, *And Party Every Day: The Inside Story of Casablanca Records* (New York: Backbeat, 2009).

24. Serge Gainsbourg originally recorded "Je t'aime" as a duet with Brigitte Bardot in 1968. It was finally released in 1986.

25. Summer, *Ordinary Girl*, 111.

26. Ibid., 108. Donna Summer was also shown in a Marilyn Monroe pose on the back cover of her LP *Four Seasons of Love*.

27. Quoted in Mackinnon, "Der Munich Mensch."

28. Lawrence, *Love Saves*, 174.

29. Quoted in Gilmore, "Donna Summer."

30. Ibid.

31. Summer, *Ordinary Girl*, 130.

32. Quoted in Howard, *Donna Summer*, 51.

33. Giorgio Moroder, e-mail conversation with author, 28 April 2013.

34. Quoted in Mackinnon, "Der Munich Mensch."

35. Ibid.

36. Ibid.

37. Quoted in Howard, *Donna Summer*, 31.

38. Shapiro, *Turn the Beat*, 109, 111.

39. Quoted in Echols, *Hot Stuff*, 112.

40. Quoted in Mackinnon, "Der Munich Mensch."

41. Quoted in Gilmore, "Donna Summer." Emphasis in the original.

42. Ibid.

43. This should not be seen as a simple equation of white Germans with "technology" and African Americans with "nature." Afrofuturist performers like George Clinton were as fully engaged with "techno" music as Kraftwerk and Giorgio Moroder in the 1970s.

44. Ibid.

45. Quoted in Howard, *Donna Summer*, 100.

46. Prostitution was also the topic of one of Donna Summer's earliest songs, "Lady of the Night."

47. Summer, *Ordinary Girl*, 173.

48. Echols, *Hot Stuff*, 275.

49. Judy Kutulas, "'You Probably Think This Song Is About You': 1970s Women's Music from Carole King to the Disco Divas," in *Disco Divas: Women and Popular Culture in the 1970s*, ed. Sherrie A. Innes (Philadelphia: University of Pennsylvania Press, 2003), 188.

50. Vince Aletti, "Electric Dreams," *Numéro* 39 (December 2002), http://homepage. ntlworld.com/clive.hocker/moroder/mor_2002/index.htm.

51. Quoted in Howard, *Donna Summer*, 142.

52. Quoted in Haskins and Stifle, *Donna Summer*, 126.

53. Downplaying the racist and homophobic elements of the backlash, Giorgio Moroder nonetheless was keenly aware that disco had run its course: "Certainly disco killed itself. And there was a terrible backlash. Too many products, too many people, too many record companies jumping on this kind of music. A lot of bad records came out. I guess it was overkill. Everybody started to come out with disco and it became . . . what's the word? A cussword." Quoted in Morgan, *Disco*, 79.

54. Giorgio Moroder earned Oscars for the soundtracks to Alan Parker's *Midnight Express* (1978) and for songs from *Flashdance* (1983, title song by Irene Cara) and *Top Gun* (1986, Berlin's "Take My Breath Away"). Moroder also contributed to the soundtracks for *American Gigolo* (Blondie's "Call Me," 1980) and *Scarface* (1983), among other Hollywood movies.

55. Giorgio Moroder produced artists as varied as Janet Jackson, Nina Hagen, Sparks, David Bowie, and Cher, wrote the theme songs for three Olympics (Los Angeles 1984, Seoul 1988, and Beijing 2008) and for the soccer world cup 1990 in Italy, and participated in designing a luxury car, the V-16 Cizeta Moroder.

56. For Daft Punk's 2013 song "Giorgio by Moroder," the producer related autobiographic tidbits to music reminiscent of his own work. His first solo album in decades, *Déjà Vu*, followed in 2015.

57. See Philip Auslander, *Performing Glam Rock: Gender and Theatricality in Popular Music* (Ann Arbor: University of Michigan Press, 2006).

58. Quoted in Pete Doggett, *The Man Who Sold the World: David Bowie and the 1970s* (New York: Harper Collins, 2012), 278.

59. Quoted in *David Bowie: Five Years*, directed by Francis Whately (BBC, 2013).

60. Nicolas Roeg had already cast another rock star, Mick Jagger, in *Performance* (1970).

61. Ibid.

62. Quoted in Marc Spitz, *Bowie: A Biography* (New York: Crown, 2009), 278–79.

63. See Tobias Rüther, *Helden: David Bowie und Berlin* (Berlin: Rogner & Bernhard, 2008), 18.

64. See Jerry Hopkins, *Bowie* (New York: Macmillan, 1985), 168.

65. Quoted in Peter and Leni Gillman, *Alias David Bowie* (New York: Holt, 1986), 426.

66. Quoted in Spitz, *Bowie*, 272.

67. Quoted in Thomas Jerome Seabrook, *Bowie in Berlin: A New Career in a New Town* (London: Jawbone, 2008), 68.

68. Ibid., 84.

69. Ibid., 165.

70. Ibid., 83.

71. Ibid., 84.

72. Rüther, *Helden*, 124–25.

73. I list Romy Haag as German here although she was born in the Netherlands and had lived in Paris and New York City before moving to Berlin.

74. Quoted in Rüther, *Helden*, 96.

75. Ibid., 132.

76. See Rüther, *Helden*, 160. There is some speculation that the song "'Heroes'" is about the affair between Antonia Maaß and Tony Visconti, but most likely Bowie wrote the song before he knew of their relationship.

77. Quoted in Seabrook, *Bowie*, 118.

78. Ibid., 117.

79. Ibid., 82.

80. Quoted in Roger Griffin, *Bowiegoldenyears*, http://www.bowiegoldenyears.com/1977.html.

81. See Hugo Wilcken, *Low* (New York: Continuum, 2005), 35. Wilcken also claims that there are similarities between *Low* and Can's *Tago Mago* "with its funk experimentalism of the first half giving way to the disturbed inner space of the second half, where not only words but music itself is more or less jettisoned in favour of textural sound." Ibid., 133–34.

82. At various points during his time in Germany, David Bowie planned to collaborate with krautrock musicians like Michael Rother, Klaus Dinger, Jaki Liebezeit, and Eberhard Froese. However, none of these collaborations ever became a reality.

83. Rüther, *Helden*, 72.

84. Quoted in Seabrook, *Bowie*, 100.

85. In addition to the "Berlin triptych," David Bowie and Brian Eno collaborated on *1. Outside* (1995).

86. The two other musicians on *Low* were Ricky Gardiner (guitar) and Roy Young (keyboards).

87. Quoted in Seabrook, *Bowie*, 103.

88. Ibid., 100.

89. Doggett, *The Man*, 324.

90. My understanding of the musical aspects of David Bowie's songs has been greatly enhanced by reading Chris O'Leary's Internet blog *Pushing Ahead of the Dame: David Bowie, Song by Song* (http://bowiesongs.wordpress.com).

91. For instance, the album topped *Pitchfork Media*'s list of the best albums of the 1970s.

92. Ibid., 316.

93. See Rüther, *Helden*, 175.

94. Rüther, *Helden*, 158.

95. See Gillman, *Alias*, 439.

96. Quoted in Doggett, *The Man*, 339.

97. See Doggett, *The Man*, 353.

98. David Bowie also revived Lou Reed's career when he produced his solo album *Transformer* (1972). Reed's follow-up, incidentally, was *Berlin*, recorded in London and New York and purely based on 1920s clichés about the city.

99. Quoted in Doggett, *The Man*, 303.

100. Nonetheless, *The Idiot* and *Lust for Life* are generally regarded as Iggy Pop's strongest solo albums. David Bowie also produced another hit record for his friend in 1986 with *Blah Blah Blah*.

101. Quoted in Spitz, *Bowie*, 297.

102. See Romy Haag, *Eine Frau und mehr* (Berlin: Quadriga, 1999), 198.

103. Klaus Nomi died of AIDS in 1983 and was later immortalized in the documentary film *The Nomi Song* (2004).

104. Quoted in Kai Hermann and Horst Rieck, *Christiane F.: Wir Kinder vom Bahnhof Zoo* (Hamburg: Gruner & Jahr, 2004), 79.

105. Ibid., 81.

106. Quoted in Andy Gill, "We Can Be Heroes," *Mojo* (April 1997), http://www.phin nweb.org/krautrock/mojo-krautrock.html.

## Chapter Six

1. Not surprisingly then, there is no scholarly account of NDW in English with the exception of Cyrus M. Shahan's *Punk Rock and German Crisis: Adaptation and Resistance after 1977* (New York: Palgrave Macmillan, 2013), which emphasizes literature over music. In the German literature on NDW, its earlier manifestations have received much more attention than its later, more commercialized forms.

2. Similar to krautrock, East German musicians did not contribute substantially to NDW, although "punk and new wave permeated the Wall and motivated parts of the young generation to consciously position themselves outside of the disciplinary regime." Like other rock and pop music, punk and new wave were suppressed by the East German government but often tolerated by Protestant churches, which were also hotbeds of the country's civil rights movement. Ronald Galenza and Heinz Havemeister, eds., *Wir wollen immer artig sein . . . : Punk, New Wave, HipHop und Independent-Szene in der DDR 1980–1990* (Berlin: Schwarzkopf & Schwarzkopf, 2005), 9.

3. See Barbara Hornberger, *Geschichte wird gemacht: Die Neue Deutsche Welle, eine Epoche deutscher Popmusik* (Würzburg: Königshausen & Neumann, 2011), 38.

4. See Jürgen Stark and Michael Kurzawa, *Der große Schwindel???: Punk, New Wave, Neue Welle* (Frankfurt: Verlag Freie Gesellschaft, 1981), 155.

5. See M. O. C. Döpfner and Thomas Garms, *Neue Deutsche Welle, Kunst oder Mode?: Eine sachliche Polemik für und wider die neudeutsche Popmusik* (Frankfurt: Ullstein, 1984), 11–12.

6. See Winfried Longerich, *"Da Da Da": Zur Standortbestimmung der Neuen Deutschen Welle* (Pfaffenweiler: Centaurus, 1989), 74.

7. See Hornberger, *Geschichte*, 51.

8. See Hollow Skai, *Alles nur geträumt: Fluch und Segen der Neuen Deutschen Welle* (Innsbruck: Hannibal, 2009), 36.

9. See Albrecht Koch, *Angriff*, 78.

10. See Frank Apunkt Schneider, *Als die Welt noch unterging: Von Punk zu NDW* (Mainz: Ventil, 2007), 8.

11. Quoted in Jürgen Teipel, *Verschwende deine Jugend: Ein Doku-Roman über den deutschen Punk und New Wave* (Frankfurt: Suhrkamp, 2001), 61.

12. See Hornberger, *Geschichte*, 287.

13. One might add that Kraftwerk had already recorded with both the most expen sive and the cheapest keyboards and synthesizers available.

14. See Teipel, *Verschwende*, 181.

15. Longerich, *"Da Da Da,"* 18.

16. See Skai, *Alles*, 65.

17. Quoted in Stark and Kurzawa, *Der große Schwindel*, 198.

18. Schneider, *Als die Welt*, 232.

19. Ibid.

20. Jewish prisoners in concentration camps were routinely stripped of the gold fillings in their teeth. The title "Herrenreiter" is difficult to translate. It is an archaic term for "jockey" but also has other connotations.

21. In 2004, East German heavy metal band Rammstein expressed similar anti-American attitudes in their hit single "Amerika," which reached number 40 on Billboard's "Hot Mainstream Rock Songs."

22. See Koch, *Angriff*, 144.

23. See Teipel, *Verschwende*, 176.

24. Quoted in Skai, *Alles*, 66.

25. Quoted in Teipel, *Verschwende*, 78.

26. Ibid., 97.

27. Ibid., 292.

28. Gabi Delgado-López has described the skinhead ideal of beauty as "big feet, small head." Ibid., 187.

29. Ibid., 306.

30. Quoted in Skai, *Alles*, 51.

31. German and British punk had also toyed with Nazi imagery. For instance, Sid Vicious of the Sex Pistols regularly wore a swastika T-shirt. For German punk and fascism, see Teipel, *Verschwende*, 42 and 51. In the final stages of NDW, the group Breslau was an unsuccessful attempt by EMI to capitalize on shock value. They paved the way for neo-Nazi bands like Landser and the early Böhse Onkelz.

32. See Jonathan P. G. Bach, *Between Sovereignty and Integration: German Foreign Policy and National Identity After 1989* (New York: St. Martin's Press, 1999).

33. See Ulrich Adelt, "Ich bin der Rock'n'Roll-Übermensch: Globalization and Localization in German Music Television," *Popular Music and Society* 28, no. 3 (July 2005), 279–95.

34. See Thomas Winkler, "Krautrock Revisited: The Rehabilitation of a Genre," *Goethe Institut* (March 2013), http://www.goethe.de/ins/za/en/joh/kul/mag/mus/10677215.html.

35. Julian Cope, "Q&A 2000ce: Krautrock," *Head Heritage* (July 2000), https://www.headheritage.co.uk/julian_cope/qa2000ce/krautrock/.

36. Quoted in David Buckley with Nigel Forrest, *Kraftwerk: Publikation* (London: Omnibus, 2012), 195.

37. Ramon Lobato and Lawson Fletcher, "Prestige and Professionalization at the Margins of the Journalistic Field: The Case of Music Writers," in *Amateur Media: Social, Cultural and Legal Perspectives*, ed. Dan Hunter, Ramon Lobato, Megan Richardson, and Julian Thomas (New York: Routledge, 2013), 116.

38. Kaya Oakkes, *Slanted and Enchanted: The Evolution of Indie Culture* (New York: Holt, 2009), 8.

39. The quotations from *Pitchfork* contributors in this section are from e-mail interviews that I conducted with them. The dates are as follows: Brian Howe, 30 July 2013; Dominique Leone, 5 August 2013; Nick Neyland, 29 July 2013; Brent Sirota, 17 July 2013; Nick Sylvester, 17 July 2013; Joe Tangari, 19 and 22 July 2013; Douglas Wolk, 21 July 2013.

40. For a comprehensive description of obscure krautrock groups, see Stephen and Alan Freeman, *Crack in the Cosmic Egg: Encyclopedia of Krautrock, Kosmische Musik, & Other Progressive, Experimental & Electronic Musics from Germany* (Leicester: Audion, 1996).

41. Douglas Wolk mentioned Ciccone Youth a/k/a Sonic Youth's recording "Two Cool Rock Chicks Listening to Neu!," as well as "Jenny Ondioline" by Stereolab, "a big hit on college radio, with a massive push behind it, and parts of it are very much like 'Hallogallo.'" Wolk also mentioned that in the 1990s, krautrock albums became "available in stores for the first time in a long time."

# Bibliography

Adelt, Ulrich. *Blues Music in the Sixties: A Story in Black and White.* New Brunswick, NJ: Rutgers University Press, 2010.

Adelt, Ulrich. "Ich bin der Rock'n'Roll-Übermensch: Globalization and Localization in German Music Television." *Popular Music and Society* 28, no. 3 (July 2005): 279–95.

Albietz, Sean, and Kyrre Tromm Lindvig. "*Autobahn* und Heimatklänge: Soundtracking the FRG." In *Kraftwerk: Music Non-Stop,* ed. Sean Albietz and David Pattie, 15–43. New York: Continuum, 2011.

Aletti, Vince. "Electric Dreams." *Numéro* 39 (December 2002), http://homepage.ntl world.com/clive.hocker/moroder/mor_2002/index.htm.

Allen, Greg. *Klaus Schulze: Electronic Music Legend.* Victoria, BC: Trafford, 2008.

Amon Düül II. "Was wir waren, was wir wollen." *Sounds* 30 (June 1971): 22.

Anderson, Benedict. *Imagined Communities: Reflections on the Origin and Spread of Nationalism.* London: Verso, 1983.

Appadurai, Arjun. *Modernity at Large: Cultural Dimensions of Globalization.* Minneapolis: University of Minnesota Press, 1996.

Applegate, Celia, and Pamela Potter, eds. *Music and German National Identity.* Chicago: University of Chicago Press, 2002.

Augustin, Gerhard. *Der Pate des Krautrock.* Berlin: Bonsworth, 2005.

Auslander, Philip. *Performing Glam Rock: Gender and Theatricality in Popular Music.* Ann Arbor: University of Michigan Press, 2006.

Bach, Jonathan P. G. *Between Sovereignty and Integration: German Foreign Policy and National Identity After 1989.* New York: St. Martin's Press, 1999.

Bangs, Lester. "Amon Düül: A Science Fiction Rock Spectacle." In *Eurock: European Rock and the Second Culture,* ed. Archie Patterson, 1–7. Portland, OR: Eurock Publications, 2002.

Bangs, Lester. "Kraftwerkfeature." In *Psychotic Reactions and Carburetor Dung,* ed. Greil Marcus, 154–60. New York: Vintage, 1988.

Barr, Tim. *Kraftwerk: From Düsseldorf to the Future (with Love).* London: Ebury Press, 1998.

Biddle, Ian, and Vanessa Knights. "National Popular Musics: Betwixt and Beyond the Local and the Global." In *Music, National Identity and the Politics of Location: Between the Global and the Local,* ed. Ian Biddle and Vanessa Knights, 1–15. Burlington, VT: Ashgate, 2007.

Blome, Rainer. "Tangerine Dream." *Sounds* 29 (May 1971): 14–16.

Borchert, Karlheinz. "Can mit neuer Platte: Zukunftstage haben begonnen." *Musikexpress* 216 (December 1973): 60–61.

Bourdieu, Pierre. *The Field of Cultural Production: Essays on Art and Literature*. New York: Columbia University Press, 1993.

Brown, Dee. *Bury My Heart at Wounded Knee: An Indian History of the American West*. New York: Holt, Rinehart and Winston, 1970.

Brown, Timothy S. "'The Germans Meet the Underground': The Politics of Pop in the Essener Songtage of 1968." In *Musikkulturen in der Revolte: Studien zu Rock, Avantgarde und Klassik im Umfeld von '1968'*, ed. Beate Kutschke, 163–73. Stuttgart: Steiner, 2008.

Brown, Timothy S. "Music as a Weapon?: *Ton Steine Scherben* and the Politics of Rock in Cold War Berlin." *German Studies Review* 32, no. 1 (February 2009): 1–22.

Buckley, David, with Nigel Forrest. *Kraftwerk: Publikation*. London: Omnibus, 2012.

*Burden of Dreams*. Directed by Les Blank. DVD. Criterion, 2005 (1982).

Bussy, Pascal, and Andy Hall. *Das Can Buch*. Augsburg: Sonnentanz, 1992.

Bussy, Pascal. *Kraftwerk: Man, Machine and Music*. London: SAF, 1993.

Canclini, Néstor García. *Hybrid Cultures: Strategies for Entering and Leaving Modernity*. Trans. Christopher L. Chiappari and Silvia L. López. Minneapolis: University of Minnesota Press, 1995 (1990).

Cavan, Ruth Shonk, and Man Singh Das, eds. *Communes: Historical and Contemporary*. New Delhi: Vikas, 1979.

"Computer-Welt." EMI press release (1981). Günther Ehnert collection, Klaus Kuhnke Archive, Bremen.

Connell, John, and Chris Gibson. *Sound Tracks: Popular Music, Identity and Place*. New York: Routledge, 2003.

Cope, Julian. *Krautrocksampler*. 2nd ed. London: Head Heritage, 1996.

Cope, Julian. "Q&A 2000ce: Krautrock." *Head Heritage* (July 2000), http://www.head heritage.co.uk/julian_cope/qa2000ce/krautrock/.

Corrigan, Timothy. "Producing Herzog: From a Body of Images." In *The Films of Werner Herzog: Between Mirage and History*, ed. Timothy Corrigan, 3–19. New York: Methuen, 1986.

Cronin, Paul. *Herzog on Herzog*. London: Faber and Faber, 2002.

Cutler, Chris. *Faust: The Wümme Years, 1970–73*. Booklet. Recommended Records, 2003.

Czukay, Holger. "Holger Czukay über das Can-Studio." *Riebe's Fachblatt* 2 (1973): 12.

Dallas, Karl. "Faust and Foremost: Interview with Uwe Nettelbeck." *Melody Maker* (March 1973), http://faust-pages.com/publications/dallas.uwe.interview.html.

*David Bowie: Five Years*. Directed by Francis Whately. TV documentary. BBC, 2013.

Dedekind, Henning. *Krautrock: Underground, LSD und kosmische Kuriere*. Höfen: Hannibal, 2008.

Deleuze, Gilles, and Félix Guattari. *Anti-Oedipus: Capitalism and Schizophrenia*. Trans. Robert Hurley, Mark Seem, and Helen R. Lane. Minneapolis: University of Minnesota Press, 1983 (1972).

DeRogatis, Jim. *Turn On Your Mind: Four Decades of Great Psychedelic Rock*. Milwaukee, WI: Hal Leonard, 2003.

Doggett, Pete. *The Man Who Sold the World: David Bowie and the 1970s*. New York: Harper Collins, 2012.

Donnelly, K. J. "Angel of the Air: Popol Vuh's Music and Werner Herzog's Films." In *Euro-

*pean Film Music*, ed. Miguel Mera and David Burnand, 116–30. Burlington, VT: Ashgate, 2006.

Döpfner, M. O. C., and Thomas Garms. *Neue Deutsche Welle, Kunst oder Mode?: Eine sachliche Polemik für und wider die neudeutsche Popmusik.* Frankfurt: Ullstein, 1984.

Dr. Rock. "Kosmische Polymath Michael Rother: Eno, Bowie & Making Peace with Dinger." *The Quietus* (3 November 2009), http://thequietus.com/articles/03128-michael-rother-of-neu-and-kraftwerk-interview.

Duffett, Mark. "Average White Band: Kraftwerk and the Politics of Race." In *Kraftwerk: Music Non-Stop*, ed. Sean Albietz and David Pattie, 194–213. New York: Continuum, 2011.

Dyer, Richard. "In Defense of Disco." In *On Record: Rock, Pop, and the Written Word*, ed. Simon Frith and Andrew Goodwin, 410–18. New York: Pantheon, 1990.

Echols, Alice. *Hot Stuff: Disco and the Remaking of American Culture.* New York: Norton, 2010.

El Kurdi, Hartmut. *Schwarzrote Pop-Perlen: Ton Steine Scherben, Keine Macht für Niemand.* Hannover: Wehrhahn, 2001.

Enzensberger, Ulrich. *Die Jahre der Kommune I: Berlin 1967–1969.* Cologne: Kiepenheuer & Witsch, 2004.

Ermath, Michael, ed. *America and the Shaping of German Society, 1945–1955.* Oxford: Berg, 1993

Esch, Rüdiger. *Electri_City: Elektronische Musik aus Düsseldorf.* Frankfurt: Suhrkamp, 2014.

"Faust (1971, Rare Footage Documentary)," http://www.youtube.com/watch?v=C6hu QHDcjWY.

"Faust Press Release," Polydor, March 1971, http://faust-pages.com/publications/poly dor.pressrelease.html.

Fellezs, Kevin. *Birds of Fire: Jazz, Rock, Funk and the Creation of Fusion.* Durham, NC: Duke University Press, 2011.

Fikentscher, Kai. *"You Better Work!": Underground Dance Music in New York City.* Hanover, NH: Wesleyan University Press, 2000.

Fischer, Ralf. "Lechts und Rinks sind nicht zu verwechseln: Aufklärung über einen weitverbreiteten Irrtum." In *Scherben: Musik, Politik und Wirkung der Ton Steine Scherben*, ed. Wolfgang Seidel, 215–27. Mainz: Ventil, 2005.

*Fitzcarraldo.* Directed by Werner Herzog. DVD. Anchor Bay, 2002 (1982).

Flür, Wolfgang. *Kraftwerk: I Am a Robot.* Bodmin: MPG Books, 2000.

Foucault, Michel. *The Archaeology of Knowledge.* Trans. A. M. Sheridan Smith. New York: Pantheon, 1972.

Freeman, Stephen, and Alan Freeman. *Crack in the Cosmic Egg: Encyclopedia of Krautrock, Kosmische Musik, & Other Progressive, Experimental & Electronic Musics from Germany.* Leicester: Audion, 1996.

Fuchs-Gamböck, Michael. "Eternal Underground." Liner notes for Amon Düül II, *Yeti.* SPV, 2009.

Galenza, Ronald, and Heinz Havemeister, eds. *Wir wollen immer artig sein . . . : Punk, New Wave, HipHop und Independent-Szene in der DDR 1980–1990.* Berlin: Schwarzkopf & Schwarzkopf, 2005.

Genrich, Ax. "Interview mit Conny Plank." *Riebe's Fachblatt* 11 (November 1974): 17–19.

Giddens, Anthony. *Runaway World: How Globalization Is Reshaping Our Lives.* New York: Routledge, 2000.

Gill, Andy. "We Can Be Heroes." *Mojo* (April 1997), http://www.phinnweb.org/kraut rock/mojo-krautrock.html.

Gillig, Manfred. "Amon Düül II: Made in Germany." *Sounds* 10 (1975): 66.

Gillig, Manfred. "Tangerine Dream: Träume von synthetischen Mandarinen?" *Sounds* 7 (1975): 36–38.

Gillman, Peter, and Leni Gillman. *Alias David Bowie.* New York: Holt, 1986.

Gilmore, Mikal. "Donna Summer: Is There Life After Disco?" *Rolling Stone* (23 May 1978), http://www.rollingstone.com/music/news/donna-summer-is-there-life-after-disco-20120517.

Gnad, Stefan. "Bloß kein Krautrock: Amon Düül II im Interview." *Zine with no Name* (April 2009), http://www.zine-with-no-name.de/musikm/amon_%20duul_%20II_ interview_john_weinzierl_april_2009.htm.

Greenfield, Robert. *Timothy Leary: A Biography.* Orlando, FL: Harcourt, 2006.

Greiner-Pol, André. "Wie die Scherben in den Osten kamen." In *Scherben: Musik, Politik und Wirkung der Ton Steine Scherben*, ed. Wolfgang Seidel, 51–60. Mainz: Ventil, 2005.

Griffin, Roger. *Bowiegoldenyears*, http://www.bowiegoldenyears.com/1977.html.

Griffiths, Paul. *Modern Music and After.* 3rd ed. New York: Oxford University Press, 2010.

Gross, Jason. "Klaus Schulze." *Perfect Sound Forever* (1997), http://www.furious.com/per fect/kschulze.html.

Haag, Romy. *Eine Frau und mehr.* Berlin: Quadriga, 1999.

Hanegraaff, Wouter J. *New Age Religion and Western Culture: Esotericism in the Mirror of Secular Thought.* Albany: State University of New York Press, 1998.

Hannerz, Ulf. "The World in Creolization." *Africa* 57 (1987): 546–59.

Haraway, Donna. *Simians, Cyborgs and Women: The Reinvention of Nature.* New York: Routledge, 1991.

Haring, Hermann. *Rock aus Deutschland West.* Reinbek: Rowohlt, 1984.

Harris, Larry. *And Party Every Day: The Inside Story of Casablanca Records.* New York: Backbeat, 2009.

Haskins, James, and J. M. Stifle. *Donna Summer: An Unauthorized Biography.* Boston: Little, Brown and Company, 1983.

Heelas, Paul. *The New Age Movement: The Celebration of Self and the Sacralization of Modernity.* Cambridge, MA: Blackwell, 1996.

Hermann, Kai, and Horst Rieck. *Christiane F.: Wir Kinder vom Bahnhof Zoo.* Hamburg: Gruner & Jahr, 2004 (1979).

Hillman, Roger. "Coming to Our Senses: The Viewer and Herzog's Sonic Worlds." In *A Companion to Werner Herzog*, ed. Brad Prager, 168–86. Malden, MA: Blackwell, 2012.

Hine, Darlene Clark. *Hine Sight: Black Women and the Re-Construction of American History.* Brooklyn, NY: Carlson, 1994.

Hoffmann, Christa. *Stunden Null?: Vergangenheitsbewältigung in Deutschland 1945 und 1989.* Bonn: Bouvier, 1992.

Hoffmann, Raoul. *Rock Story: Drei Jahrzehnte Rock & Pop Music von Presley bis Punk.* Frankfurt: Ullstein, 1980.

Hoffmann, Raoul. *Zwischen Galaxis & Underground: Die neue Popmusik*. Munich: dtv, 1971.

Holleran, Andrew. *Dancer from the Dance*. New York: Perennial, 2001.

Hopkins, Jerry. *Bowie*. New York: Macmillan, 1985.

Hornberger, Barbara. *Geschichte wird gemacht: Die Neue Deutsche Welle, eine Epoche deutscher Popmusik*. Würzburg: Königshausen & Neumann, 2011.

Howard, Josiah. *Donna Summer: Her Life and Music*. Cranberry Township, PA: Tiny Ripple Books, 2003.

Inda, Jonathan Xavier, and Renato Rosaldo. "A World in Motion." In *The Anthropology of Globalization*, ed. Jonathan Xavier Inda and Renato Rosaldo, 1–34. Malden, MA: Blackwell, 2002.

Isleib, Dankmar. "Kraftwerk." *Musikexpress* 5 (1981): 13–14.

Jameson, Fredric. "Notes on Globalization as a Philosophical Issue." In *The Cultures of Globalization*, ed. Fredric Jameson and Masao Myoshi, 54–77. Durham, NC: Duke University Press, 1998.

Jugendamt der Stadt Essen, ed. *Song Magazin 1968 für IEST 68*. Essen, 1968.

Kaiser, Rolf-Ulrich. *Das Buch der neuen Pop-Musik*. Düsseldorf: Econ, 1969.

Kaiser, Rolf-Ulrich. *Das Songbuch*. Ahrensburg: Damokles, 1967.

Kaiser, Rolf-Ulrich. "Kosmische Musik: Die Reise durch die Zeit." Liner notes for *Kosmische Musik*, LP. Ohr, 1972.

Kaiser, Rolf-Ulrich. *Rock-Zeit: Stars, Geschäft und Geschichte der neuen Pop-Musik*. Düsseldorf: Econ, 1972.

Kantner, Rosabeth Moss, ed. *Creating and Managing the Collective Life*. New York: Harper, 1973.

Kattago, Siobhan. *Ambiguous Memory: The Nazi Past and German National Identity*. Westport, CT: Praeger, 2001.

Keeling, Kara, and Josh Kun. "Introduction: Listening to American Studies." *American Quarterly* 63, no. 3 (September 2011): 445–59.

Klimke, Martin. *The Other Alliance: Student Protest in West Germany and the United States in the Global Sixties*. Princeton: Princeton University Press, 2010.

Knight, Julia. *New German Cinema: Images of a Generation*. London: Wallflower Press, 2004.

Koch, Albrecht. *Angriff auf's Schlaraffenland: 20 Jahre deutschsprachige Popmusik*. Frankfurt: Ullstein, 1987.

Koch, Arne, and Sei Harris. "The Sound of Yourself Listening: Faust and the Politics of the Unpolitical." *Popular Music and Society* 32, no. 5 (December 2005): 579–94.

Kopf, Biba. "Klaus Dinger Interview Transcript." *The Wire* 208 (June 2001), http://thewire.co.uk/articles/1042.

Kotsopoulos, Nikos, ed. *Krautrock: Cosmic Rock and its Legacy*. London: Black Dog, 2010.

*Krautrock: The Rebirth of Germany*. Directed by Benjamin Whalley. TV documentary. BBC, 2009.

*Kraut und Rüben*. Directed by Stefan Morawietz. TV documentary. WDR, 2006.

Kun, Josh. *Audiotopia: Music, Race, and America*. Berkeley: University of California Press, 2005.

Kutulas, Judy. "'You Probably Think This Song Is About You': 1970s Women's Music from Carole King to the Disco Divas." In *Disco Divas: Women and Popular Culture in the 1970s*, ed. Sherrie A. Innes, 172–93. Philadelphia: University of Pennsylvania Press, 2003.

Langhans, Rainer. "Musik ist für mich eine Form des Gebets." *Sounds* 3 (March 1973): 35–37.

Lawrence, Tim. *Love Saves the Day: A History of American Dance Music Culture, 1970–1979.* Durham, NC: Duke University Press, 2003.

Leary, Timothy. *Flashbacks: An Autobiography.* Los Angeles: Tarcher, 1983.

Lettmann, Gille, and Rolf-Ulrich Kaiser. "Star Sounds: Discover the Galaxy Sound of Cosmic Music." In *Eurock: European Rock and the Second Culture*, ed. Archie Patterson, 60–63. Portland, OR: Eurock Publications, 2002 (1975).

Lipsitz, George. *Dangerous Crossroads: Popular Music, Postmodernism and the Poetics of Place.* New York: Verso, 1994.

Littlejohn, John T. "Kraftwerk: Language, Lucre, and Loss of Identity." *Popular Music and Society* 32, no. 5 (December 2009): 635–53.

Lobato, Ramon, and Lawson Fletcher. "Prestige and Professionalization at the Margins of the Journalistic Field: The Case of Music Writers." In *Amateur Media: Social, Cultural and Legal Perspectives*, ed. Dan Hunter, Ramon Lobato, Megan Richardson, and Julian Thomas, 111–24. New York: Routledge, 2013.

Longerich, Winfried. *"Da Da Da": Zur Standortbestimmung der Neuen Deutschen Welle.* Pfaffenweiler: Centaurus, 1989.

MacDonald, Ian. "The Sound of the Eighties." *New Musical Express* (3 March 1973), http://faust-pages.com/publications/macdonald.soundeighties.html.

Mackinnon, Angus. "Der Munich Mensch Machine." *New Musical Express* (9 December 1978), http://homepage.ntlworld.com/clive.hocker/moroder/mor_1978/part01. htm and http://homepage.ntlworld.com/clive.hocker/moroder/mor_1978/part02. htm.

Mahnert, Detlev, and Harry Stürmer. *Zappa, Zoff und Zwischentöne: Die internationalen Essener Songtage 1968.* Essen: Klartext, 2008.

Manning, Peter. *Electronic and Computer Music.* Oxford: Clarendon Press, 1985.

Masters, Marc. *No Wave.* London: Black Dog, 2007.

McLeod, Ken. "Space Oddities: Aliens, Futurism and Meaning in Popular Music." *Popular Music* 22 (2003): 337–55.

McNally, Dennis. *A Long Strange Trip: The Inside History of the Grateful Dead.* New York: Broadway, 2002.

Miller, Timothy. *The 60s Communes: Hippies and Beyond.* Syracuse, NY: Syracuse University Press, 1999.

Morawietz, Stefan. "Klaus Dinger Interview 2005," http://www.youtube.com/watch?v=r32KZhgIAC0.

Morgan, Johnny. *Disco.* New York: Sterling, 2011.

Neate, Wilson. "Krautrock Deluxe: Michael Rother." *Blurt*, http://blurtonline.com/feature/krautrock-deluxe-michael-rother-part-1-2/.

"Neues auf dem Plattenteller." *Sounds* 17 (April 1970): 22–26.

Oakkes, Kaya. *Slanted and Enchanted: The Evolution of Indie Culture.* New York: Holt, 2009.

O'Flynn, John. "National Identity and Music in Transition: Issues of Authenticity in a Global Setting." In *Music, National Identity and the Politics of Location: Between the Global and the Local*, ed. Ian Biddle and Vanessa Knights, 19–38. Burlington, VT: Ashgate, 2007.

O'Leary, Chris. *Pushing Ahead of the Dame: David Bowie, Song by Song*, http://bowiesongs. wordpress.com.

Oved, Yaacov. *Two Hundred Years of American Communes*. New Brunswick, NJ: Transaction Books, 1988.

Owen, Suzanne. *The Appropriation of Native American Spirituality*. London: Continuum, 2008.

Papastergiadis, Nikos. "Tracing Hybridity in Theory." In *Debating Cultural Hybridity: Multi-Cultural Identities and the Politics of Anti-Racism*, ed. Pnina Werbner and Tariq Modood, 257–81. London: Zed Books, 1997.

Paringaux, Phillipe. "Faust: Clear." *Rock & Folk* (February 1972), http://faust-pages.com/publications/paringaux.rockandfolk.clear.html.

Patterson, Archie, ed. *Eurock: European Rock and the Second Culture*. Portland, OR: Eurock Publications, 2002.

Pflaum, Hans Günther, and Hans Helmut Prinzler. *Film in der Bundesrepublik Deutschland: Der neue deutsche Film von den Anfängen bis zur Gegenwart*. Bonn: Inter Nationes, 1985.

Pieper, Werner. "Kaiser Schmarrn süß/sauer." In *Alles schien möglich . . . 60 Sechziger über die 6oer Jahre und was aus ihnen wurde*, ed. Werner Pieper, 50–55. Heidelberg: The Grüne Kraft, 2007.

Pike, Sarah M. *New Age and Neopagan Religions in America*. New York: Columbia University Press, 2004.

Piltz, Albrecht. "Klaus Schulze, 1947–2250." Liner notes for Klaus Schulze, *Blackdance*. CD. SPV, 2007.

Pinch, Trevor, and Frank Trocco. *Analog Days: The Invention and Impact of the Moog Synthesizer*. Cambridge, MA: Harvard University Press, 2002.

Popol Vuh, "Selbstbildnis einer deutschen Gruppe." *Sounds* 25 (January 1971): 16–17.

Pouncy, Edwin. "Amon Düül II: Communing with Chaos." *The Wire* 144 (February 1996), http://www.thewire.co.uk/articles/60.

Prager, Brad. *The Cinema of Werner Herzog: Aesthetic Ecstasy and Truth*. New York: Wallflower Press, 2007.

Putnam, Michael T. "Music as a Weapon: Reactions and Responses to RAF Terrorism in the Music of Ton Steine Scherben and Their Successors in Post-9/11 Music." *Popular Music and Society* 32, no. 5 (December 2009): 595–608.

Rauhut, Michael. *Rock in der DDR: 1964–1989*. Bonn: Bundeszentrale für politische Bildung, 2002.

Reetze, Jan Eric. "Rolf-Ulrich Kaiser and Gille Lettmann." *Music, Media & More* (23 May 2011), http://janreetze.blogspot.com/2011/05/rolf-ulrich-kaiser-gille-lettmann_1460.html.

Reiser, Rio, and Hannes Eyber. *König von Deutschland: Erinnerungen an Ton Steine Scherben und mehr*. Berlin: Möbius Rekords, 2001 (1994).

Reuther, Olaf. "Polit-Rock in Deutschland." *Sounds* 2 (February 1974): 20–23.

Reynolds, Simon. "Retroactive." *Melody Maker* (November 1992), http://faust-pages.com/publications/reynolds.melodymaker.html.

Ritter, Rüdiger. "'1968' und der Wandel der Protestkultur in der Musik im Ostblock: Ausgewählte Beispiele (CSSR, DDR, Polen, Ungarn)." In *Musikkulturen in der Revolte: Studien zu Rock, Avantgarde und Klassik im Umfeld von '1968'*, ed. Beate Kutschke, 207–24. Stuttgart: Steiner, 2008.

Roberts, Ron E. *The New Communes: Coming Together in America*. Englewood Cliffs, NJ: Prentice-Hall, 1971.

Robertson, Roland. *Globalization: Social Theory and Global Culture*. London: Sage, 1992.

"Rolf-Ulrich Kaiser: Ohrenschmerzen & Pilzvergiftung." *Sounds* 9 (September 1973): 39.

Rose, Stuart. *Transforming the World: Bringing the New Age into Focus*. Bern: Peter Lang, 2005.

Rucht, Dieter. "Protestbewegungen." In *Die Geschichte der Bundesrepublik Deutschland, Bd. 3: Gesellschaft*, ed. Wolfgang Benz, 311–44. Frankfurt: Fischer, 1989.

Rüther, Tobias. *Helden: David Bowie und Berlin*. Berlin: Rogner & Bernhard, 2008.

Sawatzki, Frank. "Die Seele der Mathematik oder wie die Rockmusik zu Can kam." In *Pop am Rhein*, ed. Uwe Husslein, 91–109. Cologne: König, 2007.

Schibel, Karl-Ludwig. "Kommunebewegung." In *Die sozialen Bewegungen in Deutschland seit 1945: Ein Handbuch*, ed. Roland Roth and Dieter Rucht, 527–40. Frankfurt: Campus, 2008.

Schiller, Melanie. "'Fun Fun Fun on the Autobahn': Kraftwerk Challenging Germanness." *Popular Music and Society* 37, no. 5 (December 2014): 618–37.

Schmidt, Hildegard, and Wolf Kampmann, eds. *Can Box Book*. Münster: Medium Music Books, 1998.

Schneider, Frank Apunkt. *Als die Welt noch unterging: Von Punk zu NDW*. Mainz: Ventil, 2007.

Schober, Ingeborg. "La Düsseldorfs neu-es Kraftwerk." *Sounds* 4 (April 1979): 40–44.

Schober, Ingeborg. *Tanz der Lemminge: Amon Düül, eine Musikkommune in der Protestbewegung der 6oer Jahre*. Reinbek: Rowohlt, 1979.

Schwinn, Michael. *Klaus Schulze: . . . eine musikalische Gratwanderung*. Neustadt: Michael Schwinn, 1986.

Seabrook, Thomas Jerome. *Bowie in Berlin: A New Career in a New Town*. London: Jawbone, 2008.

Seidel, Wolfgang. "Scherben . . ." In *Scherben: Musik, Politik und Wirkung der Ton Steine Scherben*, ed. Wolfgang Seidel, 69–113. Mainz: Ventil, 2005.

Shahan, Cyrus M. *Punk Rock and German Crisis: Adaptation and Resistance after 1977*. New York: Palgrave Macmillan, 2013.

Shank, Barry. *The Political Force of Musical Beauty*. Durham, NC: Duke University Press, 2014.

Shapiro, Peter, ed. *Modulations: A History of Electronic Music, Throbbing Words on Sound*. New York: Caipirinha Productions, 2000.

Shapiro, Peter. *Turn the Beat Around: The Secret History of Disco*. New York: Faber and Faber, 2005.

Sichtermann, Kai, Jens Johler, and Christian Stahl. *Keine Macht für Niemand: Die Geschichte der Ton Steine Scherben*. 2nd ed. Berlin: Schwarzkopf & Schwarzkopf, 2008.

Siegfried, Detlef. *Time Is on My Side: Konsum und Politik der westdeutschen Jugendkultur der 6oer Jahre*. Göttingen: Wallstein, 2006.

Simmeth, Alexander. *Krautrock Transnational: Die Neuerfindung der Popmusik in der BRD, 1968–1978*. Bielefeld: Transcript, 2016.

Skai, Hollow. *Alles nur geträumt: Fluch und Segen der Neuen Deutschen Welle*. Innsbruck: Hannibal, 2009.

Skai, Hollow. *Das alles und noch viel mehr: Rio Reiser*. Munich: Heyne, 2006.

Smith, Edgar. "Neu!" *Loud and Quiet* 3, no. 17 (May 2010), http://www.loudandquiet.com/2010/07/neu-michael-rother-interview.

Spitz, Marc. *Bowie: A Biography*. New York: Crown, 2009.

Stark, Jürgen, and Michael Kurzawa. *Der große Schwindel???: Punk, New Wave, Neue Welle*. Frankfurt: Verlag Freie Gesellschaft, 1981.

Stubbs, David. "Amon Düül." In *Krautrock: Cosmic Rock and its Legacy*, ed. Nikos Kotsopoulos, 54–55. London: Black Dog, 2010.

Stubbs, David. *Future Days: Krautrock and the Building of Modern Germany*. London: Faber and Faber, 2014.

Stump, Paul. *Digital Gothic: A Critical Discography of Tangerine Dream*. Wembley: SAF, 1997.

Summer, Donna, with Marc Eliot. *Ordinary Girl: The Journey*. New York: Villard, 2003.

Sutton, Robert P. *Communal Utopias and the American Experience: Secular Communities, 1824–2000*. Westport, CT: Praeger, 2004.

"Tangerine Dream: In Münchens Benno-Kirche wurden Träume realisiert." *Musikexpress* 235 (July 1975): 38–39.

Tanner, Jakob. "'The Times They Are A-Changin'": Zur subkulturellen Dynamik der 68er Bewegungen." In *1968: Vom Ereignis zum Mythos*, ed. Ingrid Gilcher-Hotley, 275–95. Frankfurt: Suhrkamp, 2008.

Teipel, Jürgen. *Verschwende deine Jugend: Ein Doku-Roman über den deutschen Punk und New Wave*. Frankfurt: Suhrkamp, 2001.

Théberge, Paul. *Any Sound You Can Imagine: Making Music / Consuming Technology*. Hanover, NH: Wesleyan University Press, 1997.

Thomas, Nick. *Protest Movements in 1960s West Germany: A Social History of Dissent and Democracy*. Oxford: Berg, 2003.

Tomlinson, John. *Globalization and Culture*. Chicago: University of Chicago Press, 1999.

Trenkler, Winfried. "Die kosmische Reise." *Sounds* 12 (December 1972): 22–25.

Trenkler, Winfried. Liner notes for *Kraut-Rock: German Rock Scene*. LP. Brain, 1974.

UL, "Faust: So Far." *Sounds* 1 (January 1973): 34.

Upffertig, Blow. "Jürgen Irmler Interview" (2004), http://faust-pages.com/publications/jochen.blowupffertig.html.

Vayo, Lloyd Isaac. "What's Old is NEU!: Benjamin Meets Rother and Dinger." *Popular Music and Society* 32, no. 5 (December 2009): 617–34.

Von Westernhagen, Dörte. *Die Kinder der Täter: Das Dritte Reich und die Generation danach*. Munich: Kösel, 1987.

Wagner, Christoph. *Der Klang der Revolte: Die magischen Jahre des westdeutschen Musik-Underground*. Mainz: Schott, 2013.

Wahl, Chris, ed. *Lektionen in Herzog: Neues über Deutschlands verlorenen Filmautor Werner Herzog und sein Werk*. Munich: Richard Boorberg, 2011.

Waksman, Steve. *Instruments of Desire: The Electric Guitar and the Shaping of Musical Experience*. Cambridge, MA: Harvard University Press, 2001.

*Werner Herzog Eats His Shoe*. Directed by Les Blank. In *Burden of Dreams*. DVD. Criterion, 2005 (1980).

Wilcken, Hugo. *Low*. New York: Continuum, 2005.

Wilson, Andy. *Faust: Stretch Out Time, 1970–1975*. London: The Faust Pages, 2006.

Winkler, Thomas. "Krautrock Revisited: The Rehabilitation of a Genre." *Goethe Institut* (March 2013), http://www.goethe.de/ins/za/en/joh/kul/mag/mus/10677215.html.

# Index